Praise for *The Connected Mobile Family*

"*The Connected Mobile Family* toolkit takes the topic of global parenting from theory into intensely practical and pragmatic steps all parents can take to help their children (and themselves!) thrive in the chaos of global mobility. Most importantly, how they can remain strong as a family unit when the rest of the world is spinning, with these great transition and parenting tools!"

Ruth E. Van Reken
Co-author of *Third Culture Kids: Growing Up Among Worlds, 3rd edition*

Laura Giosh-Markov provides an excellent resource for Global Nomad parents seeking to optimize the benefits of the international lifestyle for themselves and their children. It is, as well, an important resource for educators and counselors who work with such families and children. The author combines a concise overview of issues inherent in the global nomadic lifestyle along with many practical "tools" to utilize in successfully navigating through the various challenges, opportunities, and potential pitfalls that will inevitably be confronted along the family's nomadic journey. An excellent contribution to the resource literature for Global Nomad families.

William G. Nicoll, Ph.D.
Co-author of *Resilience and the Internationally Mobile Family: Navigating Challenges and Transitions*

"Having worked with expat families and international schools around the world, I can confidently say *The Connected Mobile Family* is one of the most practical and insightful resources I've come across. Packed with wisdom and organized with clarity, it provides tools that are easy to apply and incredibly relevant. This book helps transform the challenges of transition into opportunities for connection and growth. I want families living the global adventure to have this book!"

Chris O'Shaughnessy
Author of *Arrivals, Departures and the Adventures In-Between*

"In *The Connected Mobile Family*, Laura Markov delivers exactly what expat parents need: a clear roadmap through the complex emotional terrain their children navigate while growing up abroad. Drawing from her extensive experience as both an international school counselor and therapist, Markov doesn't just illuminate the challenges—from identity formation and grief to transitions and belonging—she empowers parents with 55 practical, immediately usable tools to strengthen their families. This toolkit distills complex developmental concepts into accessible guidance while directing parents to deeper resources when needed. Whether you're a first-time expat parent trying to understand what lies ahead, or a seasoned global family seeking clarity on longstanding struggles, this book crystallizes experiences that can feel overwhelming and transforms them into actionable strategies. Short of having Laura herself guide you through strengthening your family one-on-one, this comprehensive toolkit is the next best thing. It's an essential companion for any parent committed to helping their globally mobile children not just survive, but thrive."

Patrick Kadian
Expat Parenting Coach and Founder of Global Family Hub
www.globalfamilyhub.com

"This book is an invaluable guide for global nomads and families navigating the challenges of relocating to a new country. With insightful tools, engaging stories, and practical activities, it provides a roadmap to building meaningful connections—within the family and with the wider community. The Tiller Family's journey adds a personal touch, making each lesson relatable and inspiring. Whether you're moving for the first time or are a seasoned expat, this book is a must-read for creating a fulfilling and connected life abroad."

Joni Kerr
TCK/International Educator
Author of *Guide to Raising Exceptional Expat Kids*

The Connected Mobile Family

55 tools for your toolkit

Laura Giosh-Markov

Summertime
Publishing

*To travelers in search of adventure and knowledge
whose vision of parenting surpasses borders.
To families who wander in awe of our world
and have taught me much about their journeys.
May the Tools within help you build more connections along the way.*

CONTENTS

Foreword

Having grown up moving across countries and cultures often, I wish my family had had access to a resource as rich and practical as this—one filled with tools to help us navigate moving with greater understanding and ease.

I was first introduced to Laura's work when she presented at the Safe Passage Across Networks (SPAN) Pre-Conference, preceding the Families in Global Transition (FIGT) conference in 2017. I was immediately impressed by her remarkable ability to weave the lessons around the Third Culture Kid (TCK) experience into creative, thoughtful activities. Her approach was inspirational, both as a teacher and as a parent.

Each member of a family experiences the joys and the complexities of transition in a unique way. Yet within these differences lies a profound opportunity: the chance to foster deeper connections and to build more meaningful relationships with our family, especially during our formative years.

By beginning each chapter with a story about "The Tillers," this book invites every family member to recognize the diverse perspectives within their own household. It offers the space to connect these stories to their own personal experience and, in turn, to one another.

Having worked with numerous families in transition, everyone benefits from developing a shared language and shared tools and resources to better support each other through times of change. *The Connected Mobile Family* and its 55 tools will empower families to embrace their unique stories and to walk forward, hand in hand, through every transition life may bring.

Valérie Besanceney

International Education and Transition Consultant
Author of *B at Home: Emma Moves Again* and *My Moving Booklet*
www.linkedin.com/in/valeriebesanceney / www.rootswithboots.com

WHO IS THIS TOOLKIT FOR?

If your family has moved so many times that you see new acquaintances as "leavers" and "stayers," and if your children have changed schools *too many* times in their young lives and can't answer the questions "Where are you from?" or "Who are you?", it's likely this Toolkit is for you.

If you're starting your journey and wondering how to keep your family connected through the craziness of working and growing up around the world, how to keep track of people and experiences from the different places you've lived in—and to make sense of it all—this Toolkit is for you.

If you want to have better communication with your children and motivate them to be more independent, confident, and resilient, and to contribute to the family and the community, this Toolkit is for you.

Throughout the book, I refer to a family consisting of two parents and their dependent children living together in one household—the nuclear family system. This is for ease of writing and is in no way meant to exclude anyone who has a different system in place such as single-parent families, blended families and the myriad of different variations of the family system. The Tools in this book are for all, whoever you are and wherever you may be on your Global Nomad journey.

HOW TO USE THIS TOOLKIT

There are three sections in this Toolkit:

1. Foundations for Global Nomads and Parents
2. Tools for the Global Nomad Journey
3. Appendix and Resources

Foundations for Global Nomads and Parents

This part lays out topics that concern mobile families and parents. The information is intentionally brief and meant to give a general framework on which the Tools are based. If you are familiar with this information, then start with the Tools. If you would like more in-depth information about these topics, refer to the *Resources* section at the end.

Foundations for Global Nomads prepares you for the journey and familiarizes you with the terms "Global Nomads," "TCKs," and "ATCKs." You'll also find an overview of topics that mobile families must continually address to help their children manage in healthy ways: social belonging, identity formation, transitioning, grief and loss, and child development in the context of mobility.

Foundations for Parents describes four parenting styles and a framework for parents of mobile families regarding: a stable family environment, a sense of attachment, significance and belonging, recognition of unique temperaments, and emotional language. Finally, a short discussion of *Control vs. Influence* gives a perspective on how to prepare our children to make good choices when outside the sphere of our supervision.

Tools for the Global Nomad Journey

If you want to jump right into the journey, start with the *Tools*: skills and activities to build more connections within the family as well as to the community and country to which you have moved.

Each Tool starts with an inspirational quote and a short story about the fictional Tiller Family, which serves to introduce a challenge they have faced. Some information about the benefits of the Tool establishes why it's important. Next, follow the steps to do the activity or to learn a new skill. All Tools end with a few thought-provoking questions to reflect on what you have learned and to connect it with other parts of your life.

You'll find Tools that direct you to look at your own journey, Tools to use with your partner, and other Tools that encourage the whole family to connect through communicating, contributing, and appreciating each other. The activities and skills you'll learn will also help you connect to experiences with new friends and places along the way.

Appendix and Resources

These sections contain supplementary templates, information, and some of the resources used when creating the Toolkit.

Disclaimer

Working with the Tools in this book is a great start to learning new information and skills. However, if you need more support, seek professional help. See the Resources *section for a list of possible places to find professional help.*

You're always welcome to get in touch with me at
www.lauramarkov.com

INTRODUCTION

If you're a family that moves around, you've got the right Toolkit! Being a parent *and* a Global Nomad are both journeys that require extra tools for you and your family. As you explore this Toolkit, my hope is that you discover strategies that reach past the pages into your life.

My first transition meetings were back in 1994 at the international school in Bulgaria, where I was teaching French, music, and theater. I had read *Third Culture Kids: Growing Up Among Worlds* by David Pollock and Ruth Van Reken as well as some other articles on this topic, and planned to share information and strategies with international families. I remember handing out photocopies to parents who were eager to learn about transitions and how to connect with the community. In small groups, they discussed the focus questions about the number of passports they had, moves they'd made, and the countries they had lived in. More in-depth questions were about what stage of transition their children were at, the difficulties and advantages of their lifestyle, and how to help their children deal with loss and grief and with any confusion they might have had about their identity. I remember that they felt supported and connected with other parents and that they learned more about our school. Hopefully, they walked away with some tools to help their family's journey.

Later, I became the first long-term counselor at that international school. Not surprisingly, my master's dissertation was about "Transitions"—a student-created musical show. My transition presentations—on a computer, by that point—were designed to share essential information in a practical way for busy parents to access. When I initiated parent workshops with programs based on principles of "social belonging," I was able to respond to parents' desires to nurture positive life skills in their children and strengthen the family unit. The activities and information in both my Transition workshops and Parent workshops were interconnected, and formed an elegant symbiosis. My experience as a counselor and therapist has also contributed to the repertoire of Tools you'll find in this Toolkit.

Since then, many more authors have shared their unique perspectives and expertise on the Global Nomad lifestyle and on ways to support families. Standing on their shoulders, and combining this information with strategies from *Positive Discipline* by Jane Nelsen, Ed.D. and Lynn Lott, *The Connected Mobile Family: 55 Tools for Your Toolkit* came into being. It's designed for busy nomadic parents to enrich and "tighten up" the family unit like a well-stocked cruise ship heading off for an adventure.

This book offers practical Tools for parents and Global Nomads to:

- Strengthen family cohesion.
- Nurture emotional intelligence and resilience.
- Increase the independence and contribution of children.
- Ease the stress of transitioning to and from places.
- Process and lessen the sense of loss and grief.
- Strengthen connections to people and places.
- Encourage self-reflection to affirm one's identity and sense of purpose.

Who Are the Tillers?

To guide you through the Tools, we will accompany Sara Darwish-Tiller, Max Tiller, and their children, a composite of the many families I have worked with over the years. Sara and Max are Adult Third Culture Kids (ATCKs) and a mixed-culture couple with different languages, customs, and experiences. Both of them lived in several countries during their childhood.

Together with their three children, Jace, Mariel, and Parul, they manage their lifestyle as best they can while on the move. Their parents raised them with the strategies they learned from their own parents, but Max and Sara need new tools for the faster-paced modern world. They are learning to use the Tools in this Toolkit to face the emotional challenges of relocating more confidently, having more fun, and feeling closer as a family. Sara and Max want their children to have the kind of skills that will help them live their adult lives richly and fully.

The Tillers' journey, although fictional, could be the story of many Third Culture Families. The challenges and joys of their mobile lifestyle are woven into a multicultural patchwork of sights, sounds, flavors, and friends they encounter along the way.

FOUNDATIONS FOR GLOBAL NOMADS AND PARENTS

Foundations for Global Nomads

*Global Nomad parents need to ask themselves
some important questions*

---

*"Wise cross-cultural parenting doesn't just happen.
Moving to a new culture far from familiar support systems
causes new stress for everyone… Parents need to ask some
important questions before committing their family to such
a major move as part of that baseline assessment."*

David C. Pollock, Ruth Van Reken, and Michael V. Pollock
Third Culture Kids: Growing Up Among Worlds

In this chapter, there are seven foundations to establish key pieces of the puzzle for Global Nomad Families:

1. Definitions of terms
2. Connection and Social Belonging
3. Identity Formation
4. The Transition Cycle
5. Grief and Loss
6. Mobility and Child Development
7. Teen Years

For the purposes of this Toolkit, they are described briefly. For more in-depth information, please refer to the *Resources* section for books and articles that offer more research, case studies, and examples.

What is a Global Nomad?

"Global Nomad" is a term coined by Norma McCaig in 1984 to describe "a person of any age or nationality who has lived a significant part of their developmental years in one or more countries outside their passport country because of a parent's occupation."

Particularly in the past few years, there has been an increase in traveling Digital Nomads who work online, often with their families in tow. This term was first coined in 1997 by Tsugio Makimoto and David Manners in their book *The Digital Nomad*. They prophesied the trend of people choosing to travel and live wherever they want while using their skills to work online. In this book, I will be using the term Global Nomads to describe both Global and Digital Nomads, but the focus of this Toolkit is for families, rather than individuals.

Whether you move only a few or many times, Global Nomad children and adults face the challenges of repeatedly leaving a life you have built and then adjusting to new communities and cultures. With the recurring cycle of leaving and settling, one of the biggest challenges is adaptation during the different stages of the transition process, as explained in more detail below.

What are TCKs, TCFs, ATCKs, and CCKs?

"Third Culture Kids" (TCKs) and "Third Culture Families" (TCFs) were terms coined by Dr. Ruth Hill Useem and her husband, John Useem, during their research on American expats in India in the 1960s. The updated description for a "traditional" TCK in the third edition of *Third Culture Kids* is "a person who spends a significant part of his or her first 18 years of life accompanying parent(s) to a country or countries that are different from at least one parent's passport country(ies) due to a parent's choice of work or advanced training." For example, this could be a kid whose parents work for an embassy, are missionaries, or work for a company, and who move to a country different to at least one of those their parents grew up in, following their parents' career choices.

The life of a Third Culture Kid includes the phenomenon of experiencing different cultures they encounter during their life abroad. The feeling of belonging "everywhere and nowhere" is common for children and adults who have assimilated aspects of places they've lived in without identifying with any single culture. This "third culture" perspective is a unifying bond with others who live the same lifestyle. Many TCKs can relate to others' "rootlessness and restlessness" and feel a sense of belonging through their multicultural experiences. Quite often, TCKs continue their mobile lifestyle through their own careers, possibly with their own families. Adult Third Culture Kids (ATCKs) are adults who grew up in different countries because of their parents' careers.

In more recent years, Ruth Van Reken coined the term "Cross Culture Kids" or CCKs who have grown up in a mixed-culture environment. This includes mixed race families, immigrants, refugees, and minorities. CCKs may also be TCKs, but without the mobility. For example, a Pakistani family that has settled in England: their children might go to a local school and experience British culture outside of the home but live a traditional Pakistani life with its values, foods, traditions, and language at home. This Toolkit is mainly for TCKs, ATCKs, and Global Nomads. However, CCK families may also benefit from using these Tools to integrate the different cultural influences in their lives.

Life as a TCK

There are all sorts of factors that shape what a child gains from growing up in a globally mobile lifestyle. Some of the standout positive qualities include:

- Adept at making friends and having short-term connections
- Culturally aware and capable of fitting into a new environment
- Used to unpredictability and "going with the flow"
- Multilingual, multicultural, worldly
- Drawn to careers of service in a community or the world

In nomadic families, kids face unique challenges and have different needs compared to their non-mobile peers. As you go through this list of common hurdles for TCKs, you might find yourself thinking of a few more to add:

- Changing people, places, languages, cultures, schools, and situations
- Adaptation period as they learn to fit in when they arrive in new places
- Disconnection from family back home and friends left behind
- A sense of loss every time they move
- Grief from compounded losses

Because of these challenges, they may also experience:

- A limited sense of belonging, feeling "rootless and restless"
- Confusion about social cues
- Identity confusion
- Feelings of helplessness and insignificance in family decisions
- Resentment of their parents for moving
- Delayed adolescence and rebellion
- Emotional "flatness," difficulty expressing emotions, unresolved grief
- Disconnection from friends and experiences they have had

To address these challenges, the Tools in this Toolkit reinforce positive aspects of the family structure and help process the emotions and feelings of disconnection. There are also Tools to build emotional expression and create awareness of their experiences as Global Nomads.

Connection

Human beings need to connect with others—for good mental health, social-emotional skills, personal growth, and a satisfying life. In an age of increased screen time and mobility, staying connected has become a skill we need to make more effort to schedule into our busy lives.

The Tools in this Toolkit address three important levels of connection during your global lifestyle:

1. Your family: your partner, your children, and between each other.
2. Communities and locations: helping disconnect from one community when leaving and connect with the next when arriving.
3. Long-term connections: staying in touch with extended family, with the friends you've made, to cultures and countries, and to the experiences and memories of your journey.

Social Belonging

In the 1940s, the American psychologist Abraham H. Maslow put forth the theory that our need to belong is a driving force in our lives. Other psychologists later built on this theory to analyze human behaviors motivated by the need to belong and form attachments. "Love and Belonging" are shown as a central piece in Maslow's Hierarchy of Needs, which is depicted as a pyramid. Once our Physiological and Safety needs are satisfied, we're driven by the need to feel Love and Belonging in our lives. This extends beyond family and community, to the whole world, including nature. In practice, there are therapeutic approaches and parenting programs founded on this theory. Once our need to Belong is fulfilled in healthy ways, we develop a feeling of Esteem about who we are. Based on the foundational pieces of the pyramid, we ultimately move toward the self-actualization of our skills and potential.

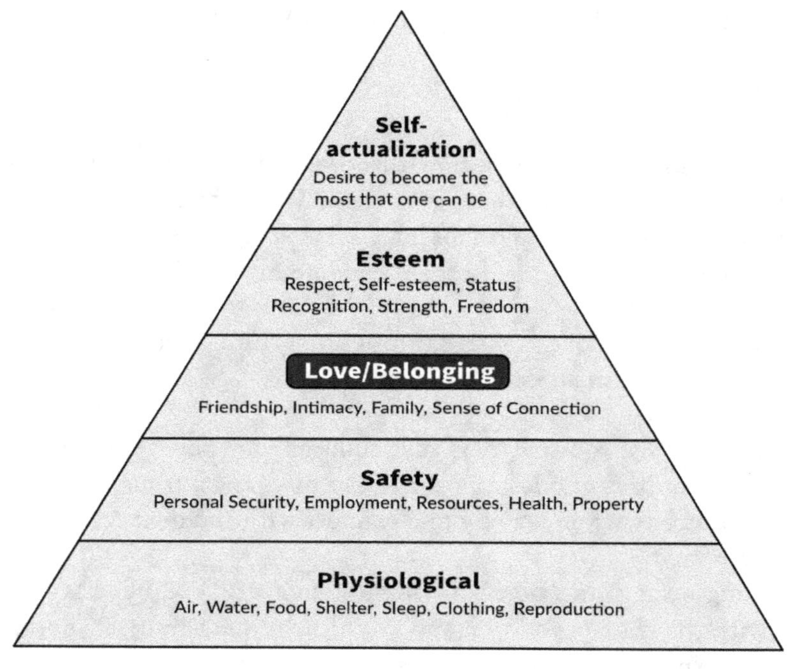

Maslow's hierarchy of human needs

Moving house and the loss of connection to a community can disturb feelings of safety and a sense of belonging. With this comes emotional disruption and a feeling of disconnection within. You may notice this while making yet another move and your child is out of sorts around the house and possibly at school. Global Nomad parents have the extra task of nurturing a sense of significance and belonging in children while changing their communities in one of the most extreme ways possible, repeatedly, and to foreign cultures with new languages, school systems, and friends.

To make the most out of this super-parenting challenge, there are ways to increase the sense of significance and belonging, as you will discover in the *Tools* section.

Identity Formation

Identity formation was described in the 1980s by Erik Erikson, a German-American psychoanalyst, as part of our psychosocial development. While the teen years are considered the most important period for our sense of identity to take shape, the influences in our lives up to the teen years also contribute to this process. As we continue to mature in adulthood, our sense of identity may expand, but it is based on a foundation established during the teen years and young adulthood. With all the changes in their lives, TCKs have a bigger challenge than their stationary counterparts when it comes to establishing their identity.

Our family is one of our earliest influences, and how it shapes our identity depends on some of the following factors: our parents' nationalities and cultural backgrounds, family customs, rituals or religious practices, different communication styles, temperaments and personalities, the number of siblings and birth order, socio-economic status, and everything else family life includes. Our family is the center of our stability. Relationships within the family serve as the foundation for our future relationships. Two other influences—community and geographical location—also contribute to identity formation, as we will see in Barbara Knuckles' "anchors and mirrors" model in the next section.

As teens pull together their values, beliefs, and experiences in life, self-image takes shape. The challenge is how to maintain uniqueness while fitting into a social group, and then, to test the perimeters of this developing self-image against the boundaries of family and society. Role models from family and society are an essential piece in this "mosaic," but establishing a separate and unique identity is a healthy and essential part of the individuation process and helps to solidify it.

Our challenge as parents is to make the family foundation as solid and as resilient as possible, especially for Third Culture Families. And then, to be a "guide on the side" as our children learn from their own experiences and mistakes (we must give up that Helicopter Parent role!). Many of the parent Tools that follow equip our children—and us—to take this momentous step.

Anchors and mirrors

Barbara Knuckles' model of "anchors and mirrors" in the development of children's identities is outlined in *Third Culture Kids: Growing Up Among Worlds*. Family, community, and geographical place are three elements that supply feedback in the form of "anchors and mirrors" that contribute to shaping the developing child's sense of identity.

Anchors "ground" me by affirming what stays constant in my life. For example, the traits and values I share with my parents and siblings are constants that affirm my place in my family group. Living in the same house over a period of years means I'll see my neighbors and the people in my community daily. I have memories and a history with them that affirms my presence there. Family and community are also references over time in the context of the geographical places we've lived in, in a similar culture and with similar values. Memories connect me to places where I've played, worked, and lived. They are constant reminders of who I am and what I have become.

Mirrors reflect how others see and experience me through our interactions and relationships. For instance, I look different from my neighbors. We eat different foods and go to different churches. The church community recognizes the musical part of me when I sing a solo in the choir and play guitar. My parents nag me about chores, but the charity group I volunteer at thinks I'm responsible. My teachers laud my academic strengths or comment on my lack of them. In an international setting, I carry my country's flag in the international parade with 40 other flags. In the marketplace, people turn their heads because I look foreign and talk with an accent. My Chinese friend and I argue about our political views.

With the feedback from anchors and mirrors about who I am and who I'm not, I adjust my perception of self and the world around me. The more "anchored" I feel in myself and in my family, the more solid my foundation is to integrate the reflections of these many "mirrors"—these different perspectives—into my self-concept.

This model of identity formation is particularly relevant for Global Nomads. A nomadic lifestyle effectively minimizes the anchors of community and geographical location and increases the number of "mirrors" that contribute to a child's developing identity. If you intend to live a mobile lifestyle, there are two questions. How do you maximize the family as the main anchor and the anchors of community and location? And how do you manage the many changing mirrors to help make sense of a developing identity?

The Tools in the pages that follow help to recognize each child's individuality and significance in the family unit. The Tools increase connection *within* the family and to the communities you live in. They reinforce family as the main anchor in your and your child's adventure into identity formation.

Supporting Tools such as the *Family Map Tool #22*, the *Life Journey Tool #32*, the *Explore Tool #20*, the *Organize Memories Tool #41*, and activities such as *Goodbye Books*, help children integrate the changing cultural "reflections" they encounter as part of their Global Nomad identity.

The Transition Cycle

If you've ever experienced a personality change in your child before, during or after a move, this section is essential for understanding what is going on in their heart and mind. Transitioning to a new location is a process that starts before the actual move and stretches into the weeks and months after arrival. The first move is perhaps the most exciting. However, as the number of moves increases, an anticipated sense of loss and grief of too many goodbyes looms over the thrill of discovering a new place. The mystery of transitions is that each child, each person, in fact, can have drastically different reactions to the upcoming move.

How your child reacts to moving may be affected by a number of factors:

- How many previous moves your family has made
- How the children were prepared for the move (were there discussions, goodbyes, connections made with the new location, were feelings processed, and were they involved in some way in the decision-making process?)
- Family closeness and time spent together on a regular basis
- Support for individual needs, activities, clubs, and classes for extracurricular interests
- Unresolved feelings of loss and grief
- Individual temperaments and resilience
- Parental support and individual time with each child
- External systems support (embassy, military, church, business)

Below are some common reactions to moving and settling in. Check them off for your family and add your own:

Excitement	Fear	Apathy
Joy	Anger	Feeling overwhelmed
Curiosity	Resentment	Helplessness
Worry	Depression	Powerlessness

Stages of transition

There's no strict timeline for the different stages of transition; it's as variable as the different temperaments of each person in your family. The number of moves your family has made and how each move was prepared for have a big impact on how resilient your children become over time. In the *Tools* section, you'll discover ways to help alleviate the stress of transition and build up emotional resilience.

The generally recognized five stages of transition are Involvement, Leaving, Transit, Entering, and Re-engagement. These are explained in detail below, along with suggestions for how parents can respond during each stage.

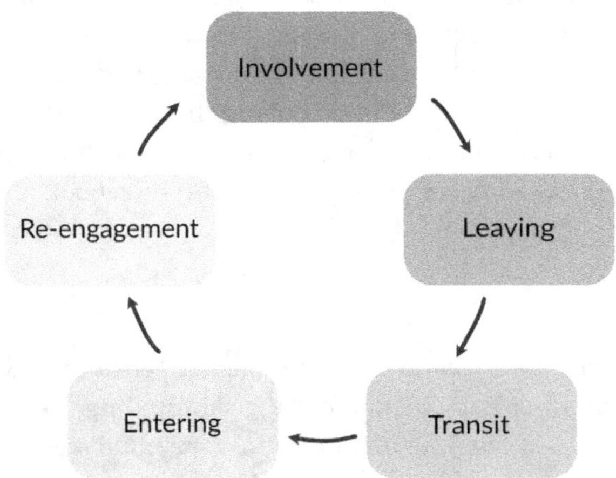

The Transition Cycle starts once you know you are leaving.
Each person transitions at their own pace.

Involvement

This is the period when a family is settled into their day-to-day life and involved in their community. With this sense of attachment comes a feeling of stability, of being known and appreciated by others. It's a time to learn, develop new skills, and nurture friendships.

Parents can use this time to reinforce family bonds, using different activities and discussions from the Tools, improving communication habits, and building up a repertoire of problem-solving strategies. These positive moments are reference points to give as examples during the more unstable moments during transition.

Leaving

Once the family knows they'll be moving, disconnection from friends, school, work, and community starts, often on a subconscious level. Whether it's the parents' decision to move or it's dictated by their employers, there are mixed feelings during this stage. After experiencing multiple moves, it's common for children and adults to mentally and emotionally "check out" of their relationships, school, and work well before their departure.

Parents can lead this shift by preparing "good" goodbyes and casting their sights ahead for a good landing in their new location. It is a time for listening to your child's concerns and giving them some choices during the preparations to leave. If you have a *Family Mission Statement Tool #2*, a *Coat of Arms Tool #13*, and a *Rituals Tool #47* in place, now is the time to call on the power of these Tools to unite your family.

Transit

Imagine a plant being pulled up from the soil where it has attached itself, its roots dangling in the air until it is placed in new soil and can start reattaching. In *Third Culture Kids: Growing Up Among Worlds*, Norma McCaig describes a family during the transit phase of a move becoming "temporarily dysfunctional, even when looking forward to the adventure."

Children may present inexplicable behaviors during this part of the transition—a lack of motivation, being unsociable, being disorganized, and a disinterest in school. There might be more sibling rivalry, careless or regressive behavior, more dependency, or disrespect. Emotional reactions can vary. Your child may be aggressive or passive, vengeful, apathetic, resentful, obstinate, confrontational, depressed, and more! Kids who are prepared beforehand with what to expect will have a relatively easier transition.

During this fragile stage, the family's bonding mechanisms are put to the test. It's a time for focusing on the positives, to listen and empathize with each other's feelings, to find fun in the challenges, and for self-care. It is a time to give structure among the chaos—put your family *Rituals Tool #37* in place and hold regular *Family Meetings Tool #23*, a format for giving kudos, problem-solving, planning, and celebrating. When traveling and settling in, give everyone a task so they feel like an important part of your "team."

Entering

The excitement of arriving in a new place can distract newcomers for a while. It may start off as a honeymoon of wonderful experiences that enchant you. However, at some point, these experiences can turn into irritating reminders of how different things are from your recent home. You may notice more emotional reactions and behaviors in your children that signal their discomfort with settling in. As new habits and connections form, things start to settle down into a semblance of normalcy.

This is the time to highlight positive things and recognize the benefits of living in your new location. Get the whole family involved in school initiatives and activities, and explore local resources. When children complain, we empathize, and we also find moments to remind them of how they have succeeded in previous transitions. Keep the "team spirit" alive. Have kids help set up the house, choose places to visit, take turns being a tour guide. Lots of positive feedback about how capable and helpful they are reinforces their place in the family as well as the family's place in their identity formation.

Re-engagement

Re-engagement is settling into your new life. Your family starts to enjoy the community, exploring, contributing, and building new relationships and skills (it may not all be rosy but staying in your comfort zone is probably *not* one of the reasons you went on the road in the first place, right?). The amount of time it takes your family to re-engage depends on the new situation, the number of moves you've made, individual temperaments, and your family's approach to relocating.

> Reinforcing the family as a successful team strengthens the foundation for other connections to happen more easily—connections with other families, the community, and the local culture. During this settled period, parents can give more attention to children's individual needs and build up the sense of stability. Feelings of loss and grief can also be processed more readily when the family feels settled.

Grief and Loss

For Global Nomads, saying goodbye on a regular basis makes it difficult to maintain satisfying friendships that endure the test of time and distance. A sense of loss and an ambiguous type of grief build up with each move. Unresolved grief is one of the hidden "travelers" that accompanies internationally mobile families. "Grief that is not dealt with directly emerges in some way—in forms that are destructive and that can last a lifetime," write the authors of *Third Culture Kids: Growing Up Among Worlds*. For this reason, taking time to process feelings of grief and loss will help keep your family resilient.

Grief and loss are a painful part of a mobile lifestyle, but with awareness and care, the negative effects of these feelings can be lessened. Finding ways to express these feelings is an important first step. Placing them in the meaningful framework of your *Family Mission Statement Tool #2* and the benefits of your lifestyle in *Pitfalls and Perks of a Mobile Lifestyle Tool #1* can help integrate them in positive ways. Many of the Tools are designed to directly or indirectly support the expression of grief and loss.

The following description of the different kinds of grief and loss that Global Nomads might experience is not meant to be an exhaustive discussion on this topic. For more information, refer to books in the *Resources* section.

Grief

One of the most important things for Global Nomads to be aware of is the "invisible travel companion," grief. There are reasons this emotional trauma gets through "passport control" undetected. Over time, children experience unresolved grief, as outlined in *Third Culture Kids: Growing Up Among Worlds*: lack of awareness, lack of permission, lack of time, lack of comfort, lack of understanding. Consider the stories below. How might parents help prepare their children beforehand and help them process their feelings to lessen the impact of grief over time?

Leslie was 11 years old when her family moved for the second time. She had thrived in the extracurricular classes, karate, and junior choir, and had developed close relationships with the instructors. When her family arrived in Cairo, the school didn't offer karate or choir for her age. Her parents attributed her sadness to the loss of friends, but weren't aware that there was suddenly a "hole" where the strong code of discipline and respect had been in those groups. Leslie joined a different extracurricular class and gradually got involved, but the next time they moved, she didn't know why she felt so apathetic.

Eric's parents are missionaries. He has lived in four countries on three different continents and gladly helps his family and their community wherever they go. Now that he is 15 years old, however, he dreams about having more choice in where he lives, with whom he can spend time, and what he does on his vacations. He believes in his parents' mission to help others through the church and respects them too much to "rock the boat." In this way, he carries a silent grief with him wherever they move.

Carmen's family moved every two years with her father's business. Just when she would get used to her schedule and started making friends, they had to pack up and leave again. No time to process her feelings. She felt like a piece of luggage being dragged around the world. Mom was always busy with her little brothers, and Dad was usually working too much. She was friendly and sociable but also didn't invest too much in friendships. When she started high school, she started having panic attacks and struggled in school.

Jae's family did not express much physical affection. He started having digestion problems after changing schools for the third time, starting high school. Jae's mother reassured him that he would adjust to the school and make new friends soon. However, Jae didn't feel so sure about this, and his stomach problems never quite went away. He needed some form of comfort to help process the emotional turmoil inside.

Kristy was starting 5th grade after her family's second move when she stopped eating, telling her mom she was too fat. The family got professional help to work through the problem, but her parents couldn't understand why their little girl had to express herself in this extreme way.

By using the Tools in this Toolkit, you can help yourself and your family to process emotions and alleviate the effects long-term grief has on your life.

Loss

Adults experience loss against a background of many more factors in their lives and an already formed sense of identity. Children experience losses differently than adults during the developmental years when their sense of identity is taking shape. With the shifting landscape of people, communities, and places, it's difficult for them to formulate what they have lost along the way.

Parents can respond to tangible losses such as teachers, activities, toys, or friends. Intangible losses such as lifestyle, system identity, status, role models, or simply the smells of a marketplace get "buried" in a pile of miscellaneous memories like a catchall drawer in the kitchen. Given no choice about moving, the loss of attachment to people, places, and things over time creates a feeling of powerlessness.

Consider the metaphor of "anchors and mirrors" from the *Identity Formation* section earlier in this chapter. With repeated loss of attachments, for your children, gaining a coherent picture of who they are becomes a puzzle of sand that cannot find a consistent shape. If you are an ATCK, you may have found ways to deal with the losses you've experienced along your journey. Or perhaps these losses affect different areas of your life in unexpected ways?

In the Tools section, there are Tools and activities within the Tools to support children to understand these losses and process the feelings that accompany them:

Pitfalls and Perks of a Mobile Lifestyle Tool #1
Connect Tool #15
Goodbyes Tool #25
Grief and Loss Tool #27
Message in a Bottle Tool #35
Organize Memories Tool #41
Rituals Tool #47
Stay in Touch Tool #51
Write Your Own Story Tool #55

Mobility and Child Development

Regardless of their age, children who move around the world frequently during their developmental years need support before, during, and after each move, as seen in the *Transition Cycle* outlined earlier.

*Children's reactions to moving reflect their level of maturity
and awareness of the world around them*

The ability of children to understand and navigate changing environments depends on their developmental level, temperament, and adaptation skills. These differences should guide our expectations concerning their reactions and adjustment time during a move: a baby will sense the emotional turmoil and need to feel safe; an older child will have their own turmoil but may not understand how to express it; a teen will have clear thoughts and feelings about moving but won't necessarily want to share them for fear of rocking the boat. Indeed, a teen's need for independence from their parents can create other challenges for parents that a toddler won't. They may show their resistance through a wide range of misbehaviors, such as anger, depression, withdrawal, rebellion against rules, and engaging in risky behaviors.

Some of the Tools that follow are intended to build communication and offer ways to allow everyone in the family to have a voice and affirm their place. Other Tools give a framework for your family's journey to help affirm the benefits of living a mobile lifestyle. As children mature, they can refer to this framework to make sense of all the experiences they had while growing up.

Teen Years

> *"[Cross-cultural] teenagers need to develop their identity while confronted by the fluid, multicultural world around them."*
>
> **Dr. Anisha Abraham** Raising Global Teens

During the teen years, identity formation comes to the forefront of a young person's development. However, even as the body is physiologically maturing at a faster rate, the prefrontal cortex, which controls higher thinking, lags behind. For this reason, teens still need parental support and guidance during this step toward their adult selves. Mobile teens moving to new locations have increased dependency on their family, which runs counter to their need for more independence.

As we discovered earlier, in the *Anchors and mirrors* section, Barbara Knuckles describes how family, community, and location serve as stabilizing and reflective factors in the creation of one's unique identity. Living in several locations during their developmental years creates an extra challenge for a teen or young adult when it comes to answering the important question, "Who am I?" The other important question is, "Who is my group?" Identifying oneself as a Third Culture Kid or Global Nomad and understanding all the multicultural influences woven into that identity is a first step to finding the answers.

*Answering the question "Who am I?" is more complex for a young person
who has been growing up living an international lifestyle*

In many ways, a mobile lifestyle creates more dependence on the family to stabilize and reflect back to the child about who they are. However, during teenage years, being accepted into peer groups starts to take precedence over belonging to their family. As part of their maturation process, they test their social skills and personalities in other spheres, such as with their peers. At home, they may argue more or insist on doing things their own way. Unfortunately, it is common for teens to experiment with alcohol, drugs, and other risky behaviors in an attempt to establish their independence, albeit in negative ways.

It's at this critical time that they benefit from a solid base from which to navigate new boundaries, risk-taking, and bigger decisions while venturing away from Mom and Dad. This is especially important when teens arrive in a new school and community. They must quickly grasp the local set of social rules at the same time as managing a new academic system. If they've moved several times, many TCK teens will have their own set of skills to join a group of students in their new place. Teens who have gone through too many moves and haven't developed skills to adapt, struggle to connect. They may reveal this in non-adaptive ways—apathy, reclusive behaviors, depression, lack of self-care.

Parents can strengthen the influence of "family" in Barbara Knuckles' identity equation—family, community, and location—by adding Tools from this Toolkit to their already established family toolkit. Many Tools increase a sense of significance and belonging in the home, as well as allowing for a burgeoning independence. With this kind of foundation, teens can find healthy ways to take risks and face challenges to assert their new autonomy. They will also be better prepared for the personal transition toward adulthood.

*   *   *

Foundations for Parents

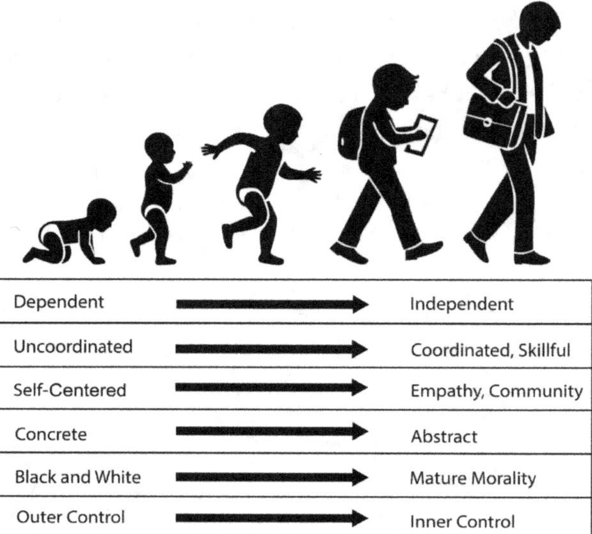

Maturation is a process that can be viewed on a continuum

"The challenge of parenting lies in finding the balance between nurturing, protecting, and guiding, on the one hand, and allowing your child to explore, experiment, and become an independent, unique person, on the other."

Jane Nelsen, Ed.D.   Positive Discipline

Parenting is a puzzle made up of several pieces that each couple will construct in their unique way. If your partner has grown up in a different culture than yours, or you were TCKs, the pieces multiply. Adding mobility puts the whole puzzle on a rotating axis that calls for stronger bonds and a higher degree of interdependence within the family to keep it all together.

The information in this section supports the use of the Tools in the Toolkit, but it is intentionally brief, as many parents may already be familiar with the topics. More importantly, the *Reflection* questions at the end of each part ask you to consider how the information relates to your family to prepare you for exploring the Tools. If you would like to learn more about a topic, please refer to the parenting books listed in the *Resources* section.

As an adult, my first significant experiences with children were through teaching French and music in international schools. I quickly realized that my expectations were out of line with their abilities. More importantly, I had no idea how transition issues affected the capacity of arriving students to jump into a new environment and function socially and academically. It was a demanding and crucial point in my career to change my approach. I learned more about TCKs, what children needed as individuals, and how to cultivate the sense of belonging that motivated students to find their place and thrive.

Later, as parents, my husband and I learned our own lessons about how to "nurture, protect and guide" our cross-cultural daughter while allowing her to become an independent and capable person. We had to face our own issues with control, aligning our expectations, developing emotional awareness, and communicating clearly—not always successfully!

I take some comfort in knowing that before Jane Nelsen created her parental life-saving guide, *Positive Discipline*, her first five children (out of seven) gave her the same challenges as the rest of us. And like us, she threatened, yelled, nagged, and even spanked her kids. Thanks to her revelations and wisdom, we can forgo wasting precious years with our (first five!) children. By understanding more about the *Four Parenting Styles*, what children need, and by using appropriate Tools (see the Tools section later in this book), we can nurture, protect, and guide them as they grow into responsible young people.

Four Parenting Styles

There are four commonly recognized parenting styles: Permissive, Autocratic, Authoritative, and Neglectful. It's not unusual to fluctuate between the two extremes: Permissive (when we allow our children too much freedom and do too much for them) and Autocratic (when we don't allow children the freedom to make decisions). In both cases, children do not learn to take responsibility. When one of these styles becomes more predominant in our approach, we encounter frustrating behaviors in our children.

Permissive

"OK, but this is the last time."

Autocratic

"No way! I'm in charge here."

Authoratitive

"We're responsible for the family. We're ready to listen to your ideas and work together, for you to learn how to contribute and become more independent."

Neglectful

"I feel overwhelmed and cannot meet your needs consistently."

A Neglectful style is when parents feel overwhelmed with their own issues and cannot adequately take care of their children. In cases such as these, it's important to reach out for support from family, friends, or professionals.

The goal of this Toolkit is to help you move toward an Authoritative approach based on mutual respect and clear limits that are set with empathy. It takes time, patience, and specific strategies to build this kind of relationship. You'll find selected Tools that help build skills to lead with a more Authoritative style. These Tools are marked "Skill." For more in-depth information beyond this Toolkit, please refer to the books listed in the *Resources* section at the end of the book.

Permissive style (minimal control)

Sometimes, we struggle to set firm limits for our children's behavior and/or follow through. I can remember regularly cleaning up after our daughter because I was tired of nagging. Or letting her stay out with friends when there was homework to do because I felt guilty that she had few companions. However, when we give in or give up on a regular basis, children have too much control, possibly beyond the boundaries of safety and age-appropriateness. Not having firm limits and expecting their parents to regularly do things for them negatively affects children's self-efficacy and self-esteem.

Children who are overly dependent on adults and unaccustomed to limits or keeping agreements lose the chance to develop inner control. Without a firm structure to guide them, they may display a variety of behaviors interpreted by others as careless, inadequate, or even unruly and disrespectful.

Examples of a Permissive style:

- Doing things for children on a regular basis that they're capable of doing themselves
- Setting a limit and then giving in to a child because they keep arguing

- Allowing a child to change an agreement you have previously made together
- Allowing a child to do something that is not aligned with your values because others are doing it
- Lecturing, then allowing a child to do whatever they want anyway
- Fixing mistakes for children on a regular basis that they can fix and learn from

Reflection

When thinking about a Permissive style, consider these questions:

- What do young children learn about "limits" from a Permissive style?
- What do pre-teens and teens learn from a Permissive style?
- How does giving children too much freedom and control affect their self-esteem?
- What skills do children learn if someone else fixes their mistakes?

Autocratic style (maximum control)

In this approach, we tend to be *too* firm, make all the decisions, and take control of situations and planning to ensure it's "done right." This was especially true for me when I was in a hurry or felt pressured to complete my endless to-do list. My poor daughter became like a piece of luggage that had to fit into my schedule and be dragged along with me. No time to listen to her needs. My way or the highway!

With strong, outer control from a parent, children have few opportunities to exercise their decision-making and problem-solving skills. There's little chance to take responsibility for mistakes and learn from them. By not developing an inner locus of control, it's difficult for children to grow confidently into their independence.

Once out of their parents' supervision, children who have lived under too much control may continue to be rule-followers or, at some point, find ways to rebel overtly or discreetly. Particularly during preteen and teen years, children who have lived with too much control in their lives may feel insecure when on their own or, at the other extreme, be prone to risk-taking in unhealthy ways.

Examples of an Autocratic style:

- Micromanaging children's schedules and activities
- Having high expectations of perfection from children
- Dictating rules and decisions that children are expected to follow without previous discussion
- Feeling challenged if a child says "no" and demanding compliance
- Seeing mistakes as problems to be avoided

Reflection

Consider these questions about an Autocratic style:

- What do children learn about responsibility from the Autocratic style?
- How might pre-teens and teens respond to an Autocratic style?
- How might not giving children the chance to make decisions and control situations affect their self-esteem?
- What do children learn from making mistakes?

Authoritative style (shared control)

With an Authoritative style, mutual respect is nurtured through meaningful discussions, building emotional intelligence, solving problems together, and encouraging each other. Children are given opportunities to contribute to the family in ways that build independence and competence. Limits are set with empathy and firmness. Mistakes are opportunities for discussion and learning. This type of foundation supports children beyond the family into the community and adulthood.

As we know from the *Anchors and mirrors* section earlier in this chapter, the influence of a TCK's family takes on greater importance in their changing landscapes of community and location. In the *Challenges and Gifts for Children Tool #3*, we will explore the positive Life Skills that are nurtured through using an Authoritative style.

Examples of an Authoritative style:

- Recognizing children's feelings and developing their emotional language
- Giving children the chance to contribute to the family in age-appropriate ways
- Holding children to previously made agreements with empathy and firmness
- Giving children limited choices to practice decision-making and independence
- Using questions to allow children to think and then act responsibly
- Recognizing effort, progress, contribution, and your child's unique qualities
- Spending fun time together as a family, where everyone has a chance to lead and contribute
- Using mistakes as opportunities to learn and grow

How to lead with an Authoritative style

To lead with a more Authoritative style takes time and awareness. There are several online and in-person workshops based on democratic principles and social belonging for parents who want to invest time and energy to move toward this. (You will find more information in the *Resources* section.) An important part of changing our approach is to first examine our beliefs about parenting to understand the style we use most often. In the multicultural parent workshops I have led, it is clear how our own parents' styles, our culture, religion, and life experiences shape our beliefs about and approach to child-rearing.

Global Nomad parents are already aware of the importance of connection due to the added phenomenon of constant moving, transitioning, and settling in. You know how mobility affects your children's needs and behavior and that you need to take extra care to stay connected as a family and help them find their place in new settings.

Once we understand the needs and behaviors of children through the lens of connection—and belonging and significance—we see their behavior in a larger context. With practice, we can use the strategies of this approach to solidify our influence by choosing our words and actions more intentionally and with more conviction. Using the selection of Tools in this Toolkit is a good start.

My own teaching and parenting shifted dramatically when I started using Tools such as *The Amygdala: Fight, Flight, or Freeze Tool #7*, the *Ask vs. Tell Tool #9*, the *Encouragement Tool #18*, the *Limited Choices Tool #33*, and the *Routine Charts Tool #48*. There were fewer arguments and more cooperation, less nagging and more engagement, more positive moments, and more fun. When I experienced these results, I started sharing the information through parent and teacher workshops.

A large part of the foundation for my own parenting, teaching, and consulting with parents is from the Positive Discipline approach by Jane Nelsen. Based on the principle of social belonging, it helps us create an environment where children feel significant and can contribute in meaningful ways. The Five Criteria for the Positive Discipline approach guides parents toward developing a more Authoritative style.

The Five Criteria of Positive Discipline by Jane Nelsen:

1. Helps children feel a sense of connection, belonging, and significance
2. Is kind and firm at the same time
3. Is effective in the long term
4. Teaches valuable social and life skills for good character
5. Invites children to discover how capable they are, and how to use their power constructively

Reflection

Consider these questions to focus on the positive aspects of an Authoritative style:

- What do children learn about responsibility and communication from an Authoritative style?
- How might pre-teens and teens respond to an Authoritative style?
- How might this approach affect a child's self-esteem?
- How will children feel about making mistakes?

Neglectful style (overwhelmed)

Life on the road adds extra stressors on parents and families with a change of location, house, culture, language, systems, and so on. Argh! It is often the mom who is at the center of this whirling vortex and must keep things together. When we feel overwhelmed, taking care of ourselves and our children is more difficult. If you identify with a Neglectful style, it is important to reach out for help from family, friends, or professionals.

Supporting Tools like the *Therapy Tool #53* might be a good place to start to look for professional support. The *Know Your Limits Tool #29* offers steps to start taking more time and care of yourself. The *Chill Out Space Tool #11* offers steps to create a personal haven at home when you need to recenter yourself.

Reflection

Consider these questions to guide your thoughts toward getting support:

1. Which family members and friends can you connect with more often?
2. Where can you find professional help in your community or online?
3. How can your partner and children understand that you feel overwhelmed and need time to recenter yourself?

4. As you go through the Toolkit, which Tools help relieve your stress? Which Tools strengthen the family to work as a team?
5. What lifestyle choices can you make to help you and your family live healthier and more fulfilling lives?

Perfect Parents?

As parents, we sometimes switch between styles at different moments. We have responsibilities and stressors that make it hard to keep the machinery consistently running in harmonious balance. As much as we would love to be perfect parents, our own challenges and needs often collide with the desire to reach perfection.

Sara and Max Tiller (our guides through the 55 Tools) realized they were not perfect parents. As you follow them on their journey through the Toolkit, you will witness the shift toward a more Authoritative style. As parents, they will learn how to involve their kids more, develop their emotional language, let them learn from mistakes, focus on strengths, work as a team, and more.

Whether you identify more with Autocratic, Permissive, or Neglectful parenting, we are all on a journey toward building a better understanding with our families. Becoming a more Authoritative parent is a process that takes time and support. If you feel the need for more support, reach out to groups and professionals online or in your community. You are also welcome to get in touch with me.

What Do Children Need?

Regardless of whether they grow up in a changing, mobile lifestyle or in a constant environment, all children need to have their physical, social, emotional, and educational needs met so that they can thrive. Outlining all their needs in detail would make for a very large book indeed. In the context of mobile families who change schools and communities every few years, this section covers five key areas of child need, each of which can be supported by the use of Tools in this book. They are:

- Stable family environment
- Sense of attachment
- Sense of significance and belonging through positive contribution
- Recognition of unique temperaments
- Emotional language

As I mentioned earlier in the *Foundations for Global Nomads* section, mobility adds extra balls for TCKs to juggle: a limited sense of belonging, identity confusion, compounded feelings of grief, the repeated loss of friends, and a smorgasbord of cultural experiences. Because of these additional challenges, TCKs will benefit from more support, as outlined in the points above and covered in the Tools that follow later in this book.

Parents who take their children on a worldly adventure can reinforce positive aspects of the family structure. By processing emotions and memories, you are building essential skills for your child's continuing journey once they leave home.

But first, let's explore the fundamentals.

Stable family environment

When you build a house, laying down a well-built foundation ensures a long-lasting, solid structure. Whereas non-mobile families will have additional long-term stability through the community and home culture, for children who have moved several times during their childhood, a stable family environment is the equivalent of that foundation. In such an environment, parents regularly spend time with each child and together as a family. There is healthy communication and mutual support, an open-minded attitude, and a growth mindset. Ideally, the family works as a team to make plans, solve conflicts, and use mistakes as opportunities for learning. With this kind of foundation, children are better prepared to adapt to different cultures and schools.

The purpose of the Tools in this book is to build more awareness and connections within the family so that children have the skills and confidence to venture bravely beyond the boundaries of home.

Sense of attachment

This section briefly covers three areas of attachment: attachment styles, family attachment, and community attachment.

Attachment theory is about one's ability to relate to others based on their earliest connection with caregivers as an infant and young child. It describes four styles of attachment: Secure, Anxious, Avoidant, and Disorganized. Infants and children depend on their primary caregivers to fulfill their physical, emotional, and mental needs. Examples of these needs include food, water, comfort, clear communication, the recognition of emotions, and positive mental stimulation. The degree to which these needs are met creates an attachment style that affects a person's relationships in life. It is important to keep in mind that a mobile lifestyle can add more stressors on parents, with fewer support networks available to easily care for children. Having a stay-at-home parent is a true gift for young children: it enables them to start off with a more secure attachment style.

Attachment theory is a topic beyond the scope of this book, but one that merits exploration to understand more about how we relate to others. If you wish to explore your attachment style to achieve more satisfying re-lationships, seek out professional support.

Family attachment merits more attention when children move around the world. Parents and siblings are a child's stable universe when communities and locations shift the scenery in the background. Once the family attachment is secure, parents can use the community they live in to expand this beyond the home. Reinforcing the family's "glue" to main-tain healthy attachment is the goal of many of the Tools: the *Pitfalls and Perks of a Mobile Lifestyle Tool #1*, the *Family Mission Statement Tool #2*, the *Coat of Arms Tool #13*, and *Family Tools #21, #22, #23,* and *#24*.

On the subject of community attachment, Douglas Ota writes, "Humans need safe attachments to community." In his book *Safe Passage: How mobility affects people & what international schools should do about it*, he proposes that international schools are in a prime position to take care of mobile families as they arrive, settle in, and leave. Ideally, a Transition Team composed of counselors, teachers, parents, students, and administrators can help families attach to a new community and build connections when they arrive. And support them when they say goodbye.

Other local communities to connect to include embassies, businesses, churches, sports clubs, volunteer agencies, and interest-based groups. Their established network allows mobile families to step into a structure where they can both receive and contribute. Children who get involved in a community are gaining more feedback "mirrors" to use when "putting together" pieces for their "identity puzzle." As we know, establishing their identity is one of the challenges preteen and teen TCKs most often face.

If your new school or community does not offer a Transition Program, the Tools in this book provide ways to create attachments within the family, the communities, and the locations in which you find yourselves. As we know from Barbara Knuckles' model of "anchors and mirrors," it takes time to create attachments within your family, to community, and geographical location, but it is an important investment in your child's sense of self. As you explore the Toolkit, you will also enter landscapes within yourself to connect the pieces of your personal journey.

In the *Resources* section, there are links to groups such as Families in Global Transition (FIGT) and Safe Passage Across Networks (SPAN) that offer support for mobile families and schools regarding transitions.

Sense of Significance and Belonging

As we saw in the earlier *Social Belonging* section, it's a basic human need to feel love and a sense of belonging—first, in our family. This "need to belong" can be expressed through Mistaken Behavior Goals and Positive Behavior Goals. Children gradually learn which behaviors (or misbehaviors) affirm their place in the family, and later, in other social groups.

What parents would label as a "misbehaving child," Rudolf Dreikurs, in his book *Children: The Challenge*, calls a "misunderstood child." He refers to "misbehavior" as a child's "mistaken goal" to belong in whatever way he can. The mistaken goals are: Undue Attention, Misguided Power, Revenge, and Assumed Inadequacy. When the environment is set up for children to belong in positive ways, they experience Involvement, Independence, Fairness, and Competence.

Maslow's Hierarchy of Needs: a template to understand the importance of Love and Belonging and the goals of behavior

Below are summaries of behaviors related to the four mistaken goals. The parenting Tools in the Toolkit are specifically selected to nurture positive goals. In fact, most of the Tools create connections within the family that nurture positive goals of behavior.

Undue Attention would include behaviors such as: whining, nagging, interrupting, talking over others, more physical touch and desire for proximity, asking for (unneeded) help, wanting more "stuff," and possibly causing problems.

> Positive ways to *Involve* a child throughout the day would include: notice what they are doing (playing, reading, working on something), comment on how responsible, independent, helpful, strong, etc., they are, ask for help with tasks, problem-solve together, take time to play together, plan a date together.

Misguided Power could be arguing, ignoring adults' requests, refusing to do required tasks such as chores or homework, and even giving the "silent treatment."

> Positive ways to nurture *Independence* on a regular basis include: give choices, use routine charts, allow children to help with decisions, let them learn from mistakes, establish reasonable limits, and use empathy and firmness to hold children to agreements. If there are conflicts, withdraw and calm down.

Revenge is the spin-off of a lost power struggle. When a child has no other recourse than to accept a demand, they will find ways to "get back" at the other person. "I hate you!" or "You're the worst parent in the world" are both common jabs we have probably all heard at some point. Other forms of Revenge could show up as something you cherish being destroyed or disappearing, a sibling being hurt, or a refusal to join in with other activities. Unfortunately, when a child feels overwhelmed with feelings of Revenge, it can lead to abuse of social media or even self-harm.

> Ways to establish *Fairness* as a standard approach: don't take Revenge personally, acknowledge your child's hurt feelings, take a chill break before responding, acknowledge your part in the problem, share your feelings, focus on your child's strengths, and include your child in discussions and decisions.

Assumed Inadequacy is when a child "gives up" trying. It may come from a lack of recognition, losing too many power struggles, having too few opportunities to contribute and demonstrate independence, or feeling overwhelmed when too much is going on around them. Sometimes children with special needs or learning differences learn this behavior if there are no reasonable accommodations or the right kind of encouragement.

> Ways to build *Competence* as a daily part of life include: recognize strengths and past successes, break down tasks into small steps, ask the child to help with things they can do, and show appreciation for your child's personal qualities and their contribution to the family.

Leading with an Authoritative style, as outlined in the section *Four Styles of Parenting*, uses strategies that help children experience Love and Belonging through mutual respect with kind and firm guidance. Once this piece is stable, a sense of Esteem naturally develops and is intrinsic to the formation of children's identity, and later, self-actualization. Children who move around the world as they grow up have the additional challenge of creating their sense of self while on the move. It could be likened to putting the final pieces on an engine while it is running.

Behavior actually stems from three main areas: developmental level, beliefs about themselves based on their environment (as seen above), and temperament. Individual temperament is described in the next section.

Recognition of unique temperaments

Temperament is a lifelong piece that influences how a person will act and respond to life events. For mobile folks, this includes the ability to adapt to new situations, meet new people, build relationships, handle strong emotions, and deal with challenges, grief, and loss. For example, a more outgoing child who has normal sensitivity to stimuli and is in good general health can make a transition with greater ease. Conversely, a more introverted child who has some hypersensitivity may feel they have no control over the situation and will respond more hesitantly.

If you have more than one child, you know they can be as different as east from west. In her book *Belonging Everywhere and Nowhere: Insights into Counseling the Globally Mobile*, Lois Bushong writes about how different personality types react to the system in which they grow up. Imagine a creative personality growing up in a family or system with strictly defined rules and expectations. Or a very organized personality growing up in an unstructured household with no outside structure from an organization such as the military. A young person in a family or system that doesn't correspond to their temperament and uniqueness is more likely to feel confused, anxious, depressed, misunderstood, or even trapped.

Even as children mature, temperament usually remains fairly constant. As parents, an awareness of each child's temperamental differences can help us know how to best address their needs during stressful times. Usually, this is most apparent during preparation for the move, the transition, and the settling-in period.

Keep in mind that the number of moves your family has made will also influence how each of your family members will respond. They might have different reactions and respond at different rates. What may be interpreted as "temperament" could also be an indication of too many difficult transitions, where a child needed more support during various phases of a move.

Using a Temperament Assessment Scale designed by *Positive Discipline* authors, Jane Nelsen, Cheryl Erwin and Roslyn Duffy, temperament can be viewed on a scale between two extremes in the following areas:

1. Activity Level (High to Low)
2. Rhythmicity of physical functions (Predictable to Unpredictable)
3. Initial Response to new experiences (Bold to Withdraws)
4. Adaptability (Flexible to Rigid)
5. Sensory Threshold (Very Sensitive to Non-Reactive)
6. Quality of Mood (Optimistic to Pessimistic)
7. Intensity of Reactions to events (Intense to Mild)

8. Distractibility (Highly focused to Easily distracted)
9. Persistence and Attention Span (Persistent to Gives Up)

In the *What Do Children Need? Tool #4*, the Temperament Assessment Scale from the *Appendix* is one piece in understanding more about your child's needs.

Emotional language

Building emotional language to understand and express emotions appropriately is one of the most important gifts you can give your children. Emotional intelligence includes recognizing others' emotions as well as your own and learning how to self-manage strong emotions. It is having empathy for other people and animals. Learning to read others' faces, body language, and tone of voice is an aspect of emotional intelligence that grows naturally throughout the developmental years. Talking about these signals with your children helps expand their emotional vocabulary to read and interpret the emotions of others.

Experts recognize the importance of emotional intelligence for us to have healthy relationships and lead a fulfilling life. Social-emotional programs are part of many school curriculums. For mobile families, developing emotional intelligence supports the healthy expression of feelings, particularly sadness, which is inevitable when changing locations. This is an important key to avoiding compounded grief that can "undercut" other emotions later in life. Remember to recognize positive emotions, and celebrate key moments as well. This builds a balanced outlook and emotional resilience.

A keep-you-on-your-toes "twist" for Global Nomads is that different countries and cultures have their own syntax and nuances for communicating emotions and needs. It is comparable to different languages having their own grammar and idioms. For instance, a child looking at an adult when they are speaking is considered respectful in some cultures, while eye contact is considered disrespectful in other places. Other examples include hand gestures, greetings, table manners, expressing emotions, and appropriate topics for family discussions.

As you go through the Toolkit, you can choose which Tools for emotional expression are suitable for your family and situation. The *Caring and Firm Tool #10*, the *I-Statements Tool #28*, and the *Reflective Listening Tool #46* provide steps for practicing how to notice and share feelings.

Reflection

With your partner or your whole family, find a quiet time to sit together and discuss ways you can:

- Create structure and consistency in your home with schedules, meetings, activities, and shared responsibilities
- Offer extra support to your children for the challenges of being a mobile family
- Offer opportunities for your children to contribute at home and be recognized for it
- Develop ways for your children to make decisions (and mistakes!), be independent, and work out problems
- Recognize each child's unique temperament, strengths, and talents
- Nurture emotional language in your communication with your family
- Have fun together, explore and learn as a team

Control vs. Influence

For parents, one of the most challenging periods in our children's development is when they are old enough to go out into the world, away from our watchful eye. They start exploring with friends, traveling with school teams, hanging out in new places, or wandering into the world of the internet, full of its own wonders and dangers. It is impossible for us to shadow their every step to make sure they don't make a bad decision or take a wrong turn along the way. The good news is that we *can* prepare our children—by nurturing Life Skills that will keep them resilient when faced with the trials of the "big, bad world." In this way, our influence accompanies them like a guardian angel on their path toward independence.

In his book *7 Habits of Highly Effective People*, Stephen Covey describes this dilemma of control versus influence using "Circle of Control, Circle of Influence." It highlights how few things we can control, and how, basically, our attitude is the most important factor. With events out of our control, our attitude has the power to influence how we experience them, and in some cases, change the situation.

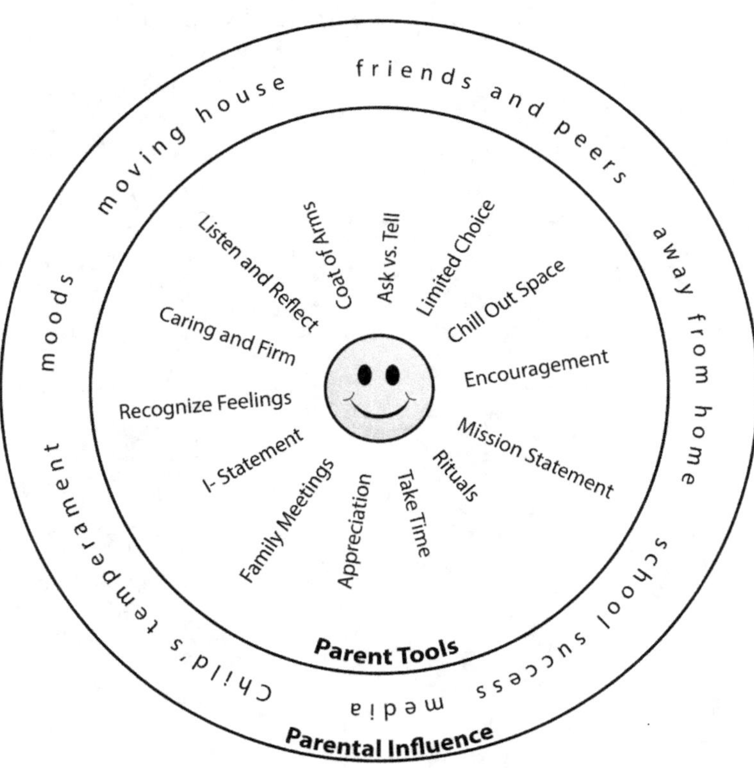

Parent Tools increase Parental Influence

As a parent, we can't control whether our child will be tempted to try cigarettes when with friends. But the close connection we nurture in our family can *influence* how they will respond and learn from the experience.

In this respect, we can control our home environment by using the Tools to tighten family bonds while building independence, thinking skills, and emotional resilience in children. Our influence is woven over time with threads of mutual respect, with caring and firm limits to guide their actions and decisions when away from home.

Be brave and persistent, have fun, stay calm, and find the positives in your adventure toward building more skills as Global Nomad parents. This influence will reach beyond the borders of your home.

TOOLS FOR THE
GLOBAL NOMAD JOURNEY

"You offer to your readers one piece at a time, thus allowing them the chance to put the jigsaw puzzle together by the end of the book."

Ashwin Sanghi The Krishna Key

The Tools

Now that you've learned about the *Foundations*, are you ready to tinker with these daily *Tools For The Global Nomad Journey?* They are a mixture of skills and activities that build connections with your own journey as a Global Nomad, within your family, and with those along the way. Put them together in your unique puzzle, suited to your family.

Navigating the Tools

If you have read the two previous sections, *Foundations for Global Nomads* and *Foundations for Parents*, the context will stand you in good stead. If not, it's still fine to jump straight in and start choosing and using the Tools.

Choosing a Tool

Different ways to choose a Tool:

1. Search for a Tool that will help with a specific challenge.
2. Try a new Tool every week or month.
3. Ask one of your children to choose a Tool.
4. Choose a random page and trust that the universe is guiding you to that Tool!

Completing the tasks

Under each Tool is a note to show whether it is an Activity or a Skill. A skill will require practice to learn something new, such as using questions instead of commands, pausing your emotional reaction before responding, or listening first.

To get the full benefit of a Tool:

1. Set aside enough time to complete some of the longer activities and skills.
2. Use a notebook dedicated to the work you will write down.
3. Post your family's creations in places they can enjoy and refer to them. Change them when appropriate.
4. Use visual and digital reminders to follow through on new skills, such as the Encouragement Tool #18, the I-Statements Tool #28, and so on.
5. Stay motivated by reminding yourself of the benefits you and your family will experience by learning new skills and doing the activities together.

Reference to other Tools

You will see other Tools mentioned in the explanation in some of the Tools. Go to those sections to learn more about them and how they support the Tool you are working with.

For instance, in the *Affirm the Positives Tool #6*, you will be referred to four other Tools: the *Encouragement Tool #16*, the *Reflective Listening Tool #46*, the *Self-Talk Tool #47*, and the *Chill-Out Space Tool #11*.

The Transition Cycle and the Tools

If we view the Transition Cycle in three phases, we can see how to support our families through each of the phases by choosing the appropriate Tools. At the center of the journey are the elements that shape identity—Family, Community, and Geographical Location. The significance of this was discussed in more detail in the section *Foundations for Global Nomads, Identity Formation*.

As your family travels through this cycle, feel free to use the graphic below as a quick reference for how to choose the Tools you need.

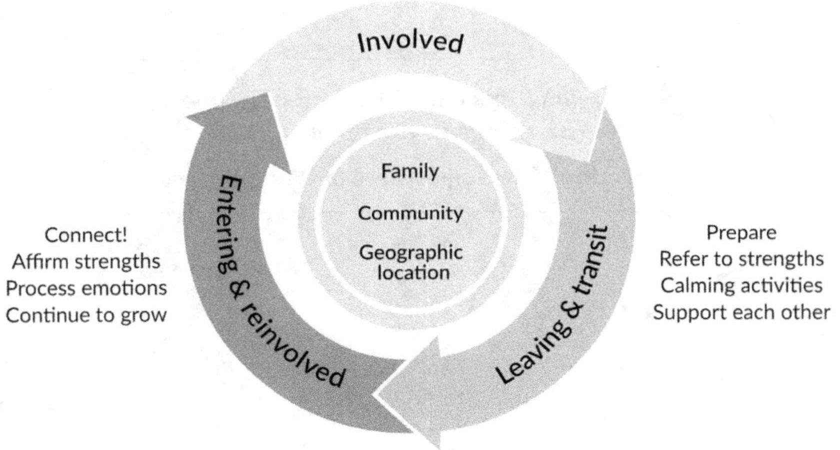

*There are different ways to support your family during
the Transition Cycle*

TOOL #1
Pitfalls and Perks of a Mobile Lifestyle
Activity

"What seems to us as bitter trials are often blessings in disguise."

Oscar Wilde   The Importance of Being Earnest

Do the Perks outweigh the Pitfalls in a mobile lifestyle?

Purpose

To identify the disadvantages and advantages of living a mobile lifestyle. To start building your Personal Toolkit.

Life Skills

Thinking, Problem-solving, Appreciation, Sense of Purpose.

Pitfalls and Perks

Sara and Max's parents had never sat down with them to talk about the disadvantages and advantages of a Global Nomad lifestyle when they were growing up. However, as the Tillers continue moving around the world, their teenage son, Jace, and ten-year-old daughter, Mariel, want to know why they can't just settle down in one place. They miss friends they have left behind in the different countries they have lived in. Jace is tired of always trying to fit into a new school every few years. As a teen, he wants independence from his parents but is constantly reminded of his reliance on them when they move to new places. Five-year-old Parul is still happy to be with her parents, brother, and sister without much concern for the moving process—yet.

Sara and Max sat with them one evening to discuss the challenges and benefits of their lifestyle. With paper and colored pens, they created their family's list of Pitfalls and Perks. They would refer to it many times over the next few years.

Do the Perks of a mobile lifestyle outweigh the Pitfalls? The authors of *Third Culture Kids: Growing Up Among Worlds* dedicate a whole chapter, *Challenges and Benefits*, to it. The act of writing out the plusses and minuses to examine, reflect on, and discuss them is one way to help each person answer this question. The parents' longer-term perspectives are essential to lead the kind of discussion that will structure the many thoughts and feelings about living around the world. This will serve as a scaffold for future family discussions and the children's own template for making sense of their mobile childhood when looking back.

What You Need

Materials: Paper, pens, colored pens (optional)

Time: 60 minutes

Instructions

Create a table like the one below. There is also a link in the *Resources* section to download a printable version.

Follow the steps below to create your family's personalized list of Pitfalls and Perks.

Step 1

Reflect on the questions below and write your answers in the downloaded table or your own version. Things you consider "challenges" go in the Pitfalls column. Things you consider to be "benefits" go in the Perks column.

- What things are difficult about living a mobile lifestyle?
- What are the wonderful experiences of such a life?
- How will the Pitfalls help prepare your children for life?
- What advantages will the Perks give you and your children later on?

Step 2

Think about ways you already address Pitfalls in your mobile lifestyle. What ways do you make the most of your lifestyle? Fill in the column for "Tools to Transform Pitfalls to Perks."

Step 3

Add more Tools to the middle column as you go through the Toolkit.

Example

Here are the Pitfalls, Perks, and Tools from the Tiller Family's discussion. Keep your list handy to refer to as you pick up new Tools throughout the Toolkit.

Pitfalls	Tools to Transform Pitfalls to Perks	Perks
Leaving friends behind.	***Ways to make the most out of our lifestyle!***	Explore different countries.
Changing schools, different systems.	We make sure we say goodbye to everyone.	Know cultures firsthand.
Having to fit in.	We stay in touch with close friends.	New recipes!
We can't have pets.		Exciting adventures.
Dependent on Mom and Dad for everything.	Kids can visit on vacations.	New languages.
Can't speak the language.	Take lots of pictures. Scrapbooks to keep memories.	Friends around the world. We can visit them!
Too many goodbyes.	Share experiences with other Global Nomads.	Make friends easily.
Staying in touch with everyone.	Find humor in our difficulties.	We can adapt more easily.
		Tight family unit.
Missing our grandparents.	Gratitude.	We talk with our grandparents more often, and they visit us.

What Happened?

Sara, Max, and the kids had a rich discussion about the pros and cons of their lifestyle. Jace felt more empowered about the knowledge and skills he had gained from growing up abroad. His parents listened to his thoughts about being more independent and set a time to talk about it in more detail. Mariel was very excited to think of herself as an international ballerina. Parul liked the fact that she could collect dolls from around the world. Sara and Max gained a stronger sense of their personal journeys that led up to this discussion with their own family. Everyone felt more clarity about who they were as a family and how to get the most out of their lifestyle.

They left the list on their refrigerator over the weeks following their discussion. Sara later put it away to take out when they had other talks about their mobile life.

Note: David C. Pollock and Ruth Van Reken have a more in-depth discussion on the comparison of Benefits and Challenges in *Third Culture Kids: Growing Up Among Worlds.*

Reflection

Use these questions to further guide you when referring to the Pitfalls and Perks list:

1. Which benefits do each of your children identify with?
2. What are some ways to increase an appreciation of the benefits?
3. In what ways might this list change over time?
4. How would a non-mobile family's values define what they consider to be Pitfalls and Perks?

TOOL #2
Family Mission Statement
Activity

"A family mission statement is a combined, unified expression from all family members of what your family is all about—what it is you really want to do and be—and the principles you choose to govern your family life."

Stephen Covey The 7 Habits of Highly Effective Families

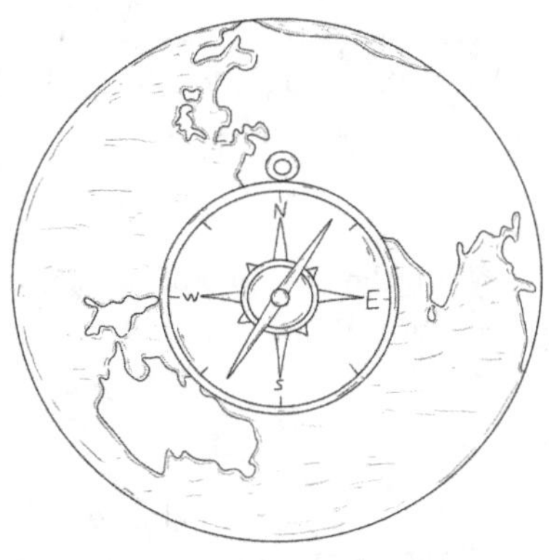

What is your family's "Why?"

Purpose

To clarify your mission and purpose for choosing a mobile lifestyle.

Life Skills

Thinking, Planning, Self-reflection, Leadership.

Why in the World?

Max got a promotion and, suddenly, the family was moving to Turkey. Sara dreaded telling their children about the change of plans. They had just spent four years in Belgium, enjoying the school, their new friends, and weekend trips to nearby European cities. Even though Sara grew up in a mobile family, leaving a place was always stressful.

One night, the reality of making another move crashed down on her. *Why in the world are we doing this*? Sara thought to herself. She felt like the ball in a pinball machine, randomly bounced around a board without any power to choose a path. As the hub of the family, she knew the emotional stress that awaited, as well as the practical things that would need her attention. Things like organizing the packing, sending school documents, saying goodbye, closing local accounts, and so on. In the middle of this list, she wondered what would happen with the yoga class she had just set up for her students.

She shared her thoughts with Max. They had a deep conversation about their lifestyle. When the question of "why" came up, they looked in the Toolkit for some inspiration.

"There are leaders and there are those who lead," says Simon Sinek in his book *Start With Why*. He tells us that the ability to inspire is not through offering external incentives, but through sharing a purpose that others feel moved to join. All successful companies and campaigns start with a mission statement. Just as Steve Jobs inspired his employees to "think different," Martin Luther King motivated a quarter of a million Americans to join his "dream" to change civil rights in the 1960s. Both had powerful "whys" that touched an inner desire to follow something meaningful.

Establishing a Family Mission Statement affirms your "why" and helps your children make meaning of the changing environments and influences.

When they understand the purpose of your wandering, they are more likely to be willing travel companions—at least until they create their own "why." Even if it's only a draft at this point, your "why" will become clearer as you live and learn along the way.

What You Need

Materials: Paper and pens, colored markers (optional)

Time: 30–60 minutes, plus follow-up sessions

Instructions

To create your Family Mission Statement, you can refer to the *Pitfalls and Perks of a Mobile Lifestyle Tool #1* for inspiration. Discuss Steps 1 and 2 below with your partner so you can lead the discussion with your children in Step 3.

Step 1

With your partner, use these ideas to start brainstorming reasons for living a global lifestyle:

1. Adventure
2. Personal growth
3. Service to others
4. Learn about other cultures
5. Have international friends
6. What your children will gain
7. Stay out of a rut
8. Career opportunities
9. Financial opportunities

Step 2

Discuss the values you and your partner hold as important. Create your own list or use some of the ones below as a starting point.

1. Family
2. Faith and spiritual life
3. Education
4. Service
5. Economic stability
6. Career
7. Work/leisure balance
8. Creativity
9. Integrity
10. Sustainability

Step 3

When you and your partner have clarified your reasons and values, include your children in the discussion. The abstract concepts in Steps 1 and 2 could be shared with your teen. Younger children will be capable of sharing their thoughts in Step 3.

Consider these questions to clarify the kind of family you want to be:

- What things are important for us as a family?
- What principles guide our decisions?
- What kinds of things do we like to do?
- What kind of feeling do we want to have in our home?
- What are our unique qualities and skills?
- How do we want to talk to each other and work out problems?
- What kind of friends do we want to have?
- What do we want to be remembered for when we leave a place?
- Who are our heroes and people who inspire us?
- How can we share who we are and what we have?

Step 4

From your brainstorming lists in Steps 1–3, choose your favorite reasons and write them on another piece of paper (or in a notebook for working on the Tools) as a basic draft. Then follow these steps:

1. Allow time for this draft to settle, i.e., sleep on it, meditate, or forget about it for a while.
2. Combine everyone's ideas and craft a statement you feel describes your "why."
3. You can create a family motto based on your discussion.
4. Post the mission statement in a visible place for the whole family to see.
5. When everyone is satisfied with the statement, create a good copy and hang it in a prominent place.
6. Revisit and review your "why" statement when making decisions or when faced with challenges such as moving and settling in.

What Happened?

Sara and Max set aside an evening after the kids had gone to their rooms, with a clear message of "This is Mom and Dad time, guys!" They discussed their reasons for living a mobile life, their values, and what kind of family they wanted to be. They made a date to look at it again in a couple of weeks. When they felt they had a strong foundation, they shared it with their children. Each child had something they wanted to add to the Family Mission Statement that Sara and Max had created.

They left the Family Mission Statement on their refrigerator for almost a month before finalizing it. Then Sara and Mariel created a poster with colors and images of the family, which they framed and posted in the hallway by their bedrooms.

Sara asked her Book Club group if they had a Family Mission Statement, but no one had heard of such a thing. She shared the idea and some of them were enthusiastic to create their own.

Here is the Tillers' Family Mission Statement:

We Are the Tillers!

We are a multicultural family living an adventure that fills our souls with rich experiences from many lands.

We learn from the wonder-filled diversity of the people and cultures we meet along the way.

We laugh, we cry, we love, we support each other, and we are resourceful and stay strong when faced with challenges.

We are grateful for all that we have and share it with our friends.

We weave all of this into our unique identity as the Tiller Family.

Wherever we go, we learn and grow!

Reflection

A mission statement is a project that may evolve over time. Reflect on these questions once you have started the process:

1. How can short-, mid-, and long-term plans help align your life with your mission?
2. Which regular practices and rituals help you stay conscious of your values?
3. In what ways do you communicate and model your values for your children?
4. Considering their ages and temperaments, what are your children's varying responses to the process of creating a mission statement?
5. In what ways might children benefit from being introduced to the idea of a mission statement early in life?

TOOL #3

Challenges and Gifts for Children
Activity

---

*"Imagine your child is now twenty-five years old
and has knocked on your door for a surprise visit.
What kind of person do you hope to see?
What characteristics and life skills do
you hope he or she has?"*

Jane Nelsen, Ed.D.   Positive Discipline

How to change Challenges to Gifts

Purpose

To identify challenging behaviors that you encounter with your
children and the Positive Life Skills you want to nurture in them.

Life Skills

Reflection, Goal Setting, Empathy, Perspective.

Challenges or Gifts?

Sara and Max were starting to realize how difficult it can be to raise three children, and more specifically, to do this while traveling around the world. Once Jace and Mariel passed their seventh birthdays, getting them to do what they were told to and help around the house became more and more challenging. Why couldn't they just listen and do what they were told? How had Sara and Max's parents done it so effortlessly? The world had changed, they realized, and electronic devices had certainly played a big role in changing the way the world works.

They decided to learn new ways to relate to their children, address problem behaviors, and hopefully, better prepare them for life. They opened the Toolkit to the Challenges and Gifts for Children Tool to start a deeper dive into their parenting journey and the Life Skills they wanted to nurture.

Jane Nelsen's quote at the start of this section highlights that all parents face challenging behaviors from their children. Some behaviors may be brought on or intensified by mobility. Like charting the route to your new country, this Tool is a map that guides you from the Challenges to the Gifts. Gifts are positive Life Skills you want your children to possess as adults—being responsible, caring, resilient, a thinker, a problem-solver, and more.

What You Need

Materials: A sheet of paper (A4, 8.5" x 11" or larger),
pens, pencils, and colored markers (optional)

Time: 20 minutes

Instructions

Create a table like the one described below. There is also a link in the *Appendix* to a template you could use.

Follow these steps to create your "map" of Challenges and Gifts for Children:

Step 1

Place the paper horizontally (landscape) and fold it into three equal parts. Label the left-hand column "Challenges," the right-hand column "Gifts," and the middle column "Parent Tools."

Step 2

Discuss the following with your partner:

- What challenging behaviors do your children display? For instance, are they argumentative?
- Write these in the "Challenges" column.

Step 3

Discuss the following with your partner:

- What Gifts (Life Skills) do you hope to nurture in your child? For instance, cooperation.
- Write these in the "Gifts" column.

Step 4

Discuss the following:

- What strategies do you currently use to address behavior challenges?
- Write these in the "Tools" column.
- Consider how they nurture the positive Life Skills you want your child to have.

Just like the *Pitfalls and Perks of a Mobile Lifestyle Tool #1*, the Challenges and Gifts for Children exercise is a map to keep parents "on course." Moving from the Challenges to the Gifts is its own journey, like crossing a gap to get to the other side.

The Tools in this Toolkit fill the gap between the Challenges and Gifts, like stepping stones. They build a stronger sense of belonging in children and a more cohesive family unit as you move around the world together. As you go through the Toolkit, add Tools that nurture the Life Skills in the Gifts column.

Keep this "map" handy to refer to, especially in particularly challenging moments. Share it with your children so they understand more about the Tools and the "destination" you are heading to—the Gifts. In doing so, they're more likely to feel involved in the process and cooperate.

Challenges	Parent Tools	Gifts (Life Skills)

Possible answers:

1. **Challenges:** Argumentative, unhelpful, moody, unmotivated, doesn't study, forgetful, aggressive, passive, too shy, too obedient, no friends, devices, sibling rivalry, etc.

2. **Gifts:** Cooperative, contributing, self-control, empathetic, communication skills, confident, articulate, resilient, responsible, respectful, thinker, problem-solver, worldview, leader, self-aware, caring, etc.

3. **Tools that work:** Spend time together, listen, caring and firmness, recognize emotions, hugs, limited choices, give responsibilities and chores, problem-solving together, express appreciation for effort and contribution, have fun together.

   Tools that don't seem to work: Rewards, time-out, nagging, distracting, bargaining, discussion, reminding, saying "no," praise.

What Happened

Once Max and Sara had created their "map" to get to the Gifts, they realized that many things they were doing *weren't* working. They referred back to *Foundations for Parents* and looked at the *Four Parenting Styles* section. They reviewed *How to Lead with an Authoritative Style* and noticed that very few of their present Tools fulfilled the *Five Criteria of Positive Discipline*. They noted that they gave too many orders, used rewards and punishment, and oftentimes, did too much for the children out of guilt. They realized they weren't always taking care of themselves, which translated into reacting impatiently toward the children when they (Max and Sara) were stressed out.

With the list of Challenges and Gifts in front of them, they set a goal to learn new Tools to offer their children the kind of gifts that would last a lifetime. They flipped through the Toolkit and wondered if they would be able to put the Tools into action and reach that goal. A different kind of journey awaited, and the adventurous souls that they were, they took the first steps. Onward!

Reflection

When considering new Tools to use with your children, consider these questions based on the *Five Criteria of Positive Discipline* in the section *Foundations for Parents—Four Parenting Styles—How to Lead with an Authoritative Style*:

1. Does the Tool you are using invite mutual respect?
2. Is it kind and firm at the same time?
3. Is it effective in the long term?
4. Does it teach valuable social and Life Skills?
5. Does your approach invite children to feel how capable they are?

TOOL #4
What Do Children Need?
Activity

"Make a conscious effort to provide experiences that increase the chances that children will develop perceptions and skills that will serve them throughout their lives."

H. Steven Glenn, Ph.D.
Raising Self-Reliant Children in a Self-Indulgent World

How do you choose schools based on your children's unique needs?

Purpose
To identify your child's strengths, challenges, and needs.

Life Skills
Perspective, Empathy, Appreciation, Sense of Purpose.

Different Needs

Before the Tillers moved to Belgium, Sara had investigated the international schools to find a good match for their children. The smallest school had 100 students and the largest school, 1,400 students. The programs ranged from British, American, French, International Baccalaureate, and various hybrids. Jace wanted a high school curriculum that would prepare him for high-ranking universities and have competitive sports clubs. Mariel was a good student but was more interested in extracurricular theater and dance. She also wanted a local dance studio where she could work with a professional teacher. Sara wanted little Parul in an early education program where children were allowed to explore and be active. Listening to her daughter's developing speech, she wondered if Parul would need a speech therapist. Not many schools had that kind of specialist available for families.

Going through the kids' interests and needs in her head felt like the weekend pandemonium in their home when trying to plan an outing they could all enjoy. Sara and Max hoped they could fulfill each child's desires and needs *and* keep the family on a unified path as they traveled the world together.

Most of us become more aware of our child's needs when there is a problem: a physical limitation, a health restriction, issues with academic learning, or other challenges. When planning a move to another location, investigate the available resources that will support your child's needs. With only one child, making decisions about new locations will obviously be simpler than with two or more children, each of whom will have their own needs.

What You Need

Materials: Two sheets of paper, pens, colored pens (optional)

Time: 30 minutes

Instructions

Refer to the sample drawing of a child's outline in the *Appendix* section or follow the steps below.

Step 1

In the middle of the page (landscape position), draw the outline of a child to represent your child. Leave room on both sides to write Steps 3 and 4. (If you are more motivated to draw the likeness of your child, then go for it!)

Step 2

Inside the outline, list your child's strengths in areas such as physical, social, emotional, cognitive, academic, and artistic. For instance, your child is friendly and caring, can express emotions clearly, is performing well academically in spite of the move, can draw well for their age, is a hard worker, disciplined, and neat, and so on. This list can contain as many strengths as you can think of.

Step 3

On the left side of the outline, list the challenges your child experiences: physical, social, emotional, cognitive, or academic. Are there any long-term challenges that require professional support or accommodation?

Examples: allergies, shy, more introverted, distractible, English is a third language.

Long-term challenges: uses a wheelchair, weak in math, physical coordination, emotional outbursts, doesn't make friends easily, depressed.

For transitioning to a new location, consider any specific challenges you have noticed. For instance, difficulty participating in sports, hypersensitivity to the reactions of others, that they are often unnoticed in a group, are insecure about school, have a rigid approach to things, any sibling rivalry that might occur, or often have emotional breakdowns before and after a move.

Step 4

On the right-hand side of the outline, list what you consider your child's needs to be, based on their challenges (left side).

Examples: Montessori, International Baccalaureate, competitive sports teams, curriculum extension for advanced students, speech therapist, wheelchair access, counselor groups, volunteer opportunities, etc.

Step 5

On the second sheet create two columns with the following headings:

1. Strategies to meet our child's needs.
2. Needs we must find support for.

For example, emotional breakdowns might be helped by taking time to talk about what's coming and then giving your child more information and choices so they have a sense of control. Since children go through different stages, some of these personal challenges may be temporary.

If they are long-term challenges that require professional support—such as occupational therapy, speech therapy, drug therapy, remedial reading, or math—you'll need to be aware of how to find that support when you move. Likewise, if your child needs special accommodations, communicating with the school before arriving is essential.

The Temperament Assessment Scale in the *Appendix* is another useful tool for understanding more about your child's needs.

What Happened

Sara and Max always knew how different each of their children were regarding strengths, challenges, and needs. Drawing out and listing these things on paper was helpful, if a bit overwhelming. With some more research, however, Sara connected with parents who shared more about the different school programs and communities. These parents also recommended local resources for supplementing what the schools offered.

It would be impossible to find the perfect school for all the kids to be completely happy. However, referring to the *Challenges and Gifts for Children Tool #3*, Sara and Max knew that learning to compromise and adjust to different environments were Life Skills they wanted their children to learn. Ultimately, it was up to them, as parents, to create as much stability as possible in their home for their children to feel connected and happy.

Reflection

If you have more than one child, this activity will highlight their individuality. You may also discover new points to think about for the same child as you go through another move. Use these questions to reflect on this process:

1. What is something new you discovered about your children and their needs?
2. What steps can you take to prepare and support each child?
3. Which of your children could benefit from discussing what you have written?
4. How can you use this information when choosing a new location?

TOOL #5
Adopt a Pet
Activity

"There is no psychiatrist in the world like a puppy licking your face."

Ben Williams   English Philosopher

Children learn Responsibility and Emotional Intelligence when caring for pets

Purpose

To enjoy the benefits of having pets in your life.

Life Skills

Responsibility, Empathy, Caring, Emotional Intelligence, Communication, Self-esteem, Confidence.

Puppy Love

Mariel came home from school one day with a picture of a puppy that was up for adoption. She begged her mom to take the puppy, but Sara knew what a big responsibility it was to have a pet, not to mention the hassle of traveling to different countries with a furry friend in the family.

She remembered how she had to leave her two cats with the neighbors in Cairo when her parents moved for the zillionth time. She had cried for months and then accepted the reality of her life.

But pets are wonderful companions and kids learn a lot about caring and responsibility, she thought. Sara doesn't want her children to miss out like she did. That night, she brought the Adopt a Pet Tool #5 to the Family Meetings Tool #23 to discuss what options might be possible for their family to include pets in their mobile life.

Having a pet is a wonderful experience for children to learn about responsibility, empathy, non-verbal communication, and the life cycle. "Developing positive feelings about pets can contribute to a child's self-esteem and self-confidence," writes the American Academy of Child and Adolescent Psychiatry in its May 2008 *Facts for Families* newsletter. Dogs are often used in therapy situations because they lift people's moods. For these same reasons, it's important to remember that having a pet can cause emotional stress when they need care or die. It can be costly and inconvenient to transport animals, and sometimes restrictions in certain countries make leaving your pet with someone else the best choice.

What You Need

Materials: Paper and pen. Colored markers, paper, and pens for everyone in the family (optional)

Time: 20–30 minutes

Instructions

First, find out your partner's thoughts about having pets. Then, call your family together to discuss ways to include pets in your life.

Step 1

Discuss the pros and cons of having a pet:

- The love and affection a pet gives, the fun, the companionship.
- The responsibilities of walking, feeding, and caring for a pet when it's sick.
- The problems of moving around the world with a pet.

Step 2

Discuss alternative ways to be involved with pets:

- Volunteer at a pet shelter.
- Help a neighbor with their pet.
- Be a pet sitter.
- Be a dog walker.
- Get involved with local pet protection agencies.
- Adopt a pet from a local pet shelter (if you're ready to commit long-term).

Step 3

Questions to consider:

- What options are available in your town or neighborhood for volunteering or helping?
- If you get a pet, who will be responsible for daily care or when you travel?
- How much will it cost?
- What if a pet gets sick? Where can you get help?
- What do you need to know about moving pets to another country?

Step 4

Decide on an option and follow through.

> ## What Happened
>
> Mariel started helping their neighbor, Mrs. Ali, walk her dog, Shazaam. She also went with Mrs. Ali to the vet when Shazaam needed his shots. When Mrs. Ali traveled, the Tiller family dog sat for her. The Tillers had the joy of including a pet in their lives and getting to know their neighbor better. Mrs. Ali and Shazaam were happy to have more friends in their lives.

Reflection

Consider the following questions to process this Tool:

1. What can children learn when caring for a pet, volunteering at a local shelter, or helping someone with a pet?
2. What cultural experience can your family gain from helping a local pet protection agency?
3. What kinds of pets travel easily?
4. What communication skills can your family learn through this discussion process?

TOOL #6
Affirm the Positives
Activity

"The more you feed your mind with positive thoughts, the more you can attract great things into your life."

Roy T. Bennett   The Light in the Heart

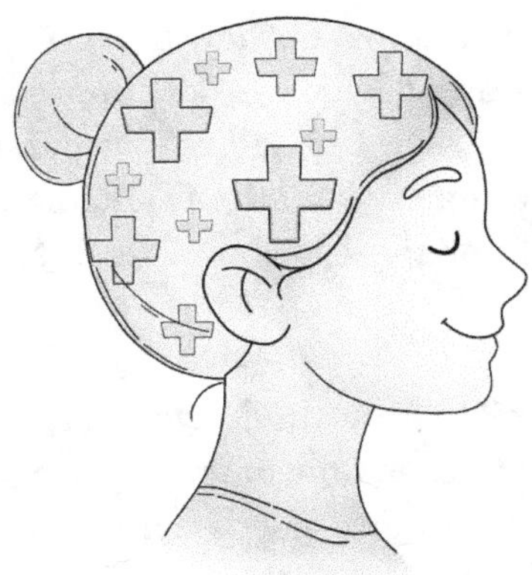

Affirming the Positives helps integrate all the experiences of your journey

Purpose

To nurture a positive growth mindset for more enjoyment of your life.

Life Skills

Appreciation, Positivity, Emotional Resilience, Self-reflection.

Off Track

It was six weeks before the Tillers' departure from Belgium, after four wonderful years. The kids' moods were like a roller coaster ride—excited about moving one minute, then irritable and withdrawn, the next. Max was overwhelmed at work and would come home exhausted and short-tempered. It felt like the family was bouncing around on some off-road track, and Sara was desperate to get them back on the "highway." She found Affirm the Positives in the Toolkit and presented it to her family.

Ideally, affirming positive things in your life is a daily practice. It guides thinking and emotions into a framework of appreciation where more difficult experiences can be seen from a broader perspective. This becomes especially important when your family is getting ready to leave a place and already preparing for the loss and disconnection that come with a move.

As a 2003 research article from the Mayo Clinic makes clear, "Positive thinking helps with stress management and can even improve your health." Combined with other Tools, such as the *Encouragement Tool #18*, the *Reflective Listening Tool #46*, the *Self-Talk Tool #49*, and the *Chill-Out Space Tool #9*, you can orchestrate a different vibration in your home.

What You Need

Materials: Paper (depending on the activity, a large piece of paper for the wall, slips of paper for writing on, colored paper to make ornaments), colored pens and markers for everyone in the family, Family Chat (a common phone app used by everyone in the family)

Time: 5–10 minutes

Instructions

Read the following options and choose the ones that are appropriate for your family's situation:

1. **Graffiti Wall:** Use a big piece of paper for everyone to write thoughts and feelings on and to draw on. Post it in a place where you can all see it and add to it as you prepare to move.

2. **Positive Pieces:** In the weeks before moving (or after arrival), write each positive statement about your time in the present location on a separate slip of paper and keep them all in a jar. Before dinner or at the Family Meeting, choose several to read out loud, or share them in a Family Chat group (see below).

3. **Celebrations:** Make colorful paper ornaments out of the above statements to hang around the house, or for seasonal celebrations.

4. **Round Table:** Before meals, each person shares something positive about their day.

5. **Family Chat:** Create a Family Chat group with your partner and children on one of your social media platforms. Use it for all members of the family to share positives in their daily lives. This can be a regular chat group that you use to stay connected wherever you live.

Prompts for Affirming Positives

- Notice daily situations and experiences from which you can affirm something positive.
- What have you learned while living in your present location?
- What positive lessons or memories will you be "taking with you" when you move?
- What have you contributed? What will you be remembered for?
- How does the experience connect with your mission statement?

What Happened

Sara used their Family Chat group to start posting her appreciation for the things she had learned during their time in Brussels. When Parul started drawing on her bedroom wall, Sara asked her to help put up a large piece of paper on the kitchen wall together with some markers. Slowly, everyone started sharing their own positive thoughts and lessons learned. Sketches and emojis appeared. The atmosphere around the house became more upbeat, with lots of humorous moments. Sara packed up the Graffiti Wall to look at the next time the family was feeling down about their lifestyle.

Reflection

Consider how focusing on positive things influences other areas in your life:

1. How does Affirming the Positives affect your brain and body?
2. How does Affirming the Positives influence your dynamic as a couple?
3. How can a positive mindset help the adaptation period in your next location?
4. How can we change our self-talk to positive statements? Also see the *Self-Talk Tool #49*.

TOOL #7
The Amygdala: Fight, Flight, or Freeze
Skill

"The workings of the amygdala and its interplay with the neocortex are at the heart of emotional intelligence."

Daniel Goleman   Emotional Intelligence

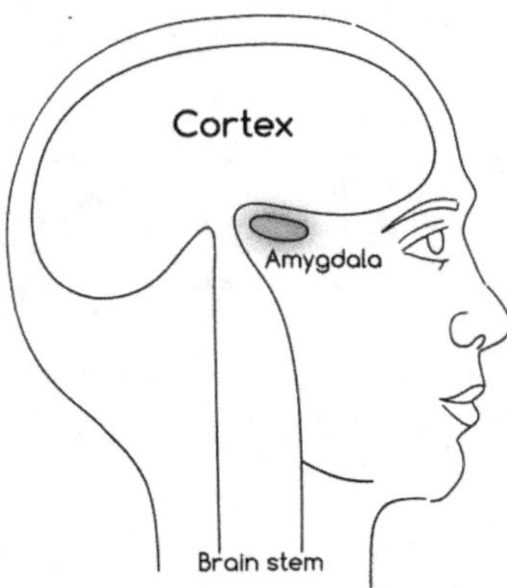

Managing strong emotions is an important skill for ourselves and those around us

Purpose

To understand the survival reaction of the amygdala and how to work with it when you have strong negative emotions.

Life Skills

Self-awareness, Emotional Intelligence, Empathy, Communication.

The Hijacking

Max came home to find toys, books, and dirty dishes in the living room one hour before his boss was coming for dinner. He felt his face flush with heat, his throat tighten, and the muscles in his hands tense.

"Jace, Mariel. Get down here, now!" he yelled. "What's this mess here? We have guests coming. I want it cleaned up, *immediately*," he commanded.

"But it's not my stuff," Jace tried to explain.

"No buts. Clean it up now."

Mariel started to cry.

Jace felt *his* face flush with heat and his throat constrict. He threw the toys in a box with too much force and broke some of them. At which point, Parul started to cry.

Sara walked in and looked at everyone's faces. "Whoa! Let's all pause for a second!"

Max and the kids looked at each other and said together, "Oh no! The Amygdala Hijacking!"

All parents should know about this small part of the brain that activates the survival instinct to protect us when there is danger. Once we understand how it works, we can help our children understand their strong emotional reactions better.

Throughout evolution, the amygdala has prepared the body for fight, flight, or freeze. It does this in the following ways:

- More blood goes to our muscles.
- Our senses become more acute and focused.
- Digestion is disrupted.
- The thinking part of our brain, the cortex, temporarily shuts off.
- We react from instinct instead of pausing to respond calmly and with clarity.

What the amygdala *can't* do is discern whether the perceived situation is a tiger, a nasty email, or a defiant child. Its purpose is survival. It disarms the thinking part of the brain, the cortex, to focus all strength on defense. When there is a strong emotion, such as anger or fear, the amygdala takes over and we are "held hostage" until the body and brain can rebalance. In the meantime, lots of damage can be done to relationships, and sometimes, physical objects.

Our first task is to recognize and work with our own strong emotions. Then, we can help children understand how to express their strong emotions and also to calm down when needed.

What You Need

Materials: None

Time: 30–40 minutes

Instructions

You may want to earmark this Tool for quick reference and refer to it often.

Step 1

Notice the sensations in your body: heat in the face or chest, tight muscles, an upset stomach, an angry voice, unclear thoughts, hyper-focused hearing and sight.

Step 2

"Pause" the amygdala's reaction with a slow intake of breath and by thinking a clear command inside your head: *Stop! Wait! Woah!* Exhale slowly.

Step 3

Engage the cortex by thinking:

- I feel angry because he's refusing to do what I want.
- I can respond in a different way.
- This is not life-threatening.

Step 4

Use your favorite calming-down strategy: breathe, tense and relax your muscles, laugh, count to ten, etc.

Step 5

Respond with one of the following options:

- I-Statement: "I feel frustrated when I see a big mess, because we're having guests."
- Caring and Firm: "I understand you want to go out and play and it's time to get ready for the guests."
- Don't argue: "I don't want to argue with you about this. I'm asking you to help us get ready for the guests."
- Agreement: "I'm counting on you to respect our agreement to keep the living room tidy. Thank you for helping."

What Happened

As soon as the family recognized it was an Amygdala Hijacking, they all paused while Sara talked to them:

"Let's take a moment.
We can work this out calmly.
We have more success when we work together."

Max and Jace used I-Statements to express their frustration:

"I feel frustrated when I come home to a messy living room because this is a family room," said Max.

"I don't think it's fair when you expect us to know you're having guests because we're using the living room, too," Jace replied.

Mariel and Parul said they didn't know about the guests, either. After this conversation, the kids felt calmer and agreed to work together to clean up the mess while Max and Sara got ready for the guests.

Reflection

Because this is a Tool that develops a skill, use these questions to guide your practice:

1. What situations trigger your fight-flight-freeze reaction?
2. Which of these steps do you already use?
3. Which physical symptoms do you notice in yourself?
4. How is the structure of an I-Statement different than other ways of expressing your feelings?
5. How does tone of voice affect communication?

Practice

Just as with any new skill, we need to create neural pathways in the brain and body for it to become more automatic. Find a time to practice when you are calm. With a partner (or with your phone to record yourself), use the steps below to rehearse this skill. With practice it gets easier and easier to stop the Amygdala Hijacking before it happens.

Think of yourself as an actor who needs to rehearse their lines over and over before going on stage.

Step 1

Call to mind a situation when you had a strong emotion.

Step 2

Recall the sensations in your body and your thoughts.

Step 3

Your partner can help act out the situation with words and actions.

Step 4

Go through the steps 1–3 above. Use a pause signal and say (or record) the statements for your situation out loud several times to prepare for your actor "debut."

Step 5

Ask your partner for feedback. Or listen to the recording of your voice and reflect on your preparation.

Reflection

After practicing this new skill, reflect on the process:

1. How many times do you need to practice for this Tool to feel natural?
2. How can recording your voice help you?
3. How different do you feel after using this Tool in real-life situations?
4. Which Life Skills can your children develop by learning to use this Tool?

TOOL #8
Animal Avatars
Activity

"An animal's eyes have the power to speak a great language."

Martin Buber Pointing the Way

What is your Animal Avatar's message?

Purpose

To identify personal strengths in a non-verbal, fun way.

Life Skills

Non-verbal Communication, Self-esteem, Tolerance.

The Wise Owl

Parul's kindergarten class was preparing a play about animals. Mariel helped Parul learn her lines. "I am the wise old owl who lives in the forest. I fly in the night and sleep in the day," Parul repeated after Mariel.

"What's your animal, Mariel?" Parul asked her sister.

"Mom, what's my animal?" Mariel asked her mom.

"Let's see!" Sara said, and they went online to learn more about animal avatars.

Identifying yourself with an Animal Avatar is a powerful Tool to support you on your journey. Sometimes referred to as animal spirits, indigenous cultures have used animals as symbols to affirm the qualities and strengths of their people through the millennia. In the Native American traditions of the Pacific Northwest and Canada, animal symbols carved into totem poles honor their history and traditions. Clans may combine these symbols as a pictograph of their unique story, and these can only be interpreted by one of their members.

In her article 'Utilizing Animal Metaphors in Child Psychotherapy: An Integrative Approach for Therapists,' Tricia A. Gordon writes that "Using animal metaphors makes it possible to discuss human situations in a symbolic way." Both children and adults can often draw strength and inspiration in a non-verbal way more effectively than through explanation.

What You Need

Materials: Paper, pens, online animal spirit resource, Animal Spirit
deck of cards (optional)

Time: 30 minutes

Instructions

Follow the steps below to discover and use the Animal Avatar Tool with
your family.

Step 1

Find Your Animal Avatar:

1. Reflect on the presence of an animal in your life or dreams, and
   research its symbolic meaning.
2. Alternatively, use an online quiz to determine your Animal
   Avatar.
3. Purchase a deck of Animal Avatar or Animal Spirit cards and
   learn to use them.

Step 2

How to Use Your *Animal Avatar*:

1. Reflect on and discuss the strengths, symbology, and messages of
   the *Animal Avatar* you choose.
2. Print or draw a picture of the animal and keep it visible.
3. Alternatively, create a collage to personalize its meaning for you.
4. Refer to your Animal Avatar to reflect on how its strengths and
   special qualities can guide or support you at different times.
5. Make a family Animal Avatar totem pole to combine everyone's
   animal, using printed pictures or drawings of them. Use the
   pictures to create your totem pole in any configuration that your
   family chooses.

What Happened

Sara and the girls chose their favorite animals. Parul chose the cat, Mariel, the horse, and Sara, the bear. They were inspired by what they learned about the qualities of these animals, and, after dinner, they helped Jace and Max determine their Animal Avatars. Jace was the eagle and Max was the buffalo.

They had so much fun that they printed pictures of their animals and placed them on the refrigerator to look like a Totem Pole. The buffalo and bear were at the base because they were big, strong, and moved more slowly. The running horse was placed above them. The cat was above the horse and the eagle soared on top of the family. They discussed how each animal's qualities and position made sense for each family member's place in the family. Sara made a mental note to use these when one of the children was facing a challenge or when they were going through their next move.

Reflection

The use of an Animal Avatar is one way to gain insight into each other's perspectives. As you answer the questions below, consider how to use these insights in different situations.

1. Which Animal Avatars of your family are the same/different, or live in the same environment?
2. How does each family member's Animal Avatar correspond to the similarities and differences between their personalities?
3. What special characteristics and strengths does each animal have?
4. How can you use this information to understand more about how each person handles change when you are transitioning to a new environment?

TOOL #9
Ask vs. Tell
Skill

"Asking enables others to lead... to bring their best thinking to the table, and demonstrate leadership regardless of their position or title."

Sinive Seely Forbes Magazine, October 2019

Asking questions engages and inspires thinking

Purpose

To inspire thinking, invite cooperation, and develop self-esteem through the use of questions rather than commands.

Life Skills

Listening, Communication, Empathy, Respect, Thinking, Problem-solving.

What's Wrong?

Max decided to take the kids to explore the park near their new home. In an attempt to speed things up, he started telling everyone what to do: "Jace, grab some drinks and bring them to the car. Mariel, help Parul with her shoes and coat and make sure she has her doll. Put the picnic in that box and close it up."

Instead of having the desired effect of speeding things up, it seemed to Max that they actually moved more slowly. Frustrated, he asked, "What's wrong with you guys? I thought you wanted to explore the park this morning?"

The kids mumbled something and started moving a *little* faster.

How do you react when someone gives you a command? In safety or emergency situations, we must obey and not object to commands. However, in everyday life, most people have a not-so-cooperative response to commands. The Fight, Flight or Freeze reaction of the Amygdala kicks in. Ask vs. Tell is a Tool that is valid at the workplace as well as at home because a question more easily bypasses resistance in the brain that a command can cause.

In her 2019 *Forbes* article 'Three Reasons Why the Best Leaders Ask Rather Than Tell,' Sinive Seely emphasizes the importance of this Tool in the workplace. Are the skills of thinking, leadership, confidence, and ability on your list of desired Life Skills for your children?

What You Need

Materials: The list of "tell" statements (see below),
a notebook, a pen or pencil

Other: A partner, or your phone to record yourself

Time: 15–20 minutes

Instructions

To use this Tool, you need to practice changing statements to questions. Follow the steps below to learn to use this skill more easily.

Step 1

Find a partner to do this exercise with, or record yourself on your phone.

Step 2

Read the following "tell" statements in your best "commanding" voice:

1. "Put your jacket on the hook."
2. "Change your shoes."
3. "Do your homework."
4. "Get ready for bed."
5. "Turn off the computer."

Step 3

Read the following "ask" statements in your best "curious" voice:

1. "Where do we hang our jackets?"
2. "Which slippers (shoes) will you change into?"
3. "What is your plan to do your homework?" "How will you get your homework done before dinner?"
4. "What do you need to do to get ready for bed?" "What do you need to do when it's 9 pm?"
5. "What was our agreement about playing games?" (Assuming you had a previous agreement in place to refer to). "Can you turn off the game by yourself, or do you need my help?"

Step 4

If you recorded the statements:

- Listen to both sets of statements.
- Notice what you're feeling, what you're thinking, and what you're deciding about the person saying them, about yourself, and the situation.

If you were the partner:

- Share what you were feeling during both sets of statements. What were you thinking about the person saying them, about yourself, and the situation?

Step 5

Change these statements from "tell" to "ask" with question words: **Who**, **what**, **where**, **when**, **how**. (Avoid "why" and yes/no questions.) Practice the questions on your own before using them with your children:

Tell	Ask
Pack your clothes!	Where will you pack your clothes?
Throw out your old toys/clothes!	*(Complete this column, then see suggestions below)*
Take pictures of your friends before we leave!	
Find out about your new school on this website!	
Make a map of our travels!	
Come here so we can talk!	

Suggested questions

Note: Avoid "yes/no" questions and "why."

- "What will you pack your clothes in?" (Choice: "This box or that bag?")
- "Who can you give these old toys/clothes to?"
- "When will you get pictures of your friends?"
- "How can you find out more about your new school?"
- "What are your ideas about keeping a map of our travels?"
- "Where would be a good place for us to talk?"

What Happened

Sara noticed how the kids reacted to Max's commands. She started asking questions to get their ideas so they would feel more involved in the process:

"Jace, what do you want to put the drinks in? Will you use this cart or carry them to the car? Mariel, what can you do to help Parul get her coat and doll? What should we put the picnic in?"

Parul chipped in, "What can I do to help, Mommy?"

Like magic, all three children got more engaged in the preparation and moved faster. Max was happy, the kids were happy, and Sara had three hours alone to work on her book.

Reflection

Once you have practiced using questions instead of commands, reflect on the following questions to consider how to make this Tool a daily habit:

1. How does your body feel when hearing a "tell" statement?
2. What makes it more difficult to use questions when you're in a hurry?
3. How can you train yourself to ask questions (instead of telling)?
4. How does asking questions strengthen the Positive Life Skills on your *Challenges and Gifts Tool #3* list?

Also, see *The Amygdala Tool: Fight, Flight, or Freeze Tool #7* for more information about how we respond.

TOOL #10
Caring and Firm
Skill

"Being kind and firm at the same time is essential to meet the primary need of all children—to feel a sense of belonging and significance."

Jane Nelsen, Ed.D. Positive Discipline

Get ready for the balancing act of being Caring and Firm!

Purpose

To find the balance between showing empathy and setting clear limits.

Life Skills

Empathy, Emotional Resilience, Understanding Limits, Cooperation, Respecting Agreements.

Five More Minutes!

The Tiller Family was in the park near their new home. It was getting close to dinnertime. Max called the kids to leave but they kept playing with newly made friends from the neighborhood. "Can't we stay longer?" the kids pleaded.

"OK, five more minutes," Max said.

"What about dinner and homework?" Sara asked.

"Let 'em have some fun, hon. It's been a rough transition for them," replied Max.

Five minutes later, Sara called them again. No response.

"Let's get going, kids," Max called. No response.

"If you want to come back to the park again you'd better get over here, *now*!" Sara yelled.

"Aww, Mom, we were having so much fun," the kids complained as they walked home.

Sara and Max also felt bad about what happened. They wanted their kids to have fun, but they also needed to go home. Setting firm boundaries with kindness was a challenge they wanted to handle more effectively.

Consider the four styles of parenting: Permissive, Autocratic, Neglectful, and Authoritative. Firmness without kindness becomes Autocratic. Kindness without firmness leads to Permissiveness.

Children need a caring attitude to know they have been heard *and* clear limits to feel safe under their parents' authoritative care. This caring attitude builds connection, without the need to "fix" the problem or make the person feel better. Once this is done, it's easier for the child to hear a "firm" statement about what you expect in the situation. "I understand you want to play more *and* it's time to go home now," recognizes the child's feelings and shows that there are also limits from Mom and Dad's side.

What You Need

Materials: The statements in the charts below, some paper, and a pen

Other: A partner, or your phone to record yourself

Time: 20–30 minutes

Instructions

Changing our language means changing our thinking—something that takes time and practice. Follow these steps to practice this skill:

Step 1

First, acknowledge the other's emotions before stating what you need. For example, "You feel frustrated because we have to move again."

Step 2

Then add, "And we will find ways to make the most of it as a family, like we always do."

Step 3

Do the following activity with a partner, or record yourself to listen to the sentences:

- First, read the statements using "but."
- Then, read the statements using "and" instead of "but."
- Notice the different feelings in your body and brain between "but" and "and."

Read these statements	Change BUT to AND
"I know it's hard to stop playing *but* it's time to go home."	"I know it's hard to stop playing *and* it's time to go home."
"I realize it's difficult to pack up *but* we need to get ready for the movers."	
"I see you are angry *but* it's better to talk when we have both calmed down."	

Step 4

For the next part, in a notebook, rewrite the statements below (see example) and then practice saying them.

Read these statements	Rewrite the statements to be both Caring and Firm
	1. Identify the feeling and 2. Calmly state what needs to be done.
"Complaining doesn't help. We need to leave now."	"You feel frustrated about leaving *and* we need to leave."
"Stop yelling at me. You need to be respectful."	
"Toma, it's time to clean up. *It's time to clean up!* Dinner's ready."	

Possible responses:

- "I understand you feel upset about leaving *and* I need your help to pack up and get home."
- "I hear from your voice that you're angry *and* we can still use respectful voices (*and* I prefer to wait until your voice is as calm as mine)."
- "I know it's hard to stop playing *and* it's dinnertime."

What Happened

After the kids went to bed that night, Sara and Max practiced using "and" statements until they felt comfortable saying them. They went to the park the following afternoon to try out their new Tool. When it was time, they called the children to go home. Since the children had already trained their parents to give in to their pleading, they tried to persuade Sara and Max several times.

"We know it's hard to stop playing," said Sara.

"*And* it's time to go home," said Max.

Each time the kids asked for more time, Sara or Max responded with a Caring *and* Firm statement. They felt more and more confident using this new Tool as they saw how the kids responded. They tried some of the following:

"You're having lots of fun *and* we can come back tomorrow."

"I see you feel frustrated *and* we can skip or walk on the way home to change your mood."

"It's normal that you want to stay *and* we want to go home together."

The children got the idea that Mom and Dad were serious about going home. Someone started a game of tag and they ran most of the way home. Sara and Max gave each other a high five, feeling like benevolent leaders instead of nagging parents.

Reflection

Use these questions to reflect on how your brain and body respond differently to "but" and "and":

1. How do you feel when you hear "but" and when you hear "and"?
2. How do children respond differently to "but" and "and"?
3. What Life Skills do children learn when there is empathy *and* clear limits in a situation?

TOOL #11
Chill Out Space
Activity

"Don't try to reason with the unreasonable."

Unknown

A Chill Out Space is NOT a punishment

Purpose

To train our children and ourselves to reset the brain and nervous system when feeling strong emotions.

Life Skills

Emotional Intelligence, Respect, Self-care.

> # Chill Out!
>
> "You're the worst mommy in the world!" Parul screamed when Sara reminded her about their agreement to clean up her toys before bed. For good measure, Parul threw some toys at her mom. Sara felt hurt that their adopted daughter would say and do such a thing. However, she recognized Parul's hurtful statement as a response to feeling powerless as well as tired, despite their previous agreement about cleaning up.
>
> Sara realized Parul's Amygdala—the Fight-Flight-Freeze part of the brain—was engaged, so she refrained from yelling back at her daughter. Instead, she got down to Parul's eye level and said, "Honey, you feel very angry right now. This is a good time to go to Parul's Parlor and settle down."
>
> "No!" screamed Parul.
>
> "Do you want to go there by yourself or do you want me to take you?"
>
> "No!" Parul screamed again.
>
> Sara put her arm around Parul's shoulder and, without a word, guided her to the tent they had set up earlier in the week, Parul's Parlor.
>
> "You can play with your dolls, draw, or just hug your pillow. It's your choice, Parul. I'll be in the kitchen when you're ready to find me."

Think of a time you felt a strong emotion that dictated that you did something you later regretted. When the Amygdala is engaged, the cortex isn't. We can reset our brain and nervous system by going to our Chill Out Space. Once we have calmed down, we're able to have a reasonable conversation with another person.

A child's personal Chill Out Space is a space where they can reset their brain. In this way, we are preparing them to separate strong emotions from behaviors that might cause more problems. See *The Amygdala: Fight, Flight, or Freeze Tool #7* for more information about emotion management. By gently insisting that your child use this space when they're upset, we can train them to take responsibility for self-regulating in emotional situations.

What You Need

Materials: Soft toys, pillow, blanket, drawing materials, clay, or other calming activity

Time: 20–30 minutes

Instructions

Create a Chill Out Space

Follow the steps in the example below to create Chill Out Spaces at home.

Mom/Dad *Find a time when you're all calm, and emphasize that this is not a punishment.*	Child
1. "Parul, you know when you feel angry or upset and can't calm down? Let's make your own quiet space for you to 'chill out' in."	"Yes. OK."
2. "Do you want to make it in this corner or under that table?" (It needs to be a permanent place.)	"In the corner."
3. "What do you want to put in there?" (No electronic devices!)	"A pillow, this blanket, my bear, my Lion books, crayons and paper."
4. "What shall we call it?"	"Parul's Parlor."

Use the Chill Out Space

Follow the steps in the example below to use Chill Out Spaces at home.

Mom/Dad	Child
1. "It looks like you're really angry. This is a good time to go to Parul's Parlor to calm down."	"No!"
2. "You can go by yourself, or I can take you there. Which do you prefer?"	"You take me!"
3. "Here we are. You can play with the things you put in your space."	"I want you to stay with me."
4. "I'll be in the kitchen when you're ready to come out."	"Hmmph!"
5. (When your child has calmed down and comes out.) "Hi there. It's nice to see your smile again. Do you want a hug?"	"Hi. Yes!"
6. "Do you want to do something together or play by yourself?"	"I want to play with my dolls."

What Happened

Fifteen minutes later, Parul came into the kitchen to show Sara how she had fixed her doll's hair in ponytails.

"It's time to get ready for bed. Do you want to tidy up by yourself, or do you want help?" Sara asked.

"Can you help me, Mommy?" replied Parul. They put on a song, dancing and laughing as they went, and had finished tidying up by the time it ended. Parul decided she wanted to get ready for bed by herself. "Maybe we can do *your* hair tomorrow, Mommy," she said.

Create a Parent Chill Out Space

As parents, we also need a space to give our bodies and brains a chance to reset to a calmer mode. Consider the following when creating your Chill Out Space:

1. It is a place to be unavailable to the family for short periods of time.
2. You can have your favorite books, music, or other items there to help you re-center.
3. You serve as a model for your children in terms of how to use it: "I feel upset right now and want to chill out before we continue talking. See you in a little while." Go to your Chill Out Space and take time to calm yourself down.
4. Your child may direct you to your Chill Out Space: "Mommy, Daddy, it sounds like you're angry. Maybe this is a good time to go to The Beach."
5. If you decide to go to your Chill Out Space but your child objects, calmly insist, using the 'I feel' statement in Step 3 or the following Tools: *Connection Before Correction Tool #16* and Caring and *Firm Tool #10*.

Reflection

This Tool is closely connected to *The Amygdala: Fight, Flight, or Freeze Tool #7*. Once we recognize the brain and body's reaction to strong emotions, we're on the right track to nurturing self-awareness and self-control in our children—and ourselves! Use these questions to reflect on this Tool:

1. How can learning to calm down help your child separate their behavior from them as a person?
2. How will this approach contribute to the development of important Life Skills for your child?
3. What do children learn when Mom and Dad take their own "chill time"?

TOOL #12
Chores Chart
Activity

> *"Never do for a child what he can do for himself. Children only become irresponsible when we fail to give them opportunities to take on responsibility."*
>
> **Rudolf Dreikurs and Vicki Stolz** Children: The Challenge

---

Creating a Chores Chart together with your child is more effective

Purpose

To structure a child's contribution to the family. To increase involvement and a sense of pride.

Life Skills

Responsibility, Teamwork, Cooperation, Organization, Self-efficacy.

Whose Job Is It?

Sara asked Jace for the hundredth time to take out the garbage. *Why couldn't he just do it the first time?* she thought to herself. His nonchalant "Sure, Mom" was as irritating to her ears as a knife scraping on stone. Frustrated, she put the garbage bag in his room.

Parul walked by, confused. "Why did you put garbage in J.J.'s room, Mommy?"

When Jace found the garbage bag in his room, he yelled, "I told you I'd take it out! Now my room stinks!"

There's got to be an easier way, Sara thought to herself. She gazed over at the Toolkit and wondered.

'The Science of Family Activities,' an article published as part of the *Listen First* series by the UN Office for Drugs and Crime, states that: "Social studies show children who do household tasks grow into happier, healthier, more generous partners and well-adjusted adults." Let's face it, where else will children learn a strong work ethic if not from their parents?

Children feel useful and important when they can do grown-up things. They also love feeling independent and respected. Everyone contributes their ideas when creating a chart to organize chores around the home. In this way, your kids can feel independent when doing chores, and the chart becomes the "boss," not you. If they don't follow through, a conversation about how they will organize themselves to get it done is a good exercise in communication.

Perhaps one of the most difficult things to keep in mind is that chores are a contribution to the family, not connected to an allowance. Getting an allowance is discussed in the *Money Tool #38.*

What You Need

Materials: Paper, pen

Time: 40–60 minutes

Instructions

There are three ways to set up and use chores to help your children be more involved and feel more independent and competent:

1. Regular chores.
2. Paid chores
3. When preparing for/settling in after a move

Regular chores

Kids can contribute to the family by helping with daily and weekly chores around the house. The discussion about setting them up gives everyone a chance to share suggestions and creates buy-in. Even with buy-in there will be moments when they forget or don't feel like doing it. Kids need time to make this a habit. Ask for their help to keep the agreement and show faith that they will.

- Discuss the different jobs and responsibilities that you, as parents, are happy to take care of.
- Which jobs around the house can your kids do? If you have more than one child, they can share and switch weekly.
- Make an agreement they can keep. For example, based on the frequency or difficulty of a task, or if it is dependent on other things.
- Discuss what they must do and a timeframe for getting it done.
- Allow your children to help create the chart with the different chores, days, and frequency.
- Place the chart in a visible place.
- Regularly thank them for their help.

- Don't do the chores for your children if they don't do them. Instead:
  - Refer to the chart.
  - Use questions and encouragement to help them feel supported.
  - Ask what help they might need.

Paid chores

In general, chores are *not* paid. However, kids can earn money by doing bigger jobs that require a lot more time and effort.

- Make a list of bigger chores you are willing to pay your kids to do. For example, washing windows, cleaning out cupboards, cleaning up the garage, and so on.
- Decide on what they can earn doing these chores, and post it on the list.

What Happened

Sara and Max discussed setting up a system for chores and extra jobs around the house. They got the whole family together and presented it as a team project. After they brainstormed their list of chores and discussed what each entailed, Mariel made a weekly chart to write the different chores in. Everyone signed up for what they wanted to do. Some of the less desirable ones like taking out the garbage were divided up and alternated week by week.

Parul was excited to be able to help out the family. Mariel enjoyed organizing it. Jace was interested in doing extra jobs to earn some pocket money. Mom and Dad felt this was a positive step toward being more connected and productive as a family.

When someone forgot to do a chore, the kids reminded each other to do it. Mom and Dad spent more time acting as cheerleaders instead of nagging. They asked one of the children about needing extra support a few times. Amazingly, the kids started asking each other if they needed help when doing a more difficult chore.

When preparing for/settling in after a move

The time before, during, and right after a move is an emotional period. When kids contribute they feel a certain degree of power. They are also building self-esteem along with practical skills.

If children have been doing regular daily chores, asking for their help when moving will be easier. If they are not familiar with a Chores Chart, it is also a good time to ask them to help the family during the moving process.

Stay caring and firm (see the *Caring and Firm Tool #10*). There's a balance between being empathetic to your children's feelings about moving and staying firm in your expectations that chores will get done and everyone will work as a team:

- Discuss the different jobs that need to be done before/after the move.
- Let the children choose which ones they will do—older children can have more responsibilities.
- Discuss what they must do and a timeframe for getting it done.
- Create a chart together.
- Place the chart in a visible place. Everyone can check off jobs once they have been completed.
- Regularly thank them for their help.
- Celebrate once a week. Focus on the teamwork and what is getting done.
- If a child is having trouble getting a job done, ask what they need for support.
- If you feel it is appropriate, do a job together with your child to show support.

Preparing for the move

Here is a short list of ideas to inspire your family when discussing jobs to be done before moving:

- Clear out old toys, clothes, books, etc.
- Kids decide where to donate some of their possessions.
- Help with packing personal items and household items.
- Plan "goodbye" outings to favorite places.
- Take pictures of memorable people, places, and things.
- Plan and organize meals for the family.

Settling in after arrival

Here are some ideas for jobs to be done to help the family settle into a new location:

- Unpack and organize personal items.
- Help parents/siblings unpack and organize household items.
- Clean up after unpacking.
- Organize and make meals.
- Connect with the neighbors.

What Happened

The Tiller family had been using their Chores Chart for several months before the move. When it was time to discuss sharing the jobs for getting ready to go, the children jumped in and started planning who would do what. Working together as a team helped everyone overcome some of their sadness, worry, and fears about the transition.

During the chaos of packing, Sara and Max made sure to have regular *Family Meetings Tool #23*. They revisited their *Family Mission Statement Tool #2* to stay focused on their purpose. Before the moving company came, the family packed up their *Family Heirloom Tool #21*, knowing it would be one of the first things to unpack in their new location.

Reflection

Every family will decide if and how they want to include children in the daily workings of their family life. Here are some commonly asked questions about this Tool:

1. What age-appropriate tasks can children do?
2. What happens when chores are paid versus unpaid?
3. What are your culture's perspectives on age, gender, and class with regard to your children doing chores?
4. How do these cultural perspectives contribute to a child's perception of their place in the family?
5. What Life Skills does this Tool nurture?

TOOL #13
Coat of Arms
Activity

"Symbols help shape and communicate the beliefs, values, and knowledge of a culture or an individual. Understanding how identities are formed helps promote understanding and respect for different perspectives."

www.terraamericanart.org

A family Coat of Arms affirms diversity and cohesion

Purpose

To recognize individual and family qualities and strengths and build family cohesion.

Life Skills

Self-awareness, Confidence, Sense of Identity, Teamwork.

Family Symbols

Mariel brought home the template for a Coat of Arms to do a school project on the Middle Ages. As she and Max worked on it, Sara remembered seeing family crests at her relatives' homes in England. Her aunts, uncles, and cousins had proudly explained what the different symbols meant. She thought it would be a fun family project they could carry with them on their journey.

We know from the earlier *Anchors and mirrors* section that "anchors" give us stability and provide feedback about who we are in our family, community, and geographical location. TCKs often face the challenge of answering the questions "Who am I?" and "Where am I from?"

Tools such as the Coat of Arms affirm both personal identity and a sense of family identity. Your family's Coat of Arms can be the *Family Heirloom Tool #21* that you hang up as an arrival ritual and pack up as part of your leaving ritual.

What You Need

Materials: A Coat of Arms template on a large (A3) piece of paper (see the *Appendix*), colored pencils and/or markers, pictures and examples of Coats of Arms

Time: 60–90 minutes

Instructions

Take time to discuss how a Coat of Arms can be a unifying symbol for your family to carry with you wherever you go. Use these discussion points to help lead this activity:

- We each have our special place in the family.
- Which symbols can we use to represent our different interests and strengths?
- How can we live together in harmony with our differences and similarities?
- What kind of theme song represents who we are as a family?

Now create your Coat of Arms by following the steps below.

1. Choose a template that your family wants to work with. See the sample in the *Appendix* or search online.
2. Divide the template's shape into enough parts for everyone in the family to have their own section to design.
3. Each person adds two or three symbols to their section that they feel represent their personality and identity (this could be an animal, a sport, a symbol, etc.).
4. Do a pencil draft at first, then everyone colors their objects and sections as they wish.
5. Create a motto that captures your family's "vibe." Include it in the Coat of Arms (usually across the top or bottom).
6. Create a chant for the motto using a catchy tune.
7. Laminate or frame the final draft and put it in a place where everyone can see it.

What Happened

Sara investigated her family name, Darwish. One meaning was *dervish*, from the Sufi religion, but she identified more with *driyosh*, a "wayfarer who travels from town to town in search of knowledge" (*Wikipedia*). She therefore drew a traveler's staff and a star.

The name "Tiller" also had two different meanings. It could mean someone who "tills the soil," which suited Max, since he was always planting things wherever they landed.

And, fortuitously, a "tiller" is the part of a boat that helps the rudder steer—a consummate symbol for their mobile family.

Parul chose the Indian flag to show her birthplace, and a cat and a dog because she loves animals.

Jace chose his Animal Avatar, the eagle, holding the Earth in one of its claws.

Mariel chose musical symbols and ballet shoes.

They arranged their symbols on a template together with their new motto, "Wherever we go, we learn and grow." They hung their Coat of Arms in the entrance for everyone to see when they entered the house.

Reflection

As you reflect on your experience with the use of symbols and the affirmation of identity, consider the following questions about your family creating their own Coat of Arms:

1. How does creating a Coat of Arms nurture a sense of significance and belonging in your children?
2. How do symbols reinforce your children's and your family's sense of identity?
3. How can a personal Coat of Arms nurture resilience?
4. As children grow, they may want to change their symbols. When would be an appropriate time to modify your Coat of Arms?

TOOL #14
Compliments and Appreciation
Activity / Skill

"We are prepared for insults, but compliments leave us baffled."

Mason Cooley Professor Emeritus, College of Staten Island

Find ways to include Compliments and Appreciation in your daily life

Purpose

To build positivity and appreciation.

Life Skills

Appreciation, Empathy, Positive Attitude.

Feeling Good!

One day, Max came home from work in a good mood. Several times he complimented one of the family. They tried to guess why he was doing it. They asked him the following:

"Did you get a raise at work?"

"Did you win something?"

"Are you going crazy, Dad?"

Max explained that there was a new initiative at work to give at least three compliments or appreciations to someone during the day. There had been a noticeable shift in the atmosphere and people were already smiling more. They were going to try it for a month and see what happened. HR hoped it would raise employee happiness and staff retention. The managers hoped that happier and healthier employees would be more productive. Max proposed they do their own experiment to see how giving compliments would help the family.

We often remember to correct or criticize but forget to compliment or show appreciation. An experiment done by the Bronfenbrenner Center for Translational Research at Cornell University in 2020 shows how people are positively affected by receiving compliments—an effect we underestimate. Results from this research show that as good feelings ripple out from the person receiving the compliment, they also return to the compliment-giver in a loop of positivity.

In addition, the Harvard Business Review shares research from 2021 that shows "expressing praise and gratitude is particularly important for keeping up morale and should be a top priority for organizations."

What You Need

Materials: Paper slips for notes, a phone to schedule reminders

Time: 10–20 minutes

Instructions

The most effective way to include more compliments in your life is to prepare them beforehand. Plan ways to show appreciation for each of your children, your partner, and yourself every day with some of the ideas below.

- Write special notes and leave them somewhere to be found.
- Schedule reminders on your phone to tell them in person.
- Wear a band on your wrist to remind you.
- Record an upbeat message to use as a ringtone.
- Leave reminders on your mirror, your fridge, your computer, and in your car.

Here are some examples of compliments you could give:

- "You always find a way to work it out."
- "I like what you did with your hair today."
- "Every time you smile, it lights up my day."
- "You're always ready to help."
- "You're really good at…"
- "I love watching you be a good friend to…"
- "I appreciate it when you…"
- "You've certainly done a lot for…"
- "You like to take your time and enjoy…"

What Happened

Max put a reminder on his phone to give everyone a compliment before he left the house.

Sara wrote out several appreciation notes for all three children and kept them in a jar in the kitchen. Once a week, she put one in each girl's lunchbox and one in Jace's backpack. Before dinner, everyone had a chance to share something they appreciated about each other or someone in their lives.

By the end of the month, the children were giving more compliments to their parents and each other. In school reports, teachers commented on how kind and polite the kids were. There were fewer problems, more achievements, and more smiles and fun. The Tillers liked this experiment so much they decided to continue it for another month. And maybe, indefinitely!

Reflection

From your own experience, reflect on the following questions to understand more about the power of Compliments and Appreciation:

1. What do you notice in others when you compliment them or show appreciation?
2. How does using compliments and appreciation create trust?
3. How can using this Tool contribute to "Gifts" in the *Challenges and Gifts Tool #3*?
4. What's the difference between a compliment and praise (see the *Encouragement Tool #18*)?

TOOL #15
Connect
Activity

"Atoms covalently bonded as a molecule are more stable than they were as separate atoms."

ACS Chemistry for Life
Energy Levels, Electrons, and Covalent Bonding

Connecting with others before a move supports a healthy transition and new friendships

Purpose

To increase ways of connecting with your family and others to support the transition process.

Life Skills

Communication, Empathy, Emotional Intelligence, Problem-solving, Responsibility, Focusing on the Positive.

Connect Ahead

Once Sara and Max found out they were moving to Turkey, Sara started investigating the international schools in Istanbul. She reached out to her international social groups to get feedback on the various options. She shared the information with the family, who began their own investigating and discussions about the upcoming relocation.

Sara and Max knew how important it was to increase their connection as a family before their move. They started taking more time with each of the kids, and together. Sara thought about ways to have fun during their trip and once they arrived. The kids planned ways to connect with friends and teachers before leaving as part of their goodbye rituals.

Connecting with others through healthy relationships and social activities directly affects physical and mental health, reducing anxiety and depression. Living a mobile lifestyle requires more effort to create connections when arriving and to disconnect when leaving a place.

The best time to build connections is when things are going well. This is when the body and brain are more relaxed and able to focus on relationships and growth. Connecting ahead to your new location is another important way to ease the stress of moving. To support your family as much as possible before, during, and after moving, consider some of the activities below.

What You Need

Materials: A notebook for planning, your Family Mission Statement Tool #2 (if you have one)

Time: Depends on the activity

Instructions

During all the phases of your transition, you can increase the connection within your family and with those in your life. Using the sections and lists below, decide which ideas work for your family.

Before a move

"Tightening the bolts" of family, friends, and community before leaving reinforces the structures you have created and prepares your family "ship" for the journey. Use the following ideas as a checklist (or inspiration) for your own options:

Connect with your family

- Review your goals and your Family Mission Statement Tool #2 as a couple.
- Referring to your Family Mission Statement Tool #2, discuss the move with your children.
- Help kids find their preferred ways to deal with their feelings about moving (see the Goodbyes Tool #25, the Grief and Loss Tool #27, and the Reflective Listening Tool #46).
- Plan times to meet as a family to celebrate, share appreciation, discuss problems, and find solutions (see the Family Meetings Tool #23).
- Plan fun time together to build your family connection (see the Family Night Tool #24).

Connect with friends

- Spend time with friends to say goodbye.
- Share gifts to remind them of your friendship.
- Plan ways to stay in touch.

Connect with the new school and families

- Ask the school if they have an ambassador program.
- Ask for connections with families in your child's class.

- Ask about extracurricular or social activities for your child.
- Communicate with the Parent-Teacher Organization.
- Notify the school of any special needs your child may have.
- Make visits (virtual or in person).
- Contact local clubs.
- Learn about your new neighborhood together (virtual or in person).
- Learn about the language, history, and culture.

During a move

When traveling to a new location, it's as if the structure of your family is loosened and jiggled so it can pass through other dimensions, arrive in a new place and time, and re-congeal. By creating your own travel rituals, you increase the amount of "sticky particles" that hold the family together on the voyage and as you arrive.

Use some of the ideas below to make the move an adventure that creates more "sticky particles" between your family members.

- Before traveling, review your *Family Mission Statement Tool #2* (if you have one).
- Create non-verbal signals to communicate while traveling.
- Plan a scavenger hunt during your trip or while waiting at the airport.
- Give each child a travel allowance to spend as they wish.
- After visiting the shops, reconvene to share what everyone bought.
  - Share what you bought as if it's an advertisement for the product.
  - Ask the others to guess how much it cost, where it's from, etc.
- Give everyone a job for which they are responsible. For example:
  - Document Master: takes care of the passports.
  - Navigator: helps with navigation or finding the gate at the airport.
  - Game Master: prepares activities and games.
  - Snack Master: brings and hands out snacks.
  - Invite your children to create jobs for everyone.

Arriving

When arriving in a new location, here are some ways to create new connections:

- Meet other parents during drop-off and pickup hours.
- Volunteer at school or join the PTO.
- Join an activity in the community. For example, a yoga class, a dance class, or get involved with local charities.
- Invite a classmate and/or their parents to hang out after school.
- Introduce yourself to neighbors.
- Find local clubs for your children to join.

After a move

There are many ways to stay connected with old friends and family. What are your favorite ways? These could include:

- Email and social media
- Regular video calls
- Visits and vacations together

What Happened

Fortunately, the school Sara chose was a member of Safe Passage Across Networks (SPAN). Sara knew her three TCKs would be in good hands with the comprehensive SPAN program in place. Jace and Mariel were assigned a student ambassador before their arrival to ask questions to and start the school year with. The PTO kindly connected families who shared a common language or a previous location before arrival. A newcomers' picnic was scheduled for the first Friday of the school year for all new families, along with the student and parent ambassadors.

The Tillers visited their favorite places in the last months of their stay in Belgium and spent time with friends. During their family meetings they planned the trip to Turkey, with everyone choosing a job: Max was the Document Master, Jace was Navigator, Mariel was Game Master, and Parul and Sara were the Snack Masters. Things seemed to be falling into place. Max and Sara decided to go on a weekend date to have time to reconnect before things got crazy.

Reflection

Staying connected with your family and friends is one of the biggest challenges for a nomadic family. Use the questions below to consider how to expand your use of the Tool.

1. What other resources are available in your present and future locations that can help you and the family prepare for your move and settle in?
2. How is your *Family Mission Statement Tool #2* strengthened when you connect beforehand and maintain older connections?
3. In what ways can older children become more proactive in connecting before, during, and after a move?
4. What other ways are there for your family to connect before, during, and after a move?

TOOL #16
Connection Before Correction
Skill

"When a student is feeling an intense emotion and behaving in direct response to that emotion... the logical part of the brain is 'out to lunch.'"

Lee Ann Jung
Association for Supervision and Curriculum Development

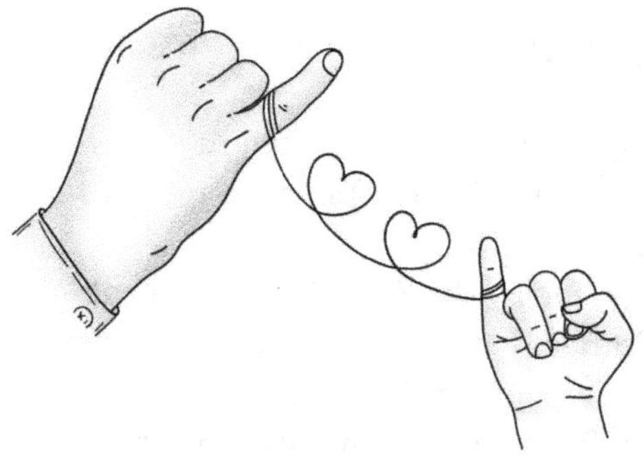

Showing empathy first builds the relationship

Purpose

To reinforce the connection between you and your children before correcting them. To allow children to participate in the problem-solving process.

Life Skills

Empathy, Respect, Listening, Verbal and Non-verbal Communication, Patience.

Testing the Limits

Soon after the Tillers had arrived in Belgium, Jace began testing the limits of his parents' authority. He started going to a local park with his classmates to play basketball until dinnertime, even though Sara and Max had told him (several times) to come home from school first. They talked about grounding Jace, but keeping him home seemed contrary to helping him settle in to his new social circles. After looking through their Toolkit, they decided to connect with their son and work together to create guidelines, using some of the Tools they already felt comfortable with.

"Transformational leaders listen first and speak second," writes Greg Trueblood, a consultant for the organizational transformation company Insigniam. According to Greg, it's because "once people are listened to, they're more likely to listen in return and be open to what you have to say."

"Connecting" with a child before "correcting" them means you're all ears, i.e., your whole body and mental focus are present to hear not only the words but, more importantly, the emotions being expressed. This also models listening and empathy, two important Life Skills from the *Challenges and Gifts for Children Tool #3*. Children who feel this connection will be ready to listen—once they have had the chance to share what's going on from their perspective.

What You Need

Materials: Patience and Self-awareness

Time: Indefinite

Instructions

Connecting with a child before correcting them on something requires more effort from our side, as parents. By curbing our tendency to over-protect children, solve their problems, or overreact emotionally to the situation, we allow them to take more responsibility for themselves and their problems. Consider trying one of these ways to connect:

Ways to Connect

- Give your full physical and mental attention to your child.
- Go to their level: get eye-to-eye.
- Use calm, physical touch (if appropriate).
- Listen to their words, body language, and feelings.
- Paraphrase what you have heard; check for understanding.
- Recognize their feelings and intentions. For example: "I can tell you're angry about... What were you expecting?"
- Avoid judging your child's reactions or statements while listening.

Ways to Correct

- "I understand how you made that choice. How did it affect others and the situation?"
- "We had an agreement. How does this behavior fit with that?"
- "What ways are there for you to help fix the problem? Can you do it yourself or do you need help?"
- "What you did was not OK. We trust you can make better choices in the future."
- "What can you do next time this happens? Who can you ask for advice or help?"

Finish

- Focus on: "We work together as a family team."
- Reconnect with a smile and/or a hug, or do something together.
- Show your appreciation: "Thank you for sharing, for listening, and for helping work it out."
- Plan a fun activity to do as a family within days of the conversation.

What Happened

Sara and Max practiced going through the steps of Connection before Correction. They asked Jace whether he would like to talk with them before or after dinner (*Limited Choices Tool #33*). After dinner, they sat in the living room. Jace and Sara sat on the couch, and Max sat on the floor next to them (to be at the same level as Jace).

Max: "Jace, we had an agreement that you would come home from school before going out with your friends. When you don't come home, it causes us to worry. We'd like to understand what is going on after school when you don't come home."

Jace: "I'm fine. I just want to have fun with my new friends after school."

Sara and Max: "Mm-hmmm." (Listen)

Jace: "You don't get it because you have your job and Mom has her groups. I have to make new friends every time we move. I didn't want to move in the first place, but here we are."

Sara and Max: "Mm-hmmm."

Jace: "I know how to take care of myself. Besides, we play basketball in the complex by their houses. Their parents are around. They don't make their kids check in with them after school."

Sara: "You feel angry because we've moved a lot. It's hard to keep changing schools and making new friends." (*Recognize Emotions Tool #45, Reflective Listening Tool #46*)

Jace: "Yeah. It's not fair."

Max: "And you feel frustrated about checking in with us because you feel you're old enough to take care of yourself." (*Recognize Emotions Tool #45, Reflective Listening Tool #46*)

Jace: "Hello! I'm not a little kid anymore."

Max: "We realize you're able to look after yourself in many situations, Jace. We feel nervous when you don't check in with us after school because this is a new place for all of us." (*I-Statements Tool #28*)

Jace: "You don't have to worry about me."

Sara: "We understand that your independence is important *and* we're still responsible for you (*Caring and Firm Tool #10*). We also had an agreement about this. What's a solution we're all comfortable with?"

They discussed different solutions and agreed that Jace would call his mom when he arrived at a friend's place. She would text him 30 minutes before dinner and he would let her know he was coming home. They agreed to try this for the next week and see how it worked. They thanked Jace for his participation in reaching an agreement and ended the meeting with a group hug.

Over the next couple of months, Sara would connect with the other parents and kids to get to know them better. Max, Sara, and Jace agreed to review this plan after two months.

Reflection

Connecting before correcting children models an important lifelong skill in both personal and professional realms. Consider these questions:

1. How does this Tool contribute to building trust, as well as helping kids make future decisions when away from our direct influence?
2. What other ways help a child (or adult) feel respected and like they're part of the team?
3. What Life Skills are reinforced with this Tool? (See the *Challenges and Gifts for Children Tool #3*.)

TOOL #17
Date Night
Activity

---

*"In the happiest of our childhood memories,
our parents were happy, too."*

Robert Brault   Short Thoughts for the Long Haul

Keep the magic in your relationship

Purpose

To strengthen the connection with your partner.

Life Skills

Self-care, Work-leisure Balance, Appreciation.

What's the Occasion?

Max was traveling for work more than usual, as well as putting in extra hours at his office. Sara was managing the home front like a many-armed goddess who doubled as a personal chauffeur for their three children. Their time together as a couple was filled with rushed conversations about finances, their to-do lists, issues with the kids, and complaints about getting things done in the bureaucracy of a new country. Even worse, they started having arguments about things that normally wouldn't even register a bump on the Richter scale of their marriage.

Terence, an older mentor at work, noticed a change in Max. He and his wife invited Sara and Max to go out for drinks one night. The older couple were remarkably calm and affectionate with one another, and the conversation that evening flowed easily from one interesting topic to another.

"What's the occasion?" Max asked.

"Date night," Terence replied. He chuckled at the Tillers' confused look. "Once a week, whether we need it or not." He winked at Max and smiled warmly.

By the end of the evening, Max and Sara felt very different. They started laughing, holding hands, and even played "footsie" under the table a few times. *We should do this more often*, they both thought.

"Keeping a regular date night is an important part of staying connected while raising a family," writes Helene A. Miller for the *Journal of Family Psychiatry and Therapy* in her article 'The Essential Nature of Date Night for Parents.' She also lists other reasons for making this special time important: "Everyone in the family is happier... a 400% increase... It makes the relationship stronger... Women show even higher satisfaction... Sex lives improve."

What You Need

Materials: A list of local restaurants, theaters, clubs, spas, hotels, outings

Time: Once a week or more

Instructions

A solid bond with your partner is at the center of a strong family unit that can better withstand the stresses in life, especially those of a mobile lifestyle. Here are some ways to use this Tool:

- Plan a Date Night once a week for you and your partner.
- Plan trips for just the two of you once a month (or a few times a year).
- Meet for lunch on random days.
- Set bedtimes (or "in-the-room" times) so you and your partner get to have quiet time together in the evenings.
- Focus discussions on positive and interesting things.
- Create surprises for your partner.
- Keep problem-solving for family issues separated from Date Nights.

What Happened

Sara invited Max to help plan a regular Date Night. "Did you see how happy they were after so many years?" she asked him. They decided on Wednesday evenings, with Friday as an alternative if Wednesday didn't work. When Max was traveling, they would meet online for an hour, with their favorite drink in hand. The ground rules were simple: it would be a time to relax and enjoy each other's company without conversations about the kids. They also scheduled a regular time to talk about more serious issues and fix problems.

After two months of Date Nights, the Tillers felt reconnected and renewed. Even their children were having fewer arguments and seemed happier. The essence of their *Family Mission Statement Tool #2* felt stronger than ever.

Reflection

If you and your partner are considering setting up a Date Night, here are some questions to inspire your discussion:

1. What makes spending time together difficult?
2. How can setting your priorities as a couple help overcome some of those blocks?
3. How does this Tool support your *Family Mission Statement Tool #2* (if you have one)?
4. What positive Life Skills will your children learn when you and your partner regularly take this special time together?

TOOL #18
Encouragement
Skill

Encouragement blossoms into self-esteem and motivation

Purpose

To create an atmosphere of recognition and instill a can do attitude.

Life Skills

Self-esteem, Motivation, Self-efficacy, Perseverance.

Crumpled Up

It was two weeks after the start of the school year in their new school. While cleaning out Mariel's backpack, Sara found a crumpled-up flyer about auditions for a dance show. She was surprised Mariel hadn't mentioned anything.

When Sara asked her about it, Mariel mumbled that she didn't feel like it. A tiny alarm went off in Sara's head. "But you're so good, probably the best! What a shame!" Sara said in hopes of raising her daughter's spirits, but the pep-talk didn't have the desired effect.

"I'll see," said Mariel. Sara wondered if Mariel's hesitation was part of transitioning to a new place or if she was feeling unsure of her dance abilities. Perhaps it was a combination of both.

"Encouragement provides opportunities for children to develop the perceptions, 'I am capable, I can contribute, and I can influence what happens to me or how I respond,'" Jane Nelsen writes in *Positive Discipline*. Compared to "praise," which is like an evaluation from the person saying it, "encouragement" acts as a mirror that reflects the child's own effort, progress, and contribution.

Encouragement is the perfect "gift" that can be given on any occasion. Ideally, it's a regular part of the positive environment in your home (see the *Compliments and Appreciation Tool #14*). For instance, if your children use the *Chores Chart Tool #12* or the *Routine Charts Tool #48*, you can use Encouragement to comment on how responsible and capable they are.

This essential Tool nurtures a sense of self-esteem and self-efficacy that serve as a cornerstone when your household gets disassembled and whizzed off to another location. It is reinforced within other Tools, such as the *Family Meetings Tool #23*, where giving kudos for effort and progress open the meeting.

What You Need

Materials: Paper, pen, a partner (or a recording device)

Time: 45 minutes

Instructions

Experience the difference between Praise and Encouragement as you read through the following sentences. Notice how you feel, what you're thinking, and consider when or to whom you might say these things (and vice versa):

Praise

- "You're so smart! And talented!"
- "Great job!"
- "You're the best."
- "You did it exactly right."
- "I'm so proud of you."

Praise is a judgment from the perspective of the person giving it. Short term, Praise feels good, but it motivates children to do things to please adults. In the long term, children become dependent on outside approval and may feel less motivated to do something where they might struggle or fail.

Encouragement

- "You put a lot of time and effort into that project."
- "Look how far you've come since you started."
- "I appreciate your help."
- "You really like building things, don't you?"
- "You should be proud of yourself."

Encouragement directs children to appreciate their own *effort, progress, contribution,* and *personal qualities.* In both the short-term and long-term, children learn to focus on their sense of accomplishment and are better prepared to face new challenges.

Practice

Like other skills in this Toolkit, we need to practice language and phrases that create new patterns in the brain. Work with a partner or use your phone to record and listen to the difference between Praise and Encouragement. The more you include Encouragement in your daily repertoire of phrases, the more natural it becomes to use it.

Step 1

Practice with a partner or record the sentences below that focus on different ways to encourage someone. Process how you feel when saying them and listening to them.

Areas of effort and progress
For example: hobbies, music, dance, theater, sports, school, and helping others.

- "You worked hard on that project. Look at the progress you've made!"
- "It used to be hard to make new friends but you kept trying. That's a strength."
- "You got 6 out of 10 correct. How did you figure them out?"
- "You jumped right in and learned a new way to do math. How does that feel?"

Areas of contribution
For example: helping the family, volunteering, clubs, and leadership.

- "When you help out, we have more time for fun together."
- "Cleaning the garage is a tough job but your help made it much easier. Thanks."

- "Those kids are lucky to have you helping their group."
- "You're learning lots of new skills in that club."
- "Running for student council president shows a lot of courage."

Personal qualities

For example: interests, hobbies, and strengths.

- "You really like to build things, don't you?"
- "It's unusual to see a young person so dedicated to…"
- "You've got a lot of perseverance and a strong will to succeed."
- "It's thoughtful to help the elderly group. It looks like they really appreciate your time."
- "It's clear you love animals and helping them."

Step 2

Create and use Encouragement statements with these ideas:

- Prepare statements for each of your children.
- Write them out and practice reading them.
- Plan reminders to share them with your children daily (Post-its, telephone reminders, notes in backpacks, etc.).

What Happened

Sara found a calm time to sit with Mariel in her room. "I'm wondering what's bothering you about auditioning?"

"It's a different style of dance. I don't want to look stupid," Mariel replied.

Sara resisted the urge to say, "You're not stupid! You're talented and smart!" Instead, she used Encouragement along with other Tools she had learned:

She put her hand on Mariel's shoulder. (*Connection Before Correction Tool #16*)

Sara: "You feel unsure because it's new and you're new." (*Recognize Emotions Tool #45*)

Mariel: "Yeah! Everyone else knows the steps."

Sara: "And yet, you've joined new dance groups before. What has helped in the past?" (*Encouragement* and *Ask vs. Tell Tool #9*)

Mariel: "I got to know some of the girls, but I'm tired of always having to start over."

Sara: "I remember when you started ballet lessons in Brussels. You were so determined to join the dance show. You practiced every day. Your hard work really paid off." (*Encouragement*)

Mariel: "I was only in the chorus, though."

Sara: "You were the only *beginner* in the show!" (*Encouragement*)

Mariel: "Yeah, that's right."

Sara: "Dance is an important part of your life. Let me know how I can help you feel more settled so you can move forward." (Show trust)

Mariel: "Thanks, Mom."

"Wherever we go, we learn and grow!" said Sara, reminding Mariel of their family motto from their *Coat of Arms Tool #13*.

Sara allowed her daughter to work out the solution to her problem but with a clear display of emotional support. Mariel *did* audition and she got a part she felt good about. More importantly, she pushed past her self-doubts to a new level of confidence as the new kid on the block.

This confidence was *earned* due to her own efforts, and not because her mom told her to do it.

Mariel felt an increased sense of power that carried her into friendships with students she normally wouldn't have reached out to. Observing her, the dance teacher started to think of ways to highlight Mariel's talent in future shows.

Reflection

Consider the following questions about Encouragement and ways to include it in your life:

1. How does transitioning to another country affect your children's motivation to engage in activities?
2. How do your children respond differently to Praise and Encouragement?
3. In what other areas of your life can Encouragement be a positive addition?
4. What positive Life Skills (see the *Challenges and Gifts for Children Tool #3*) does Encouragement nurture?

TOOL #19
Exercise
Activity

"Just Do It."

Nike slogan

Exercise is an important part of self-care

Purpose

To create a personal and family habit of self-care and enjoyment through physical activity.

Life Skills

Self-care, Planning, Perseverance, Teamwork.

Doing It

Max was overworking and too tired to spend quality time with his family. Evenings were spent with Max zoning out in front of a movie and Sara taking care of the kids' needs. Going out together became less and less frequent, and there was less affection between them as a couple. Sara recognized the symptoms of too much work and not enough self-care. She sat with Max one evening and asked him to go through the Exercise Tool with her.

She used the three-list format from the *Pitfalls and Perks of a Mobile Lifestyle Tool #1* to guide their discussion. They talked about the Challenges that were stopping them from exercising and wrote them in the left column. Then they focused on the Benefits of exercising and wrote them in the right column. Thinking of the Benefits motivated them to brainstorm several Solutions, which they wrote in the middle column.

The Mayo Clinic Staff shares several reasons to "Just Do It" in their Healthy Lifestyle Fitness article 'Exercise: 7 benefits of regular physical activity.' Apart from the more obvious reasons—weight control and reducing disease—other benefits are also listed: mood enhancement, increased energy, better sleep, and better sex. Beyond that, exercise is also a fun way to spend quality time with close friends and family.

Even though research has shown that regular exercise enhances the quality of life and increases lifespan, more and more adults and children lead increasingly sedentary lives. Unfortunately, when the work-leisure balance gets out of whack, the instinct of many overworked people is to conserve energy. Finding the right balance is important for your personal health as well as for your relationships.

What You Need

Materials: A sheet of paper

Time: 30 minutes

Instructions

When you sit down to do this activity, draw three columns on your piece of paper, like in the example below. Feel free to use Max and Sara's ideas and then come up with some of your own.

Challenges to Exercising	Solutions	Benefits of Exercising
Schedule	Find something you like to do	I feel so good when I exercise
No time	Focus on a goal	My metabolism increases
Availability of classes	Take small steps toward it	I feel more toned
Location of classes	Schedule it	I can lose some weight
Too tired	Get a buddy	It's a good stress reliever
Weather	Online, home options	More oxygen to the brain
	Apps	
Kids	Family exercise	I feel more resilient
Other	Organize a teacher	Other

What Happened

Max cut down the number of hours he spent working at the office every day. Early mornings were best to fit in some exercise, so he committed to walking for half an hour with Sara three times a week. Sara joined a gym and did classes every other day. After a couple of weeks, Max noticed a big difference in his energy levels, mood, and motivation to do some of his hobbies. His family noticed these improvements too and enjoyed having interesting conversations with him again.

Sara proposed they create a list of physical activities the family could do together. Jace and Mariel did some research on local places to go hiking, climbing, bike riding, traditional dancing, and kayaking. They planned different activities for two weekends every month and got to visit scenic places in their new country.

Eventually, Max got involved in regional marathons. Sara helped organize a charity event at school for families to do a "Walk for Water" fundraiser.

Reflection

Consider these questions about exercise and how staying active instills positive habits in your children:

1. What values are you modeling for your children by taking care of yourself?
2. What do children learn about the work-leisure balance when you set the example?
3. What Life Skills do children gain when helping plan activities?
4. What opportunities are available for your family to do exercise together in your community?

TOOL #20
Explore
Activity

"Not all those who wander are lost."
J. R. R. Tolkien The Lord of the Rings

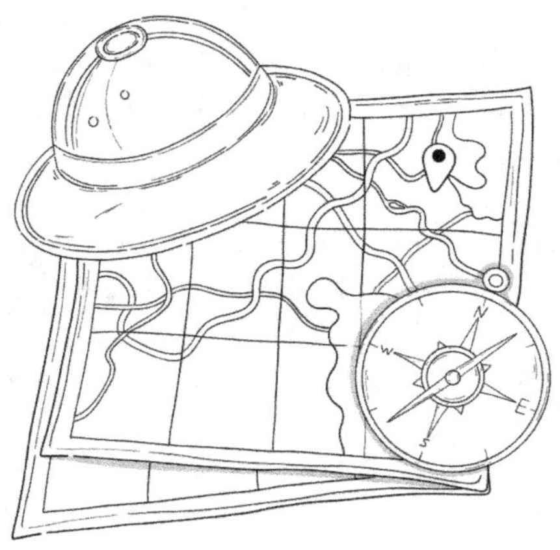

Explore and expand together

Purpose
To fill your soul with adventures.

Life Skills
Risk-taking, Being Comfortable with Ambiguity, Problem-solving.

To-do List

Soon after they moved to Turkey, the Tillers started planning to visit places. Their Turkish friends in Belgium, the Yilmaz family, had made a list of must-see sites. One evening, Max sat with Jace, Mariel, and Parul to go through the list. Once they had chosen several places, Sara investigated hotels and made reservations for the next few months.

Sara also wanted to see historical sites in the city. She printed out some of the train and bus maps for Istanbul and planned some navigation challenges for the kids.

Your family's reasons for living and working abroad most likely include wanting to explore other cultures. You can reinforce this by having adventures together wherever you live, from your local neighborhood to the more exotic locations and experiences a country has to offer.

What You Need

Materials: Online resources, maps and access to local information, a calendar

Time: One to two hours for planning, days and weeks to explore.

Instructions

Making plans to explore can start as soon as you know where you'll be moving to. It's one way to keep your family in a positive mood about changing locations. Use the suggestions below to help plan. How many of these ideas have you already tried? What can you add to the list?

Which activities can your children help plan?

- Use maps and apps to plan and educate.
- Plan weekly or monthly outings in the new town or country.
- Ask your pre-teens and teens to help plan outings.
- Learn how to use the public transportation system.
- Encourage teens to explore on their own or with friends.
- Invite other families or friends to join you.
- Investigate planned tours that highlight local history and offer cultural events.
- Create your own "discovery" outings.

What Happened

Once a month, the Tillers explored places close to Istanbul. Sara discovered there was a tour service recommended by the parents at the school. On one of their trips, they met other parents from the school. When there was a week-long break in October, they traveled to Cappadocia for hot-air balloon rides and visited the cave churches and underground cities. Jace and Mariel took tons of photos and shared them with their friends in Brussels.

Twice a month, the family went to visit something in the city center. Jace and Mariel took turns being the family navigators. The public transportation system turned out to be easy to use, efficient, and a fun way to get to know Istanbul. They even started picking up Turkish by reading the signs and asking for directions.

As if to affirm the Tillers' new adventure-filled agenda, Sara came across a quote by one of her favorite actresses, Jaime Lyn Beatty: "Jobs fill your pockets but adventures fill your soul." She wrote it out and posted it on their refrigerator. A week later, she saw that the quote had been decorated with Mariel's colorful images.

Reflection

Exploring involves much more than just seeing new places. Consider the following questions to make the most out of your trips:

1. What Life Skills can your child develop through leading and participating in these activities?
2. What ways are there to document new discoveries and experiences?
3. How can you reference such adventures to support your family's mission as Global Nomads?

TOOL #21
Family Heirloom
Activity

"It would be an existence rife with difficulties... but of a pleasurable kind, difficulties they could take pride in, possess, value, as one would a family heirloom."

Khaled Hosseini A Thousand Splendid Suns

Choose an object that has meaning for your family

Purpose

To affirm identity. To initiate or continue your family heritage.

Life Skills

Communication, Self-esteem, Sense of Purpose.

The Traveler

As they were packing their belongings, yet again, Sara reflected on the masks, pottery, and sculptures she had carried with her from her time in Africa as a child. She remembered the stories her father had told her about these different pieces, about their significance, how he came by them, and why he cherished them.

One of his favorite vases was from Ghana. The hand-painted design portrayed a common theme—a stranger or traveler—which the tribal leader had felt was an appropriate gift for this stranger who had come to know and help their tribe.

When she read about Family Heirlooms in the Toolkit, Sara realized this vase was an apt piece of art that identified her present family, as well as the one she grew up in. After dinner, she shared her thoughts with everyone about making this vase the Tiller Family Heirloom.

An heirloom is an object that passes through the different generations of a family, connecting the past with the present, and into the future. It's usually something of value that had meaning for the original owner and has carried its story (and the stories of its owners) over the years.

Whether you've already been traveling with Family Heirlooms or not, you can designate an object to start the tradition with your own family. By highlighting its origin and meaning, your children, grandchildren, and great-grandchildren will have a special object to connect them to you. Perhaps it's an object that symbolizes the different lands you have traveled to and that will inspire stories to be told around your descendants' dinner tables for years to come.

What You Need

Materials: Meaningful objects for your family to choose from

Time: 30–60 minutes

Instructions

Use these suggestions to guide your choice of a Family Heirloom:

- The whole family takes part in choosing an object that will be the Family Heirloom.
- Talk about the symbolism of the object and its significance for the whole family.
- When you move, pack the Family Heirloom with a ritual. When you arrive in a new house and are settled in, place the Family Heirloom in an arrival ritual.

What Happened

The Tillers liked the idea of having the vase as their Family Heirloom. Parul wanted the *ghanti* (bell) from India to be together with the vase since it was one of the items she had when the Tillers adopted her.

They found a glass case to put them in and placed it on the buffet by their dining room table. At the end of their packing, they gathered around the vase and the bell and said, "Goodbye for now." Weeks later, when their shipment arrived, their new Family Heirloom was unpacked with care and placed on the buffet by the dining room table. The family welcomed it by lighting a candle and having their first meal at the table together. Using their family motto from the *Coat of Arms Tool #13*, "Wherever we go, we learn and grow," they started the meal with this recognition of their family's identity.

Reflection

Whether you already have a Family Heirloom or want to create one, the following questions may help you to create a more intentional connection with the various aspects of your mobile journey:

1. How does designating such an object and using it in rituals support the transition process?
2. Which known rituals might serve as models to create your own ritual?
3. How might this activity contribute to family cohesion?
4. Would each child benefit from designating their own special object?

TOOL #22
Family Map
Activity

"Of all the books in the world, the best stories are found between the pages of a passport."

Saber Ben Hassen   CEO, Carthage Magazine

A Family Map is a record of your children's mobile lifestyle

Purpose
To "connect the dots" of your journey with a visual representation.

Life Skills
Reflection, Appreciation, Map Reading.

Where Are We From?

Mariel's class was doing a map project to show where each student was from. "Where are we from, Mom?" she asked.

Sara chuckled and said, "From nowhere and everywhere!"

"Mom! I can't write that," replied Mariel, sounding annoyed.

"But it's true," Jace chimed in.

"I'm from India," Parul announced.

"You guys aren't helping!" said Mariel. "I'll ask Dad when he gets home."

In Barbara Knuckles' Anchors and Mirrors model (see the earlier section on *Identity Formation*), family, community, and geographical location are the three influences that give feedback for a developing sense of identity. As we have already discussed, family is the constant factor that anchors a child in a life of mobility. Family can also reflect how a child is different, but people in the community and location give a wider range of reflections that a child must one day fashion into a self-image. A Family Map organizes the different locations of a mobile life into a more cohesive perspective of your family's journey.

Beyond the educational benefits of learning geography, a Family Map is a concrete reminder of your lifestyle and the many adventures it encompasses. In effect, the world becomes the neighborhood your children will look back on in their adult years. A physical map will help them reminisce about various cultural experiences in their childhood and how these contributed to their unique "Third Culture" identity.

What You Need

Materials: A sturdy, portable world map or an online version, pens or pins to mark locations

Time: 30–60 minutes

Instructions

Once you've decided which map you'll use, set aside time with your family to start marking the places of your journey. The following steps are just one way of organizing the process:

Step 1

- Each parent chooses a color.
- Mark your countries of origin, places where you both lived before you were a couple, and where you met.
- Use numbers or dates to keep track of the order.

Step 2

- Mark places where you lived together as a couple.
- Mark where each child was born, using their own colors.
- Mark each place where you lived as a family (use the same color for these places).

Step 3 (optional)

- Decide as a family if you want to include countries you have visited or perhaps want to visit (use a different color for these places to differentiate them from the places you've lived in).

Step 4

- Revisit the map when preparing for a move.
- Discuss your global journey.
- Enjoy the memories and celebrate your lifestyle.

What Happened

Max ordered a large world map that came rolled up in a handy cardboard tube. The family laid it out on their dining room table and had fun looking at all the places they'd been. They used green stickers to mark the countries where they'd lived and blue stickers for places they had visited or gone on holiday to. Parul stuck a small picture of herself in Mumbai, India, to show where she had joined the family.

The whole evening turned into a storytelling time and the reliving of memories. They discussed who they were as a family and where they "were from." Identifying as Third Culture Kids and as being part of a Global Nomad family felt reassuring for the kids.

The fun continued as they started dreaming of where they'd go next. They put yellow stickers on those destinations and got inspired to start researching them. Then Max gave the family a riddle: What is one of the few things you buy that can make you richer? When they were unable to answer, he smiled and said, "Travel." Max and Jace put up the map on the living room wall so they could refer to it easily.

Later that month, Jace shared a cool online option to create a personalized family board game: *Make-Your-Own-Opoly*. They used places where they had lived and places they wanted to visit and began moving around the board. Buying and selling places from their world brought up memories and dreams that reinforced their lifestyle's sense of adventure.

Sara decided to find a way to organize all the memories they had just shared. *There must be something in the Toolkit,* she thought.

Reflection

To help understand how this Tool can support your family's journey, reflect on these questions:

1. How can this activity help children keep a sense of connection with the family?
2. How does it contribute to cohesiveness in their developing psyches?
3. What else can children learn from this activity?
4. How can using such a map support your values and the advantages of your global lifestyle?
5. In what ways do you organize the memories from the different places your family has lived in?

TOOL #23
Family Meetings (ages 5+)
Activity / Skill

"It is a safe place where everyone is free to say what they think and feel as they cooperate to make decisions and solve problems."

R.J. Fetsch and B. Jacobson
Colorado State Education Extension Journal

Family Meetings nurture positive Life Skills

Purpose

To build cohesion in the family through a structured format where each person has a voice and a chance to lead the group.

Life Skills

Communication, Connection, Responsibility, Teamwork, Self-confidence, Leadership.

Get it Together!

Winter vacation was only weeks away. The Tillers were finalizing their plans to go to Cairo. Sara wanted her family to meet the Muslim families she spent several years with during her time there. The Tillers would celebrate the Christian New Year and experience the Muslim New Year on January 7.

As Sara drove around doing her errands, she started panicking about all the things she needed to do to prepare for the trip. First, there was a hotel deposit to pay, but Max wasn't answering his phone to confirm dates. Jace had proposed an agenda of places to visit, but it wasn't in the family online chat group. When was Mariel's ballet concert? There were puppet theater performances for Parul, but would Sara be free to take her? She still needed to book the airplane tickets and finish her Christmas shopping.

Sara pulled the car over and slammed the steering wheel with her hand. "I'm tired of getting so frazzled every time we take a trip!" she yelled out loud in the solitude of her SUV. Finally, she took some deep breaths. She had recently skimmed over the Family Meetings Tool in the Toolkit. When she got home, she revisited it in hopes of finding a better solution for working together as a family.

Life gets crazy, even without moving your family around the world. Holding regular Family Meetings is an excellent way to strengthen your family's communication, problem-solving skills, and teamwork. It's the perfect time to reinforce positive interactions when things are going well. The sense of stability from this foundation will also help your family weather the storms of hard times, such as transitioning to a new country.

What You Need

Materials: A notebook, an agenda sheet, a place where everyone can sit comfortably without distractions

Time: 20–30 minutes

Instructions

Once your family establishes the guidelines for these meetings (see the steps below), the meetings can take place quickly and efficiently, depending on the agenda items you need to discuss.

Step 1

When you start to hold regular Family Meetings, consider the following:

- Discuss guidelines for sharing, taking turns to lead, timekeeping, and note-taking.
- Focus on one topic and solving one problem at a time.
- Use the *I-Statements Tool #28* to share thoughts, feelings, and opinions.
- Schedule a regular 20-minute slot, once a week.
- During the week, prepare an agenda. Everyone can add things they'd like to be addressed.

Step 2

Use the following format to help meetings remain positive, productive, and engaging (also see the *Appendix*):

1. Each child (over the age of five) gets a turn to lead the weekly meeting.
2. Use a "start" signal or a family ritual to begin the meeting.
3. Give kudos, recognition, and appreciation for efforts and achievements from that week. Avoid complaints and criticism.
4. Follow up on action items from the previous meeting.

5. Address one new issue on the agenda.
6. Use problem-solving steps: identify the problem, brainstorm solutions, choose a workable solution, try it for a period of time, review and adjust, if necessary.
7. Discuss or plan for upcoming family events.
8. Show appreciation for the leader and others who contributed to the meeting.
9. Finish with a family handshake or signal.

Note: If children are under five, parents can still meet and set the model while the little ones are present or wait until they are asleep to hold the meeting.

What Happened

The first Family Meeting took almost an hour. Everyone wanted to talk at once until Sara insisted on following the protocol. By the end of the meeting, they had established a start signal, a list of who would fulfill each role every week, a place to post the agenda, and a family handshake to finish the meeting.

Everyone enjoyed giving kudos and showing appreciation for each other. Most importantly, Sara had a chance to express her frustration about being the organizer for all their trips. Following the problem-solving steps, they came up with ways to distribute the responsibilities for planning future trips.

Thereafter, when an issue came up during the week, Sara would respond, "That sounds like a good topic for our Family Meeting. Let's put it on the agenda." Gradually, the kids started doing this without a reminder. Thanks to Sara's near meltdown, she was able to steer the family to a new path that brought them closer together. She and Max were once again amazed at how capable and responsible their children were. The kids felt closer to each other and had a new sense of respect for their parents, who were also learning their own lessons.

Reflection

Take a moment to reflect on these questions if you are thinking of starting Family Meetings:

1. How is a regular Family Meeting in this format different from talking at the dinner table or in the car?
2. How might pre-teens and teens benefit from this format? What will younger children learn?
3. What Life Skills do children develop when a family uses this Tool regularly?

TOOL #24
Family Night
Activity

"Never, ever underestimate the importance of having fun."

Randy Pausch   The Last Lecture

Weekly family fun builds long-lasting bonds

Purpose

To create an environment of fun and connection through leisure activities

Life Skills

Problem-solving, Cooperation, Sportsmanship,
Self-confidence, Resilience.

What Happened

Sara read about the 'Science of Family Fun' in an article on the website of the United Nations Office on Drugs and Crime. It stated: "Quality family time builds stronger, connected families. Family group activities such as cooking, painting, or playing music together promote bonding. Trust, love one another, and create more resilient and self-confident children."

The Tiller Family liked to do things together, so she decided to share this idea with everyone and see how they could have even more fun.

You may have heard the saying "The family that plays together stays together." Having regularly planned family fun time strengthens the bonds that unify you and builds resilience that comes in handy when life puts extra pressure on things. The positive moments and memories from these times together create a treasure trove of resources children can dip into when they are faced with challenges outside the home, especially during moves.

What You Need

Materials: Paper, pen, and ideas!

Time: 30 minutes

Instructions

Follow these steps to start building your Family Night:

Step 1

First, as a family, decide on one night of the week to have fun together. If once a week feels like too much, you can meet two or three times a month. It's good to have a second choice of day in case some of your family members can't make the scheduled one.

Step 2

Make a list of activities to choose from. Here are some examples:

- Board games
- Crafts
- Build something
- Movies
- Karaoke
- Musical instrument jam
- Cooking
- Dance
- Exercise
- Explore something new in your town/city
- Help others
- Scavenger hunts
- Challenges with other families

Step 3

Now that you've planned, have fun and keep the following in mind:

- Put Family Nights in your calendar with reminders.
- Take turns to decide who will choose the activity each week.
- You can use your list of planned activities for several months, and then find new ones to add some variety.

What Happened

The Tillers liked this idea and decided to get together at least three times a month. Jace said he might have other things to do with his friends on Family Nights but would try to join in. The family chose an alternative night in case something did come up.

Everyone contributed ideas to the list of activities. On their first Family Night, Jace chose the activity. They made pizza together and watched a video clip he had made with his friends. Mariel and Parul were already planning what they would propose to the family when it was their turn to choose and lead the night.

After two months of Family Nights, the Tillers had so much fun that even Jace looked forward to them. When his friend Ash joined them once, he went home and told *his* parents about Family Nights.

Reflection

If you're wondering whether to use this Tool with your family, here are some questions to guide your decision:

1. How could such activities build stronger bonds in your family?
2. In what ways might each child benefit in their own, individual way?
3. How might Family Nights help older children deal with peer pressure?
4. What Life Skills does this Tool nurture?

TOOL #25

Goodbyes

Activity

---

*"If you're brave enough to say goodbye, life will
reward you with a new hello."*

Paulo Coelho   The Pilgrimage

Goodbyes are the hardest part of a mobile lifestyle

Purpose

To give children tools for saying goodbye to people, places, and things.

Life Skills

Communication, Empathy, Reflection.

NOT AGAIN!

"I'm not moving," Mariel screamed, throwing her book across the room. The book hit one of Sara's favorite vases, which broke into pieces. Parul started crying and climbed into Max's lap. Jace braced himself for the news with his arms crossed over his chest, his expression as hard as steel.

"We know how hard it is leaving, guys," said Max. "We've been here for three years and we've all got friends and connections to this place."

"It's the hard part of our lifestyle *and* it comes with the good stuff, too," said Sara.

"I don't want to leave my friends again. I hate saying goodbye," Mariel said.

"Me too, Mariel," Sara agreed. "And we're going to make sure we do it in the best possible way," she added, thinking about some of the Tools in the Toolkit.

"You have to say a clear 'goodbye' to say a clear 'hello,'" is one of the basic tenets in David Pollock and Ruth Van Reken's magnum opus, *Third Culture Kids: Growing Up Among Worlds*. When leaving, Global Nomads may display a whole range of behaviors and emotions. They may be overwrought or excited; they may let go too easily or too quickly; or they may display emotional flatness. Some of these reactions can cause someone to shut down emotionally, and this can create difficulties later when it comes to intimacy and long-term relationships.

Many families are familiar with the acronym R.A.F.T. in *Third Culture Kids*—a process that helps "leavers" say a clear "goodbye." It stands for: Reconciliation of any problems; Affirmation of the positive things you have learned in the place you are leaving behind; Farewells to people, places, and things; and Think Destination to prepare you for the next step of your journey. Most families already have ways to create their own R.A.F.T. The activities in this Tool are a good place to start the preparation for saying goodbye.

What You Need

Materials: Various materials, depending on the activity

Time: 30 minutes for the planning, activities can vary in length

Instructions

The suggestions below will help your family say a clear goodbye. They include activities that support children to express their thoughts and feelings.

Affirm connections

Cards and notes

- Help your children prepare cards with thoughtful notes to teachers, neighbors, friends, and others.
- Include a small memento or personal item from your child.

Small get-togethers

- Have several small get-togethers for quality time rather than big bashes where the time spent is less personal.
- Give your family friends something to remember you by.
- Help your child share out items they want to give away to specific friends.

Reflect and express

Feelings Jar

- Put out a big jar with paper and pens for everyone to write feelings they have during the preparation period.
- Decide as a family if you want to share them or leave them in the jar.

Graffiti Wall

- Put a big piece of paper up where the whole family can write or draw what they will miss from the people and places they're leaving behind.
- Include emojis to express emotions simply.
- Use specific phrases to model for your children how to say goodbye. For example:
  - "My best friends here are…"
  - "I'll miss the park by our house."
  - "I'll always remember the corner store."
  - "We made amazing meals in this kitchen!"

Pictures and words

- Print pictures of your favorite places at your present location and stick them onto a piece of paper.
- Everyone can write down their memories, thoughts, and feelings about the places listed.
- Keep the final product in a box that stores your memories, or make a video of it.

Goodbyes

Goodbye Book

- Make a book on an app, such as Canva or another such program, with several pages for pictures and classmates' signatures.
- Ask your child (or their teachers) to take pictures of their classmates.

- Your child can also bring the book to school for classmates, friends, and teachers to sign.

People, places, and things

- Visit people and places to say goodbye.
- Take pictures and organize them in folders for each location.
- Offer pictures of your family or small gifts to your friends so they might remember you.
- Ask forgiveness or forgive others for problems that arose while living there.

Build communication skills

Expressing emotions

- Here are some examples of the *Reflective Listening Tool #46*, which you can use when talking to your children about the move:
  - "You feel sad because you're saying goodbye to friends."
  - "You feel angry because you want to stay longer."
- You or your kids might also want to use the *I-Statements Tool #28* when sharing feelings about moving:
  - "I feel (upset) when (we move) because (we say goodbye to friends)."
  - "I feel (excited) when (we pack) because (another adventure is waiting)."

Conversation starters

- "Things I'm (excited, worried, frustrated) about are..."
- "Things I'm (sad, happy) to leave behind are..."
- "Things I look forward to when we move are..."
- "Things I'll always remember are..."
- "Things I want others to remember about me are..."

Connecting ahead

Explore the new location

- Find out as much information as you can about your new location online.
- Contact the school or other organizations your family will have a connection with. For example, sports clubs, art clubs, local expat groups, the local embassy, and so on.
- Plan a pre-visit.
- Make plans for activities to do once you arrive.

The Family Map

- Put up your *Family Map Tool #22* and review all the places you've been to.
- Look at your new destination and start dreaming about places to explore.

What Happened

Sara and Max used one of their Family Meetings to discuss how they would prepare for saying goodbye in the best possible way. They started the meeting by recognizing the kids' feelings: "You feel sad because you have to say goodbye to friends," and "You feel angry because you don't have any say in our moving," and "Maybe you also feel some excitement about discovering a new place."

"I feel frustrated because I have to leave my friends—again," said Mariel.

"Shall we put up a Graffiti Wall or a Feelings Jar?" Sara asked the kids.

They preferred a Graffiti Wall, which she put up in the living room. The kids soon started filling the big piece of paper with their thoughts and feelings about moving.

Everyone made a list of places they wanted to visit in the next few months before they left. They also made a list of people they wanted to say goodbye to. Jace and Mariel made a schedule of how to organize the visits.

Mariel set up a photo folder on the family computer where everyone could upload their pictures. It filled up over the following weeks and Mariel started organizing subfolders for everyone in the family.

Sara helped each child decide how they wanted to say goodbye to friends, either with cards, gifts, parties, or outings. She asked them to help her make cards for their teachers and to design a Goodbye Book for their classmates to sign.

The next part of the discussion was about affirming all the wonderful experiences and things they'd learned while living in other countries. They looked at the *Family Map Tool #22* and reminisced about the people and places from their journey. Jace added Turkey to the map and said he wanted to check out the best places to see. He'd heard about the hot-air balloons in Cappadocia and was eager to explore. Max encouraged everyone to start making their wish-list of places they wanted to explore. They wrote these on the right side of the Graffiti Wall and soon needed extra paper.

Sara and Max told the kids that when they found options for their new house, they'd discuss them together at a meeting to decide as a family. After that, each of them could decide what color they would paint their rooms—with permission from the landlord, of course!

Reflection

Goodbyes are probably the biggest challenge of a mobile lifestyle and require lots of awareness, care, and time to process. Consider these questions:

1. What activities does your family already use to prepare for saying goodbye?
2. How can learning to say "good" goodbyes develop emotional intelligence in children?
3. What will be the most important things to include in a Goodbye Book for your child or children?
4. How can your *Family Mission Statement Tool #2* support this process?

TOOL #26
Gratitude
Activity / Skill

"When I started counting my blessings, my whole life turned around."

Willie Nelson   Singer/songwriter and musician

Regularly expressing Gratitude affects all areas of your life

Purpose

To create awareness of positive things in your life.

Life Skills

Gratitude, Reflection, Self-awareness.

Counting Blessings

Although her family wasn't Muslim, Sara grew up with the traditions and rituals of Islam during her 12 years in Africa. Five of those years were in Egypt. The *Sujud Ash-Shukr* ritual—a prostration of thanksgiving for some benefit or blessing—had made an impression on her. Her friends' families also practiced other ways of expressing gratitude to Allah. For example, when they got in the car, her friend Wafaa's mother would say a prayer of thanks to Allah that they had a car. When they passed a woman with children walking along the road, Wafaa's mother would offer them a ride. She explained to Sara that this was the practice of showing gratitude beyond saying the prayer.

Sara still said some of these prayers in her daily spiritual practice and was also conscious of showing gratitude in her life. Her family expressed gratitude before dinner and bedtime. She put out a Gratitude Jar several weeks before the family made a major move and also thanked the people in their community before leaving.

After reading an article in the *Positive Psychology Journal* about the results of "Gratitude Experiments," she looked in the Toolkit and was inspired to start her own experiment with the whole family.

In her article 'The Science and Research on Gratitude and Happiness,' Erika Stoerkel writes:

"Researchers in Positive Psychology have found that gratitude and happiness are always strongly correlated. A possible theory is that gratitude moves people to experience more positive emotions, to thoroughly enjoy the good experiences, better their health, face adversity, and develop and maintain relationships of strength, which in turn makes you happier."

Stoerkel also quotes from Sonja Lyubomirsky's book *The How of Happiness*: "The more you practice and express gratitude, the more self-worth and self-esteem you feel, whether it's thinking about what others do for you, or what you have done (for yourself or others), it adds to your confidence and how effective you are at this thing called life."

What You Need

Materials: Paper, pen, jar

Time: 29 minutes (set up), one to five minutes (usage)

Instructions

Here are some ideas to discuss with your family on how to start including more gratitude in your life:

- **Gratitude Jar:** Keep slips of paper and a jar handy. When you think of something to be grateful for, write it on a piece of paper and put it in the jar. Everyone gets to read one at dinner, during a *Family Meeting Tool #23*, or when having a hard time.
- **Meal times:** Take a moment for everyone to express gratitude before a family meal.
- **For a problem or conflict:** When focusing on a problem situation, take time to express what you are grateful for in the situation.
- **Write notes:** Send a note to someone who deserves your appreciation.
- **Personal prayer:** Create your own and/or a family Gratitude Prayer.
- **Stay Positive:** The *Affirm the Positives Tool #6* and the *Compliments and Appreciation Tool #14* can help us stay positive and focus on gratitude.

What Happened

Even though the Tillers already expressed Gratitude in many ways, at the next Family Meeting, Sara proposed they experiment using it when there were problems. When they discussed how to keep the living room and dining area orderly, they brainstormed the possible benefits of tackling this problem. They discovered they would become more organized, work more closely as a team, and gain respect for these shared spaces.

Sara suggested they express gratitude for the problems they would face in the next two weeks and report back to the family. They created a phrase to remind them of this Tool: "I am grateful for the gift this problem holds."

In the coming weeks, Mariel had the honor of being invited to work with the choreographer in her dance troupe. Parul was invited over for playdates with two new friends. The Student Council nominated Jace for president, and he also became more popular with several of the girls in his class. Max was more positive when he came home from work. Sara felt more connected than ever with their family's mission and the people in their lives. She started thinking about how to use this Tool during the hectic time of moving and settling into a new location.

Were all these positive events for the Tillers the result of their Gratitude Experiment? You and your family can try your own experiment to find out.

Reflection

Consider these questions when adding more gratitude to your family's traditions:

1. In what ways could this Tool help your family prepare for moving and during the transition process?

2. Which of your children would agree to or not agree to participating in a Gratitude Experiment as outlined above? What can you do when children don't want to participate?
3. What changes in your life do you notice when you express more gratitude?
4. In what ways can you express gratitude to yourself for all you do and for your unique qualities?
5. How can this Tool support your *Family Mission Statement Tool #2* (if you have created one)?

TOOL #27
Grief and Loss
Activity / Skill

---

*"You can't truly heal from a loss until you allow
yourself to really feel the loss."*

Mandy Hale   The Single Woman

Grief and Loss are invisible travel companions

Purpose

To recognize and address feelings of Grief and Loss and
build emotional resilience.

Life Skills

Emotional Intelligence, Self-expression, Communication, Resilience.

Hidden Grief

Sara was driving in a residential area when a cat unexpectedly ran out into the street. There was no way to avoid hitting it; fortunately, it was killed instantly. When Sara got out of the car, she gasped when she saw how closely it resembled her cat, Rafiq, that she had been forced to leave behind in Cairo as a girl. Her throat tightened and tears spilled onto her cheeks. With her face in her hands, great sobs of sadness gushed from her heart. *What's going on?* she thought. *That was more than 25 years ago.*

When she got home, Sara took some time to look at pictures from that period in her life. Lots more tears and sobs came out until she felt she had cleared out the sadness. In that moment, she realized with greater clarity the impact of unexpressed grief from the repeated loss of friends, community, and a way of life. Thinking of her family, she wondered how she could keep "hidden grief" a minimal part of their "luggage?" For their upcoming move, Sara looked in the Toolkit for more ideas.

When moving, a sense of loss is unavoidable, and feelings of grief are inevitable. In his book *Safe Passage*, Doug Ota talks about the repeated disruption of a child's environment and explains that: "The fuses of the attachment system burn out, giving rise to a flattened, detached affect in the child." He connects this feeling of detachment with a student's ability to learn: "If attachment alarm bells are ringing, students will not be able to hear the teacher."

Lois Bushong's book *Belonging Everywhere and Nowhere: Insights into Counseling the Globally Mobile* provides clarity about the unique nature of the challenges faced by TCKs and ATCKs and how to approach them. "Trauma therapists believe that emotional wounding takes place in the right brain, the feelings and creative part. Therefore, to help healing, the use of the arts shows amazing results in the client." With the knowledge that art and music are non-verbal approaches that reach this part of the brain, more and more therapists are utilizing arts-based techniques to help clients work through challenges.

It takes time and sensitivity to navigate these feelings in a way that allows each "traveler" to know how to "pack" and "unpack" them. It's also important to have a counselor or therapist for extra support if needed. See the *Resources* for more information and help about this important topic.

Ways to Connect and Express

The more connected you are as a family, the more solid your core of stability will be to help withstand the losses you encounter on your journey. For example, the loss of friends, communities, and ways of life. Help your children process feelings and find coping strategies before, during, and after a move.

Preparation for the move

- Refer to the *Family Mission Statement Tool #2* as part of your conversations.
- Build your family's emotional language by talking more about feelings on a daily basis.
- Help process thoughts and feelings with some of the following Tools and activities:
  - **Coat of Arms:** Keep your family's *Coat of Arms Tool #13* and motto visible in your home.
  - **Graffiti Wall:** Put a large piece of paper up on the refrigerator (or in another central spot). Include a Feelings Chart (see *Appendix*), on which everyone can add their thoughts, feelings, and/or drawings during the days of preparation. Parents can discuss these at *Family Meetings Tool #23* or use them to understand the unspoken thoughts and emotions that are happening in the family unit.
  - **Gratitude:** Express *Gratitude Tool #26* and appreciation before meals and/or bed.

- o **Feelings Jar:** Set up a jar for everyone to add thoughts and feelings to on slips of paper during the weeks before moving. Choose some of them to start a discussion at *Family Meetings Tool #23*. Alternatively, a person can write on the paper "not for sharing" if they don't want them to be shared publicly. Here are some "starters" for expressing thoughts and feelings:
    - "I feel… when… because…"
    - "I feel… because… and I wish…"
    - "I think…"
- o **Map:** Put up a large map of the country/region you're moving to and that shows places of interest. Before leaving, everyone can add comments, questions, notes, and places they want to visit. Alternatively, use your *Family Map Tool #22*.
- o **Pictures**
    - Draw some of your favorite things from your present location, what you'll miss, and the things you'll take with you (physical, emotional, psychological).
    - Draw, sketch, or paint to express feelings and experiences for which you have no words.
    - Create goodbye cards for friends and the people who have helped you.
    - Several weeks before your departure, go through photos with your children to organize favorite memories in a family album.
- o **Stories**
    - Read books about moving (see *Resources*) and about inspiring travelers, heroes, and adventurers. Highlight what is hard for the characters and what they learn.
    - Children can create their own stories about moving (include pictures and/or photos). These self-created stories can be part of a collection to reread during subsequent moves.
- o **Write**
    - Journal to express thoughts and feelings.
    - Write your own stories and encourage your kids to write as well.

   o   **Animal Avatar**
- Each family member chooses an *Animal Avatar Tool #8*. Discuss how the Avatar's qualities can help respond to the move and to the sense of grief and loss.

During the move

- Increase family time (despite the hectic schedule and preparation). Make reference to the following Tools:
  - *Family Night Tool #24*
  - *Family Meetings Tool #23*
- Schedule more one-on-one time with each child.
- Listen to and validate each other's feelings.
- Express *Gratitude Tool #26* before meals and/or bed.
- Give more hugs and other comfort to each other.
- Distract with special treats, surprises, and experiences. For example:
  - Give your child (or children) a new book, journal, or toy for the journey.
  - Plan a scavenger hunt at the airport or while on the road.
  - Explore something new and different.

After the move/arrival at the new destination

Many of the same Tools that can be used preparing for or during a move can also be useful after the move. For example:

- Put up the *Family Heirloom Tool #21* with a welcoming ritual.
- Continue *Family Meetings Tool #23*.
- See also the *Family Night Tool #24*.
- Refer to your family's *Coat of Arms Tool #13*.
- Emphasize your *Family Mission Statement Tool #2*.
- Put up a Graffiti Wall.
- Use a Feelings Jar.
- Express *Gratitude Tool #26* before meals, at bedtime, or throughout the day.

- Read stories about settling in.
- Journal and write your stories.
- Refer to the *Animal Avatars Tool #8* to reflect on the move and what lies ahead.
- Stay in touch with friends from your previous location.
- Allow different adjustment times for each child, but observe how they're expressing their feelings. Find time to connect with each one of them.
- Get professional help from a school counselor, or a local, online, or embassy psychologist.
- What other resources can you add to your list?

What Happened

To reinforce her family's stable foundation in the months before their move, Sara put up a piece of paper for a Graffiti Wall and placed a Feelings Jar near their family's Coat of Arms Tool #13. The Family Meetings Tool #23 and one-on-one time with each child gave opportunities to listen to their thoughts and feelings. They also made more of an effort to practice Gratitude.

At dinnertime, Max and Sara started sharing more stories from their own Third Culture Kid experiences. Somehow, they would link their experiences and challenges to a positive perspective about their mobile lifestyle.

Everyone chose an Animal Avatar to reflect on the strengths they could tap into during the transition. While traveling, everyone had special tasks. For example, Jace was responsible for the passports, Mariel carried the arts and crafts bag, and Parul was Snack Master. Max and Sara used the family motto several times during the journey, "Wherever we go, we learn and grow."

After arriving in Istanbul, Sara referred to the Toolkit often as she stayed vigilant about the kids' settling-in process. She benefited from several meetings set up by the school's Transition Team comprised of counselors, several teachers, administrators, and parents. They shared the ways in which all children had the opportunity to process feelings of loss and sadness within the program. She met other new families and learned more about the people and resources available to support her family if needed.

Even though her kids were becoming more skilled as Third Culture Kids, Sara knew it was a lifelong task to recognize and process her own feelings about moving and to keep a positive outlook. For more resources about grief and coping strategies related to it, refer to the *Resources* section at the end of the book.

Reflection

When considering ways to support your family to process Grief and Loss, use these questions to guide your planning:

1. How many moves has your family made over the past three, five, or ten years?
2. What are the signs (or lack of signs) that your children are experiencing the effects of grief and loss?
3. In what ways does each member of your family express their feelings?
4. What are the phrases you use to help develop your children's emotional language? See other Tools, such as the *I-Statements Tool #28* and the *Reflective Listening Tool #46*.
5. Which other Tools reinforce your family's stable foundation to be more resilient when they experience the effects of grief and loss during their transitions and beyond?
6. What resources are available locally and abroad to support you and your family?

TOOL #28
I-Statements
Skill

"When you point a finger at someone, three fingers point back at you."

Unknown

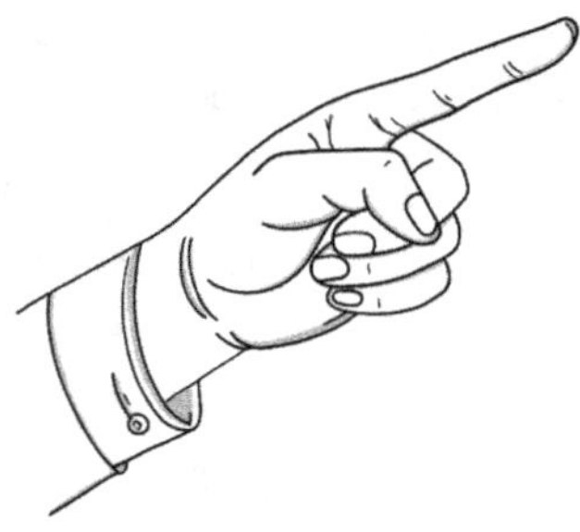

*Using I-Statements (rather than You-Statements) models
Emotional Intelligence for children*

Purpose

To express strong emotions in an appropriate way.

Life Skills

Emotional Intelligence, Communication, Self-care.

You, You, You!

Sara arrived home after a busy day of helping the PTO prepare for the Spring Fest at their school. She managed to buy groceries and was mentally preparing herself to make a quick dinner for the family. However, when she found dirty dishes lying everywhere, food left out, and a bin in the kitchen that was overflowing with garbage, she flipped.

"You left a mess everywhere! Why can't you guys clean up after your-selves? You treat me like I'm the maid. I've had it!" she yelled in frustration.

Jace, Mariel, and Parul listened to their mom, their heads hung in shame. She left the bags of groceries and stomped off to her room to calm down. After a while, she replayed this scene over in her head and felt worse and worse. She could see that the kids felt discouraged by her reaction. She would have preferred that they got defensive and argued with her. How could she share her frustration and move for-ward with her kids to find a solution together? She looked in the Toolkit and decided to try using I-Statements.

Don Dinkmeyer, Sr., Don Dinkmeyer, Jr., and Gary D. McKay write the following in *The Parent's Handbook* from the *Systematic Training for Effective Parenting* series: "Children who hear too many you-messages begin to feel discouraged. They may fight back, feel worthless, stop lis-tening. I-Statements focus on you; they don't label or blame. When you use an I-Statement, you simply tell how you feel."

If you are addressing a problematic situation by expressing how *you* feel, rather than blaming the other person, it's more likely your words will bypass a defensive reaction in the listener's brain, and the message will be heard.

You can use *positive* I-Statements to reinforce your child's effort or contribution in a situation. This formula allows you to state your feelings in a clear, objective way. See the *Encouragement Tool #18* for more insight into the power of a positive I-Statement.

What You Need

Materials: Paper, pen, something to record your voice, or a partner

Time: 40–60 minutes

Instructions

Go through these steps to learn more about the power of I-Statements:

Step 1

Read aloud (or record) the two statements below. The first is a "you-statement" and the second is an "I-Statement."

- "You make me so angry. You always walk away when there's a problem."
- "I feel angry when you walk away because I want to work out the problem. I'd prefer to find a way to talk about it calmly."

How do you feel like responding to each of the two statements above? What sensations do you have when reading them? Where do you feel them in your body?

Step 2

How to formulate an I-Statement:

State your feeling	**I feel...** *angry, sad* (problem) *happy, encouraged* (positive)
Connect it with a specific behavior or situation	**When you...** *walk away, hit, come home late* (problem) *help out, join us for dinner* (positive) **When...** *the phone breaks, the music is loud* (problem) *the kitchen is clean, it's quiet* (positive)
Give a reason. Place it in a bigger context.	**Because...** • *I want to connect calmly.* • *We are respectful in our family.* • *It has happened three times.* • *We want to support each other.* • *You're helping the family.*
State what you prefer (optional—if there's a problem).	**Preference** • I'd prefer to find a solution together. • I'd prefer to talk when we're both calm.

Practice

Just like actors rehearsing for a performance, we need to prepare and practice new ways of saying things before we say them to another person. Follow these steps to practice using I-Statements:

1. Think of situations in which to use both "problem" and "positive" I-Statements with your children or partner.
2. Write out your I-Statements using the formula above.
3. Practice reading them out loud several times.
4. Record and listen to them several times.

5. Find a time when you feel calm enough to tell your statements to the people involved.
6. Notice how they respond and listen.

What Happened

Sara took a chill-out break and then got her notebook to write a couple of I-Statements to share with her children. After practicing the statements out loud several times, she felt ready to talk to them. "I feel frustrated when I come home to a messy house because we already talked about helping each other to keep it clean," she told her kids. "I wish you would respect our agreement."

"We got busy," said Jace.

"I know you get busy *and* I also need your help to keep things in order," said Sara. (*Caring and Firm Tool #10*)

Miraculously, the kids didn't continue defending themselves. They quickly got moving to clean up the kitchen. Parul helped put the groceries away. Mariel helped with the cooking and set the table. Jace made a fruit dessert.

When Max arrived, he had his own I-Statement. "I feel energized when the house is orderly and everyone's helping each other because we are a team."

Sara and the kids looked at each other with a secret smile.

Was this the last time there were messes in the Tiller household? No, but the whole family was learning how to communicate feelings in an appropriate way. They were working together to solve problems. The children were becoming more independent and responsible. Their family bonds were strengthened and ready to be tested by the next challenge.

Reflection

Using and hearing I-Statements develops emotional intelligence. Consider these questions to build awareness around the effects of this strong Tool:

1. Which situation was easier to think of, the problematic one or the positive one?
2. Which I-Statement (problem or positive) was easier to share with the other person?
3. What surprised you about the listener's response to your I-Statement?
4. Which I-Statements will build more cohesion in your family?
5. Which positive Life Skills will your child develop by hearing and using I-Statements?

TOOL #29
Know Your Limits
Skill

"Your personal boundaries protect the inner core of your identity and your right to choices."

Gerard Manley Hopkins   Victorian poet and Jesuit priest

Setting limits means saying no at times

Purpose

To recognize the signs of being overextended. To create habits of self-care and establish boundaries for others to respect your limits.

Life Skills

Self-care, Respecting Limits, Empathy, Communication.

Out of Bounds

It was March, and the calendar of upcoming events was already over-flowing. Sara had invited friends to stay with them for the spring break and she needed to plan their time together. She had also volunteered to make costumes for Mariel's dance troupe. And somehow, she had signed up to visit the elderly home with the PTO. Also, as a new member of the Transition Team that had helped their family settle in, Sara was asked to start connecting with leaving families.

At home, Sara was committed to spending individual time with each of her children, but mentally, she was stressing about how to get all her tasks done. Evenings were often exhausting, even when the kids helped out with dinner. When Parul needed help with reading, the phone interrupted them several times. Sara finally snapped and put the phone on mute and threw it onto the couch. She wanted to cry when little Parul put a gentle arm around her shoulder and said, "It's OK, Mommy. I'll do it by myself."

Parents who move their family around the world have to make extra effort to ensure their children are safe, settled in, connecting with others, and thriving. Parents have their own needs for connection and contribution in the community, which requires additional time and effort outside the family. Traditional roles, communication styles, and family models contribute to how we accept responsibilities and balance them with personal well-being. In some cases, children overextend themselves and experience burnout based on their parents' model.

Setting clear limits communicates to other people in your life what you can and cannot take on. Establishing clear limits is also a form of self-care. The problem we usually face is how to communicate this in an assertive way—kindly and firmly.

What You Need

Materials: Paper, pen, the *Personal Mission Statement Tool #37* or the *Family Mission Statement Tool #2* (if you have created them)

Time: One hour

Instructions

The goal is to find balance and well-being, to focus on priorities, and to stay healthy. Go through each of the following steps and decide how to start setting your personal limits:

Step 1

Use this checklist to take note of how your body is responding to the stress in your life. Do any of the following apply to you?

- Overly tired
- Short-tempered with your family
- Tense muscles
- Confusion
- Digestion problems
- Low immunity
- Sleep disruption

Step 2

Choose from the following strategies to set limits and to communicate them clearly, and with respect.

Learn to say "No!"

- "I'm sorry but I can't help you move your boxes right now."
- "I'd love to help you but I need a break."
- "I can help you with your homework when you give me a heads-up the day before."

- "I'm feeling overwhelmed and I can't add another thing to my to-do list."
- "This is not a convenient time for me. Thank you for your understanding."

Take a break

- Create and use your own *Chill Out Space Tool #11*, in which your kids will know you're unreachable for some time.
- Take time for your hobbies.
- Go away for a weekend—on your own, with your partner, or with friends.

Reflect on your Personal Mission Statement Tool #37 and Family Mission Statement Tool #2

- How do you choose activities and situations in regard to your bigger purpose?
- Who are the people in your life with whom you can affirm your values and goals?

What Happened

Sara read through the Know Your Limits instructions and immediately recognized her body's signals for being overwhelmed. After the kids were in bed, she took out her notebooks and colored pencils, put on some music, and started drawing. An hour later, she felt calmer and went to bed.

In the morning, she called a local travel agency and gave them the dates for her friends' visit. She also called a seamstress whom several of the mothers had recommended to order the dance costumes. She contacted the PTO organizer and told her she was sorry, but her calendar was too full and she wouldn't be able to help with the elderly home this year. Lastly, Sara offered to help the Transition Team after spring break, when she would have more time.

After she shared her decisions with Max, they decided to go away for the weekend. Relaxing at the spa together, she realized it *is* possible to maintain a healthy balance between helping others and taking care of herself, in order to be at her best with her family. They had a good laugh when Sara read the "kismet" (fortune) that came with her coffee. She unrolled the tiny scroll and read: *"Lack of boundaries invites lack of respect."*

Reflection

Setting limits can sometimes feel selfish. Consider these questions to help you guide your decisions about setting limits in your life:

1. How can setting limits in some areas of your life help you do more?
2. How can your *Personal Mission Statement Tool #37* or *Family Mission Statement Tool #2* (if you have created them) be reinforced by setting your limits?
3. What do children learn when they see their parents modeling how to set limits?
4. What cultural and past models in your life determine your role in doing things for others?

TOOL #30
Learn the Language and the Culture
Activity / Skill

"Language is the road map of a culture. It tells you where its people come from and where they are going."

Rita Mae Brown   American feminist and writer

The best way to get to know a place

Purpose

To integrate into your new location and experience the culture as much as possible.

Life Skills

Communication, Perspective-taking, Tolerance, World-view.

Multilingual or Sublingual?

Max was in the living room doing his online Turkish lessons.

"Not another language!" complained Mariel. "I don't want to learn Turkish."

"I feel like I'm *sub*lingual," Jace said. "I know six languages but all of them are subpar."

"You poor children," Sara said with mock sympathy. "How many kids do you know who get to travel around the world and learn new languages and cultures? And Turkey has a very different culture from all the others we have lived in," she reminded them.

Parul sat on the carpet, playing with her dolls—Miss India, the Belgian one, and her new Turkish doll—and listening to everyone.

Learning a new language and getting to know a new culture helps build excitement for your upcoming move and helps you settle in more quickly. It's also a great way to build more brain cells. In Steven Bartlett's September 2023 podcast, *The Diary of a CEO*, Dr. Tara Swart, a neuroscientist and MIT professor, highlighted the benefits of learning a new language. "With foreign languages, your brain will not only get the benefits of being able to speak French or Portuguese, but will also be able to regulate your emotions better, solve complex problems, think flexibly and creatively, and override any conscious or unconscious biases you may have."

Experiencing new languages and cultures is at the heart of the Global Nomad life. In the discussion about "anchors and mirrors" in the section on *Global Nomad Foundations*, culture and geographical location are two of the three key elements that contribute to identity formation in young people. Family is the third piece of that discussion. Taking time to deepen your knowledge of the cultures and places you live in affirms your *Family Mission Statement Tool #2* to live a mobile lifestyle. When you give attention to what children discover about themselves in each location, you're facilitating their understanding of who they are on this journey.

What You Need

Materials: Your choice of language resource (book, lessons, app), resources to learn about the country and culture (books, internet, friends), a planner to organize your information and plans

Time: Ongoing

Instructions

Work through each of the sections below to choose ways you and your family can start accessing the language and culture of the place you're living in now, or of the one you're moving to.

Language

Some people pick up languages more easily than others; the goal is not perfection, but rather an exploration into a new cultural "territory." It's a gesture of respect for the host country where you live to attempt to know their language. Increasing your brain's neuroplasticity may also give you another reason to give it a go.

There are several ways to learn a new language. It's important to find a way that suits your learning style and available options. Some examples are:

- Use phone applications.
- Arrange online or in-person lessons, or investigate your embassy's training programs.

- Make friends with local folks (who preferably don't speak your language).
- Do a language exchange with someone who wants to learn your language.
- Get children's books and learn simple words and phrases with the help of a dictionary.
- Join a club or do activities that require you to listen to and use the new language. For example, yoga, cooking, art, or volunteering.
- Learn songs and memorize the lyrics (performing them for family and friends is optional!).

Country

There are many ways to get to know more about a new country before you get there:

- Online information is plentiful.
- Print out a map and plan places to explore.
- Add your new country to your Family Map.
- Share your plans with friends and family and invite them to explore together.
- Get to know how the roads work, as well as the train and bus systems.
- Find local families in your new area and ask for information.
- Join hiking groups, bird watching groups, seminars, or other events.

Once your family is there, you will also enjoy many options to get to know the place firsthand. Just start exploring.

Culture

The colors, sounds, tastes, and smells of a place are an intricate part of the culture that will become part of your family's memories as well as your identities as Global Nomads. There are many ways you and your family can explore the culture of your new country:

- Learn about traditions, holidays, arts and crafts.
- Take a cooking class and learn local recipes.
- Go to local markets and buy spices.
- Learn traditional songs.
- Join a local dance group.
- Take music or art lessons.
- Go to local concerts and events.
- Explore the museums and events halls.
- Connect with families from the new country, and plan meetings.
- Share your own traditions with local families.
- Volunteer for charity groups.

What Happened

The Tillers went to a market in Istanbul to buy some local pottery. As Max haggled over prices using the Turkish he had recently learned in his online lessons, his family listened and watched in wonder. After ten minutes of back and forth, lots of hand gestures, and even some joking, Max was pleased to seal the deal at a middle price. With a smile and a handshake, the seller wrapped up the bowls and, for good measure, also put some chocolates and bright pencils in the bag. "For your children to do well in school! *Tanrı aileni korusun* [God bless your family]," he said.

Parul repeated with perfect pronunciation and accent, *"Tanrı aileni korusun."* Now it was the seller's turn to be surprised by this little girl's ability to pick up Turkish so adeptly. Her family was just as surprised that Parul had magically learned Turkish.

When they unwrapped the bowls at home, the kids talked about how their dad had managed to negotiate in a new language. Max told them it was part of the culture to enjoy the back and forth of haggling over prices. He said the seller was very friendly and hoped they would meet more people like him while in Turkey. Suddenly, they all wanted to learn some phrases in Turkish so they could talk with people and get to know more about the culture.

Reflection

Use these questions to inspire your thinking about learning a new language and getting to know a new culture:

1. How can your children help arrange ways to learn the language and find out more about the culture?
2. Are there ways to combine these activities with your children's school?
3. How can you organize the cultural information you're learning to refer to it easily when you want to revisit it?
4. What are your family's ideas for keeping track of all the languages they know?

TOOL #31
Learn a New Skill
Activity

"Intellectual growth should commence at birth and cease only at death."
Albert Einstein

Keep tinkering with those brain cells

Purpose

To keep the brain and body active through learning.

Life Skills

Adaptability, Flexibility, Lifelong Learning, Curiosity.

New Neurons

Parul was learning how to ice skate at an indoor rink. Sara marveled at her daughter's balance, strength, and coordination. It looked so fun and effortless that she thought about trying it herself, but she knew how much easier it is for kids to pick up new skills compared to adults. The last thing Sara wanted was to embarrass herself by falling and carrying around some bruises as painful reminders.

While getting a hot tea in the reception area, Sara saw several posters advertising different activities: salsa and bachata, oriental dance, aerial yoga, pole dancing, Tibetan bowls, and more. So many choices to keep her body and brain active. How to decide?

In Steven Bartlett's September 2023 podcast, *The Diary of a CEO*, Neuroscientist Dr. Tara Swart talks about maintaining neuroplasticity after the brain stops physically maturing at the age of 25. She says, "It could be learning to play a musical instrument, making a new habit in your daily life, or interacting with people who have had a different life from yours." Science-backed research proves that adults can improve their brain power and health with continued learning, and decrease the chance of diseases such as dementia and Alzheimer's.

When was the last time you had to learn something new, either alone or in a group? Apart from the skill and the content, what did you learn in the process? This Tool will have you tinkering with new neural networks to keep your brain flexible!

What You Need

Materials: Internet, local resources, paper and pen

Time: Ongoing

Instructions

As with Sara, you may come across resources while doing something around town. Perhaps a conversation with someone will open up new ideas, or a search on the internet will yield a plethora of possibilities for learning.

As you read through the ideas below for yourself, find ways to include family members to build your family's inner network of cohesion.

- Sports and fitness
- Dance
- Yoga (or meditation)
- Art
- Music lessons
- Ceramics
- Jewelry making

- Flower arranging
- Learn a new language
- Become a wine sommelier
- Writing
- Photography
- Aromatherapy
- Life coaching

What Happened

Sara had recently received her certification to be a yoga instructor. She had never been a teacher and shied away from putting herself in the role of leading a group. Thinking about Parul learning to skate, Sara challenged herself to work on her teaching skills and started a class for parents at the school. It was a challenge to keep the sessions accessible and interesting for the different levels of students.

Sara realized she had a knack for explaining the poses in a way that non-native English speakers could easily understand. She felt her own yoga skills expanding to new levels as she developed her teaching skills. It was also a great way to get more yoga time for herself. The class quickly became popular with mothers, and she also found a new social group of appreciative and like-minded friends to spend time with.

Sara joined one of the other mother's aromatherapy trainings in a fascinating foray that was both fun and practical and which she enjoyed sharing with her friends and family. It had the added benefit of helping her take care of herself when feeling overwhelmed or stressed.

Reflection

Learning a new skill takes time. It also takes courage to step out of your comfort zone. Consider these questions to help motivate you:

1. What self-talk comments inhibit us from learning something new, or encourage us to learn something new?
2. What positive side effects do you notice when learning a new skill?
3. How can learning something together, as a family, help you all get more out of living in a different location?
4. What are you modeling for your children by learning something new?

TOOL #32
Life Journey
Activity

---

*"Not everyone will understand your journey. That's fine.
It's not their journey to make sense of, it's yours."*

Unknown

Looking at your journey as a whole creates a new perspective

Purpose

To view the events in your life as parts of a whole journey.

Life Skills

Reflection, Connection, Perspective, Mindfulness.

Sara's Journey

When the Tillers lived in Brussels, the transition counselor at the international school had offered a Life Journey workshop. To Sara, it had sounded like an interesting exercise to look at where her life had led her up till then, but she had been hesitant to attend. Why would she want to track her journey and analyze it? Her parents had moved their family a lot, just as Max and she were doing, but nothing monumental had happened along the way. If anything, it might be embarrassing to share personal experiences with strangers.

Now in Istanbul, the opportunity came up again, with one of her yoga cohorts. She decided it was the right time to explore her life journey up till that point.

In his book *Safe Passage*, Dr. Douglas Ota speaks of how mobility affects life stories: "The personal sense of continuity that one's self-narrative affords undergoes a massive rupture when the majority of the strands that make up 'who you are' get cut." He highlights that it's the mothers and children who most often experience this drastic "chop," while the dads feel a sense of continuity through their work.

This Tool, Life Journey, offers an overview of the various landmarks in your life in a visual format. When you take time to reflect on them, you also have a better perspective on the lessons and strengths gained over the years.

What You Need

Materials: Sheet or sheets of paper to make a line, colored pencils/ markers, selected objects, glue (optional), a partner to share with (recommended)

Time: 60–90 minutes

Instructions

Create your Life Journey with a group or on your own. This Tool requires enough time to reflect on your journey up to the present moment, and then to calmly reflect on what you have discovered. If possible, sharing with other participants is a great way to find support and connect. Put on some music and let your heart and mind wander through the steps.

Step 1

Draw a line to represent your journey up until now. It can be straight, curved, or winding. It's up to you how you choose to draw it.

Step 2

Decide on several important events in your life you would like to mark on the line you have drawn.

Step 3

Write these important events on the line in a way that makes sense to you. For example, brief notes, consecutive years, landmarks, general time period, etc.

Step 4

Reflect on (or share with a partner) the events on your map.

- What was difficult during specific events?
- What did you lose or gain?
- What did you learn?
- How did you become stronger because of it?
- Is there a common theme or thread you notice that connects with other pieces?

Step 5

Symbols surpass the mundane and give higher meaning to an event, allowing us to link otherwise unconnected events and experiences. Choose which events to create symbols for and draw them next to those events. For example, reaching a goal might be represented by a star, or a move to another country could be shown by a symbol that denotes resilience. (If in a group, you can share your symbols with the others.)

Step 6

Create a motto or a chant, or choose a song, to represent your journey.

Step 7

Post it somewhere and reflect on it for the next few weeks. Focus on your strengths.

What Happened

Six other Global Nomad mothers and one father came to the session and mapped out the important landmarks in their lives: births, deaths, successes, traumas, important moments, spiritual revelations, and the many moves they had made were sprawled out over each of their maps.

Sara pulled up several painful memories as well as some of the joys of her many successes:

- The various moves she had made with her family
- Rescuing two cats from a well, which became her pets
- Being introduced to Islam, learning Arabic, and practicing its rituals
- Caring for her mother during a serious illness while studying
- Meeting a partner to share the excitement of a mobile lifestyle with
- Getting an online business degree while working part-time, with a young child
- Adopting Parul against all odds in a system that discouraged foreigners from adopting

When she viewed the different events together, Sara felt like an explorer who finds so many riches along the way that the destination becomes less important than the trek to arrive there. Somehow, the disparate pieces made sense in the context of her unique story and her Global Nomad identity.

The group shared their maps and the "gifts" they had gained, adding several tears to the cartography of their Life Journey. Listening to the other participants, Sara reveled in the commonalities of their experiences, despite the differences. When the facilitator offered a follow-up workshop to create their Coat of Arms, Sara readily signed up. What else might she discover about herself and her journey?

Reflection

Once you've created the visual of your Life Journey, these questions can help you debrief the process:

1. What is something that surprised you in this activity?
2. How does telling your story give cohesion to the events?
3. What will be important to take with you from this activity?
4. In what ways can you add to this depiction of your life journey as you continue?
5. What ways are there to record experiences and memories for your children on your family's journey in different locations?
6. Where can you find support if you feel overwhelmed by reflecting on your Life Journey?

TOOL #33
Limited Choices
Skill

"Share control on your terms, or kids will take control on their own terms."

Foster Cline and Jim Fay   Parenting with Love & Logic

Giving Limited Choices affirms an Authoritative Parent style

Purpose

To establish firm limits while respecting your child's need for independence and control.

Life Skills

Communication, Setting Limits, Being Respectful, Decision-making.

Taking Control

It was right after they told their children that they were moving to Istanbul that Sara and Max were faced with learning a new skill: Limited Choices.

Jace was angry that he would have to leave his friends and start in a new school with a different program. He began staying out after his curfew and didn't call his parents to let them know where he was.

Mariel gave her parents the silent treatment for several days. She stopped helping out with chores and isolated herself in her room.

With older siblings as role models, Parul started acting out when it was time to turn off her favorite videos. She refused to help with chores and often "forgot" to clean up her toys.

"A misbehaving child is a misunderstood child," wrote Rudolf Dreikurs, a 20th-century Austrian-American psychiatrist and educator. As we learned earlier in the *Love and Belonging* section, in referring to a child's need for a sense of significance and belonging, Dreikurs asserts that children resort to misbehaving to fulfill this need. Dreikurs calls these misbehaviors "mistaken goals." They are: Undue Attention, Misguided Power, Revenge, and Assumed Inadequacy (giving up). Particularly when there is a power struggle, offering Limited Choices allows children to exercise some power within a secure structure. As part of your daily interactions, it's one way to build healthy independence in all children to avoid having constant power struggles.

In mobile families, where children have no real voice when it comes to moving, giving them Limited Choices can counterbalance some of the feelings of powerlessness and resentment. In addition to a daily diet of choices, the intentional use of choices before, during, and after a move reinforces a sense of power and contribution to the family. These kinds of experiences create "reflections" that also help construct a child's sense of identity, as discussed earlier in the *Identity Formation* section of this book.

What You Need

Materials: Paper or notebook, pen

Time: 40 minutes

Instructions

Limited Choices can be used for everyday situations as well as before, during, and after a move. To become more adept at making Limited Choices in the moment, use the guidelines below.

- Give two choices that are acceptable to you.
- The two options allow the child to choose when, where, with what, how, and possibly with whom to do a certain task or activity.
- If the child offers a third choice, repeat your choices: "We can consider that next time. For now, the choices are..."
- Avoid these kinds of questions: open questions, "yes" and "no" questions, "why" questions: "Where do you want to eat? Do you want to eat at the Thai? Why not?"

General use of Limited Choices

As an everyday practice, providing your children with Limited Choices can help to support your children's sense of independence and control. Here are some examples:

- "Will you do your homework now or after your snack?"
- "Shall we meet in the living room or the library?"

- "Will you pick up the blue or red blocks first?"
- "Do you prefer to take a walk or ride bikes?"
- "Do you prefer to help me now or in 20 minutes?"
- "Would you like help or do you want to do it alone?"
- "Will you turn off the computer or do you need help?"

Before the move

After you've told your children that you'll be moving and they've had a chance to absorb this fact, use Limited Choices to get them involved in the move. Here are some examples:

- "Do you prefer to contact new classmates now or wait till we arrive?"
- "Do you want to have a party at school or here at home?"
- "Would you prefer to visit the beach or the mountains before we leave?"
- "Would you prefer to pack things by yourself or would you like help?"
- "Would you like to lead our Gratitude prayer tonight, or should I?"

During the move

Depending on your situation and the stage of your move, you can offer choices while in transition. These examples will get you started on creating your own:

- "Do you want to stay at this hotel or that hotel?" (Assuming you're OK with either hotel!)
- "Do you prefer the window or the aisle seat?"
- "Do you prefer to wait here for the flight or walk around?"
- "Do you want to un/pack your room first or help with the kitchen?"
- "Shall we eat at the Thai restaurant or the Mexican restaurant?"

After the move

As your children feel more settled, continue giving them Limited Choices:

- "Do you prefer to take the bus on the first day or do you want me to drive you?"
- "Will you do after-school activities once or twice a week?"
- "Do you want to help plan our weekend activity or would you like us to decide?"
- "Do you want to have a Family Night on Tuesday or on Thursday?"

What Happened

When Max and Sara had decided on two housing options, they invited the kids to help choose where they would live. There was a lively discussion about the number of bedrooms, the proximity to school and to parks, the benefits of the neighborhood, the ease of public transportation, and the views from each of the two places. When the kids finally decided on a large fourth-floor apartment with a park close by, they started vying for their choice of bedroom.

Sara connected with the school and looked at the programs the kids could choose from. She said they could contact the student ambassadors or wait till they arrived. They could take Turkish lessons or choose not to.

While preparing to leave, Max and Sara gave their kids lots of Limited Choices—which items to donate, which things to ship, and which to take with them, where to visit before leaving, and how to say goodbye to friends. This was reinforced during the move when each child chose a job to do. Jace took care of the passports, Mariel created a bag of travel activities, and Parul was the Snack Master.

When they arrived, Sara and Max continued giving Limited Choices—when and how to set up their rooms, helping with the apartment, and choosing family activities. The kids got to choose whether to go by bus or car for the first week of school, which restaurants to try, and when to schedule the Family Night Tool #24. With lots of Encouragement Tool #18 about how responsible and helpful the kids were, both parents reinforced the positive contribution that is so essential to feeling appreciated.

By the time they had settled in, Max and Sara could see how giving Limited Choices empowered their children. They handled the transition more confidently and the family felt more connected. It was at one of their Family Meetings Tool #23 that they took a moment to revisit their Family Mission Statement Tool #2 and remember why in the world they were living this lifestyle. The family motto, "Wherever we go, we learn and grow," felt more apt than ever.

Reflection

Giving Limited Choices can be interpreted as being permissive. However, it's a Tool that is both *Caring and Firm Tool #10*, giving the child some control, within an acceptable framework. This is a quality of an Authoritative style of parenting.

Using the questions below, reflect on the use of Limited Choices.

1. How does giving Limited Choices support your parenting style?
2. When we give a Limited Choice, which other Tools are reinforced?
    a. *Caring and Firm Tool #10*
    b. *Connection Before Correction Tool #16*
    c. *Know Your Limits Tool #29*
3. How can using Limited Choices in your communication help your children develop other positive Life Skills?

4. If your child usually does what they are told to do, how can this
    Tool help them feel they have more control in their lives?
5. When are there times you might not be able to give a choice?
    Which activities are non-negotiable?

TOOL #34
Make Local Friends
Activity

"Friendship is the only cement that will ever hold the world together."

Woodrow Wilson   28th US President

A recipe for friendship can always be made with local ingredients

Purpose

To affirm the importance of friendship with local and expat communities.

Life Skills

Tolerance, World-view, Friendship, Communication.

The Challenge

With their move to Istanbul, Sara and Max would add a completely new culture and language to an already impressive list of life adventures. Sara thought back to Japan and Singapore when Jace and then Mariel were born. It had been hard to enjoy the local culture with new babies. Their network of friends and activities had been primarily with other Global Nomads who had babies. However, in India, Jace and Mariel were already in school, and the house helper and nannies became a bigger part of the Tiller family than in previous postings. When they adopted Parul, Sara and Max worked closely with Indian friends and professionals who helped them navigate the twists and turns of the adoption process. As the children grew, it became easier to make local friends in Belgium, where they were at the time, and to get to know the culture and country more than as "tourists." What new friendships awaited them in Turkey?

Is it possible for Global Nomads and TCKs to develop true friendships with local folks or only "assimilate elements from each culture," as described by the authors of *Third Culture Kids*? If the "sense of belonging is in relationship to others of similar background," then what can a mobile family gain from investing time and energy in friends who are firmly planted in their home culture? The answer is: some settled expats can be a bridge to the local culture.

Making friends with local families and long-term expats may not always be easy, but there are usually many things to share that can be mutually enriching and encouraging—their experience and view of the culture and country, and your adventures as a mobile family. This kind of friendship establishes a level of consistency that helps your children connect the various faces and places you move to and from.

What You Need

Materials: An open mind!

Time: Ongoing

Instructions

There are many ways to make local friends. Brainstorm with your family and make a plan for how you'll do this. Try these ideas to start with:

- Meet your neighbors, even if you don't speak the language (yet).
- Invite neighbors for a tea or drinks, or something that your culture does.
- Learn the language.
- Go to local parks to meet other families.
- Share your traditions and experiences for holidays and celebrations.
- Join local clubs.
- Connect with local people associated with your children's school, your embassy, or your work.
- Volunteer your services with local businesses or interest groups.
- Get to know your local community centers.
- Start a language conversation group.
- Offer a workshop.

What Happened

Sara was looking for ingredients in their neighborhood shop to make a special cake to celebrate their first six months in Turkey. She asked the shopkeeper, but apparently, condensed milk was not an everyday item on the local shelves. As Sara was wondering about using a substitute, another woman in the store spoke to her in French.

She explained how Sara could make condensed milk with one of the Turkish products, or even just by using heavy cream with added sugar.

The two women started sharing recipes and moved on to sharing their stories about how they came to live in Istanbul. Ebru was from Izmir. She had married a Frenchman and moved to Istanbul for his work. They lived close to the Tillers, and the two families started getting together. The parents and children became good friends, and by extension, the Tillers also gained a closer connection to the Turkish culture through Ebru's family and friends.

Reflection

Consider these questions to reflect on the importance of making local friends:

1. How can your children's sense of identity benefit from making local friends, and also, sharing your family's traditions?
2. What difficulties do Global Nomad children have when making new friends in a new location? How is it different for a toddler, young child, pre-teen, or teen?
3. Who or what can help you and your children make friends? A transition program? Student ambassadors? The Parent-Teacher Organization?
4. How does this Tool support your *Family Mission Statement Tool #2* (if you have one)?

TOOL #35
Message in a Bottle
Activity

"Hundred billion bottles washed up on the shore
Seems I'm not alone in being alone
Hundred billion castaways looking for a home."

The Police   Message in a Bottle

What do you want your future self to know?

Purpose

To connect wisdom and experience with your future self.

Life Skills

Communication, Reflection.

Message From the Past

Sara was helping her aunt Rachel move after living 30 years in the same house. Up in the attic, Sara found a box of stuff she'd stored there when she stayed with her aunt back in her high school days. It was a treasure chest of memories and moments that encapsulated Sara's life and personality during a difficult but "rich" time of her teen years: her mother's illness, winning awards for speech and debate, and for tennis, a breakup with her boyfriend, finishing the International Baccalaureate with top marks, losing a classmate, and making a major move with her family.

She leafed through the pages and pictures of her past self with awe. How had she kept herself together and moving forward? She discovered an unopened envelope addressed to "The future Sara" tucked into the back pages of a journal. Sitting in the dusty calm of the attic, she was transported back to the teenager who had penned these wise words about strength, hope, vision, the power of love, and the importance of following your dreams at any cost. Had she stayed true to that young woman's ideals along the way?

"A diary is a personal journal where you can reflect on your thoughts, experiences, and emotions. Making this a stable part of your daily routine can help improve mental, emotional, and physical well-being," writes Kevin Bennett in *Psychology Today*. Research has shown that regular journaling can help relieve stress, depression, and anxiety, and help with emotional regulation. It gives the writer an insight into their own thoughts and emotions, which supports self-awareness and provides insights for personal growth and innovative problem-solving.

Perhaps you have rediscovered the thoughts and feelings of your former self in an old diary, or maybe you've found an auspicious message that had lost its way and is now in your hands, as if by the universe's design? The Message in a Bottle Tool offers you an opportunity to express something meaningful to an older, more experienced, and hopefully, wiser self.

What You Need

Materials: A bottle or container with a sealable cap, slips
or sheets of paper, a pen

Time: 30–60 minutes

Instructions

Create your Message in a Bottle using the steps below.

Step 1: Write your message

On a piece of paper or other material, write your message using some of
these prompts:

- Your thoughts and feelings at this time of your life.
- Reflections on your time in this location.
- Wisdom you've gained from experiences and life events.
- A positive, encouraging message.
- Warnings or lessons learned.
- Your eulogy—what you might want to hear at your funeral.

Step 2: "Send" your bottle

Consider how to get your message out there. Options include:

- Pack the message in a special place to find later.
- Leave an anonymous message somewhere for a stranger to find.
- Send it out in a body of water to be found.
- Use an app such as *www.futureme.com* to write a letter to
  yourself and schedule the delivery date in the future.

What Happened

Sara came down from the attic uplifted by this visit with her former self. Yes, she had stayed on course throughout the years and was living her dream, but she hadn't taken the time to affirm it. *What a gift to share with my family*, she thought. That evening, she read the letter to her husband and children, stopping a couple of times to get through the tears.

The discussion about growing up, facing challenges, and staying on course was enriching for everyone. It also inspired the whole family to write their own messages to their future selves. Jace and Mariel chose to open theirs when they finished high school and middle school, respectively. Parul wanted to read hers in one year. Sara and Max planned to open theirs in three years (when they intended to make their next move).

Reflection

This Tool can be fun, as well as being a more serious reflection on life and the changes we go through over time. Consider these questions when writing your message and encouraging your children to write theirs:

- What are the ways you might leave future messages for your children to discover?
- Which of your children do you think will enjoy this activity the most?
- Do teachers in your child's school offer this kind of activity?
- Which Life Skills could this Tool support?

TOOL #36
Mindfulness and Prayer
Activity

"The family that prays together, stays together."
Pope John Paul II
Address to the Plenary Assembly of the Pontifical Council

*Mindfulness and prayer can be practiced
in so many different ways*

Purpose

To include a spiritual practice in your life.

Life Skills

Reflection, Gratitude, Respect.

Which Practice?

When Jace and Mariel were still preschool age, Sara started wondering about their spiritual education. Both she and Max were raised Christian and prayed, but their common spiritual practices were irregular. Sara had also gained so much from her experiences with Islam while living in Egypt. She loved many of the traditions and prayers and continued to use them, but they were in Arabic, a language no one else in her family knew.

Max agreed that solidifying their spiritual practice could only strengthen their family as they faced life's challenges, especially with all the transitions they would face in their mobile lifestyle.

In an interview with Nicole Spector for NBC News, Dr. David Spiegel, Medical Director of the Center for Integrative Medicine at the Stanford University School of Medicine, shared his research on the brain. His team used MRIs to show how prayer affects the parts of the brain associated with self-soothing, self-reflection, and the reduction of the "fight-flight-freeze" survival instinct. The release of oxytocin, the "feel-good" hormone, allows the person praying or meditating to reach another level of awareness about themselves and their surroundings.

In triple-blind experiments, results also showed significant (positive) effects on the health of both the person praying and those they were praying for. For more examples of this, see the work of Chittaranjan Andrade and Rajiv Radhakrishnan in their article on 'Prayer and Healing' in the *Indian Journal of Psychiatry*.

With this Mindfulness and Prayer Tool, parents nurture a connection with the "self" and with something bigger than the individual. By making this a part of your daily practice, children gain a sense of significance and belonging within the family and beyond. Nowadays, there are many ways to "pray" or practice mindfulness that can suit your family's beliefs.

What You Need

Materials: A variety of mindfulness and
prayer practices to choose from.

Time: 5–15 minutes.

Instructions

Here are some suggestions for how to incorporate a level of mindfulness
and prayer into your daily life:

- Use prayers from your spiritual upbringing or create your own.
- Create meaningful affirmations as a family to use for specific
  occasions. For example, to use before, during, and after moving,
  or during hardships, to celebrate successes and affirm
  connections.
- Seek spiritual guidance from someone you respect.
- Build friendships with other families that have a spiritual
  practice.
- Join a church or group that prays or uses mindfulness in their
  practices.
- Express gratitude regularly throughout the day, or before
  dinner.
- Plan a few minutes of silence as a daily practice.
- Use breathing practices.
- Practice Yoga Nidra, relaxing and promoting an awareness of the
  body.
- Get phone apps with guided practices on them.
- Set reminders on your phone to schedule mindfulness moments
  in your day.

What Happened

Sara shared with Max more about the Islamic practices she had learned. There were prayers for all parts of the day—when waking up and going to sleep, before and after meals, before going to the bathroom and after, and even before and after sexual intimacy.

Max shared prayers he had learned for guidance, gratitude, and staying connected with his faith. Together they defined the common themes in their spiritual practices—gratitude, alignment with a higher power, trust, and service to others—and began to create prayers and rituals for who they were as a couple and a family. It would be an ongoing process, but with each of them renewing a daily personal practice as well, they felt certain they were heading in the right direction.

Reflection

Mindfulness and prayer are very personal ways to connect to yourself and to a higher power. Although there are different ways to do this, consider the following questions about how such practices affect you and your family:

1. Which practices (spiritual or other) help you handle the stress of everyday life, especially during the transitions of moving and settling in?
2. What conversations have you had with your children about a spiritual practice?
3. Which practices would be suitable for your whole family to do together?
4. What are we modeling for children when we regularly incorporate such practices into our daily lives?
5. How does practicing mindfulness and prayer support your *Family Mission Statement Tool #2* and your *Personal Mission Statement Tool #37*?

TOOL #37
Personal Mission Statement
Activity

"Knowing our personal mission further enhances the flow of mysterious coincidences as we are guided toward our destinies."

James Redfield   The Celestine Prophecy

Follow your star

Purpose

To clarify or define your purpose in life.

Life Skills

Reflection, Thinking, Communication.

Sara's Mission

When Sara finished a seven-day yoga retreat for her teacher training and certification, she was convinced she had made the right decision. Doing yoga and sharing it with others felt very connected to something deep inside her. One of the other trainees offered a session to her fellow yogis to create a Personal Mission Statement. Even though Sara felt she had a strong idea of her mission in life, she decided to participate in this session with her new friends.

What You Need

Materials: Paper or notebook, pen, colored pens (optional)

Time: 60–90 minutes initially, plus reviews (ongoing)

Instructions

To start creating your Personal Mission Statement, use the following steps as a guide:

Preparation

- Plan a quiet time to focus.
- Gather whatever you need to spend this time productively. For example, relaxing music, candles, special scents, a soothing beverage, and so on.

Step 1

Choose your favorite way to brainstorm and use these prompts to get your ideas flowing:

1. Identify your core values. These could be things like self-realization, autonomy, adventure, balance, service, creativity, faith, learning, meaningful work, wealth, etc.
2. List your passions, skills, and talents.
3. Identify your goals and dreams (short-term and long-term).
4. How would you like people to remember you after you have moved from a place?
5. What do you want to contribute to your community and to the world?

Step 2

1. With the ideas from your brainstorming in Step 1, write out a draft of your Personal Mission Statement.
2. Read through it and let it settle in for a few days, or longer.
3. Revisit your Personal Mission Statement after it has settled in and make any changes you feel are necessary.

Step 3

1. Create a final draft as a poster or a digital copy on your phone.
2. Refer to it regularly, or as a reminder when needed.

What Happened

Catalina, the facilitator, set up a calm space with gentle music to help the participants settle into their thoughts and work with focus. She led them through a short relaxation exercise and then read through the prompts for brainstorming. The smell of sage that filled the room created an atmosphere for self-reflection and clarity as everyone began to write out their ideas.

Ninety minutes later, Sara had a good first draft, which she took home. A week later, she reread it and made some minor changes before making a final copy.

On a sheet of paper from her sketchpad, she wrote out her statement and decorated it with colors and designs. She posted it above the mirror in her bedroom and also took a photo of it to look at on her phone.

Reflection

Once you have created your Personal Mission Statement, reflect on these questions:

1. How does your Personal Mission Statement coordinate with your *Family Mission Statement Tool #2*?
2. What do you imagine your partner's personal mission might contain?
3. How often should your Personal Mission Statement be revisited and revised?

TOOL #38
Money
Activity / Skill

"Teaching your kids about money is never just about money."

Dave Ramsey   The Total Money Makeover

Start teaching kids about money early on

Purpose

To clarify your values about giving your children money, and to develop your children's relationship with money.

Life Skills

Decision-making, Managing Money, Responsibility, Independence.

Cash Machine

"Can you give me another 20 euros, Dad?" asked Jace.

"What happened to the 50 I gave you?" replied Max.

"Inflation, Dad!" quipped Jace.

"Mom, look at this cute makeup bag. It's only 39 euros," said Mariel.

"Cute price, too!" said Sara.

"Mommy, I need that bear. He's got the same heart t-shirt as my bear from Prague," Parul said.

"Don't you have enough bears, sweetie?" Sara replied.

The Tillers were waiting for their flight at Schiphol Airport in Amsterdam. Sara and Max wanted to have a calm cup of coffee. However, the kids were drawn into the well-designed flow of shopping options for travelers, with so many things they desperately "needed" calling for their attention.

Up until now, when the kids asked for money or wanted to buy something, Sara and Max would decide in the moment whether to be the benevolent financier or not. When they traveled, they gave each of the kids some cash to shop in the airport stores during layovers. If they didn't spend it all, they could add what was left to their savings. If they overspent, Mom and Dad were the family cash machine.

"It's important to introduce the concept of money early. Letting kids manage an allowance teaches them to think in terms of choices, alternatives, and consequences," write advisors on the Scholastic website for parents. They caution against using money as a reward for good grades.

This approach disconnects children from the love of learning and doing their best and puts the focus on receiving the reward. Likewise, a weekly allowance is not payment for household chores, which are simply a way children can contribute to the family.

Considering how dependent TCKs are on their parents when living in foreign countries, developing their financial skills encourages a sense of independence and responsibility. As with all such Life Skills, the most valuable part is the discussion. Whether you find solutions together or allow your child to explore, make mistakes, and learn on their own, it all adds up to learning about financial responsibility.

What You Need

Materials: Paper, pen, notebook, calendar, and money!

Time: 30–45 minutes

Instructions

There are different beliefs and thoughts about giving children a weekly allowance. Parents must decide what they can afford to give on a regular basis, either weekly or bimonthly. When using the Money Tool, consider the guidelines below.

Guidelines

How to set it up:

- An allowance is separate from basic household chores (which are a contribution to the family and unpaid).
- Decide if you will give cash or set up a bank card for kids over 12. A bank card also allows you to track spending.
- Kids can earn extra money for bigger jobs (see the *Chores Chart Tool #12*).

- Kids need information about saving, budgeting, investing, and borrowing.
- Be empathetic when your children overspend or want something outside their budget, but *don't* give them extra money. Direct them to choose bigger jobs to earn extra money.

Money savvy

What kids will learn:

- Managing and budgeting money teaches children financial aptitude.
- Children become adept at working with different currencies and systems.
- Using local currency integrates them into the culture and local economy.
- Add pictures of the different notes and bills of different countries to your photo album of memories.

Discussion

Here are some ideas for starting the discussion with your kids when introducing the idea of getting an allowance:

- "We are a team and you can help by contributing in these ways." (Name chores and bigger jobs that kids can do to earn extra money.)
- "You can learn how to manage your own money."
- "You can save money for bigger items."
- "Where will you keep it?"
- "How will you decide what to spend it on?"
- "What will we, the parents, buy or share the costs on?"

What Happened

Max and Sara were already using the "50-30-20" rule: 50% for necessities, 30% for wants, and 20% for savings. They adjusted the amounts of "necessities" and "wants" to include their kids in this plan. The formula they used for monthly allowances was 10 euros multiplied by each child's age. Jace would receive 160, Mariel, 120, and Parul, 60 euros a month.

Once this was decided, they called a "financial planning" meeting with the children. "We've noticed you're all very capable of doing so many things: helping around the house, managing school, adjusting to new places, developing your interests, and working out problems," said Max.

The kids waited expectantly...

"Are we moving again?" asked Jace.

"No!" said Sara. "We want to talk about giving each of you an allowance."

"That means money, honey!" Mariel whispered to her little sister, who suddenly perked up.

Max explained their calculations and the monthly formula for each child. The kids asked if this was for doing chores.

"No, chores are separate," said Mom and Dad together. But there would be a list of bigger jobs that any of the kids could help with to earn extra money. They asked if they would get a raise on their birthdays. "Yes," said Max and Sara.

The first task for the kids was to convert the amount in euros to Turkish lira. Jace and Mariel calculated theirs and showed Parul hers. "Wow! I'll be rich," she exclaimed when she saw the money conversion showed a much bigger number.

The next point of discussion was whether the kids wanted this amount monthly, bimonthly, or weekly. They also discussed how to budget and save their money, as well as what to do if they ran out of money before their next allowance. "No more Bank of Mom and Dad!" Max and Sara chanted together. "If you don't have enough, you'll have to work it out."

They clarified what they would pay for and what the kids would have to spend their money on. For example, the kids would use their money for personal interests, going out with friends, extra expensive clothes and shoes, or sharing the cost of phones and laptops.

From several articles and podcasts, Sara and Max got the idea of setting up investment accounts for their children to pay into using some of their allowance. It was a valuable lesson that would have a practical payoff later. The discussions about money also clarified Sara and Max's values as a family and strengthened their connection as a couple.

At the end of their first meeting with the kids, they decided to go out for dinner to celebrate, and Parul asked, "Who's paying?"

Reflection

If you decide to use this Tool, consider these questions:

1. How does your present "money system" allow your children to learn financial skills?
2. What beliefs and values do you have that support or go against giving your child an allowance?
3. How does a child's motivation change when receiving an allowance that is *not* dependent on doing chores, and when the allowance *is* dependent on doing chores?
4. How can this Tool help children integrate into the country where you are living?
5. What Life Skills can managing money develop?

TOOL #39

Music

Activity

---

*"My Brain is 5% names, 3% phone numbers,
2% stuff I should know for school, and
90% song lyrics."*

Jane Holmes
Morning Show Radio Host, Station 3AW, Melbourne

You don't have to be a musician to make music

Purpose

To harness the power of music to increase a sense of well-being
and connection.

Life Skills

Emotional Intelligence, Non-verbal communication, Self-care,
Teamwork.

Musical Crossroads

Parul was listening and dancing to her favorite Disney song for at least the hundredth time when Sara finally broke down and asked her to change the song or turn off the music. Parul reluctantly turned it off, but as she left the living room, she started singing and dancing happily again.

Mariel soon entered, singing along to a song that was booming from her phone, oblivious to her mom, who was working at the desk. When she twirled off to the kitchen, Jace came along rapping to a song that was playing so loudly that Sara could hear it from his earbuds. She tapped him on his shoulder.

"Mom! What are you doing?" he screamed as he pulled off the earbuds.

"Turn it down!" she yelled.

"You don't have to yell." Jace stomped off to his room and soon after, his music was amplified on his speakers.

Sara put on *her* headphones and chose a selection of focus music. Soon she felt more centered and was able to work on her blog for an hour, until Max arrived, and country music started blasting in the kitchen. *There must be a way to harness the power of all this music!* she thought.

In 'Why and How Music Moves Us,' a wellness article on the Pfizer drug company's website, Jennifer L.W. Fink shares research about how listening to and making music has a direct effect on the body, brain, and emotions. Blood flow increases and the "feel-good" chemical, dopamine, starts circulating through our brains and bodies. Oxytocin is also produced when we play or sing music in a group, helping us to feel more connected. Getting in sync with others through the regular beat of music and breathing in rhythm are natural stress relievers that reduce levels of the stress hormone, cortisol, in the blood.

The power of music to improve, or even heal, a range of physical, mental, and emotional ailments across all age groups has become more accepted as scientists and doctors see the results. "Oldies" songs help Alzheimer's patients tap into memories. Playing instruments helps in the rehabilitation of stroke patients. Listening to and playing music helps with mood regulation in cases of depression or stress, and helps autistic children develop language and social skills. With the present-day understanding of how music affects the brain, new styles of music are used to increase brain power for working and studying.

Listening to, singing, or playing music together is a unifying experience. In Global Nomad families, music is a Tool to be used for expressing and affirming emotions and creating better connections between people. For these reasons, it is fitting to use music in many situations as a family. For example: when there's work to be done, to relax, to celebrate, or to mark special occasions.

What You Need

Materials: The favorite songs of everyone in your family, a platform to create playlists, hand percussion or other musical instruments

Time: 30–40 minutes

Instructions

Gather your family together and propose putting everyone's favorite songs into playlists for different occasions. Also, suggest finding ways to have fun making music together.

Favorite songs

Collect everyone's choices for eventual playlists: everyone creates a list of their top five (or ten) favorite songs and shares them with the family.

Create playlists

Ask everyone to create playlists for different occasions:

- Songs for moving and settling in
- Celebrations
- A family theme song or personal theme songs
- Dance breaks
- Other ideas for your family

Making music

You don't need to be a musician to tap, shake, strum, and beat musical instruments.

- Invest in simple hand percussion instruments. For example, hand drums, triangles, shakers, bells, tambourines, claves, and so on.
- Encourage your family to learn to play instruments like the ukulele, guitar, piano, violin, etc.
- Create texts to chant during improvisations or write lyrics to create your own songs.

Musical moments

Start using your playlists and instruments regularly.

- Use your playlists before, during, and after a move.
- Use music to highlight any celebrations your family has.
- Have dance breaks to get everyone active and feeling upbeat.
- Organize family jam sessions for fun, special times, or to express yourself non-verbally.
- Use instruments on your own for relaxation and self-expression.

What Happened

Shortly after the musical "crossroads" occurrence in the Tiller home, Sara walked her family through the steps of the Music Tool in the Toolkit. It was to be expected that not everyone would be thrilled with each other's musical selections. However, they finalized a playlist to use for celebrating special occasions. It included one song from everyone's favorites and a couple of epic songs they all liked. They were given the task of researching more songs the whole family could enjoy when moving house, and also some upbeat songs for dance breaks.

Max got excited about the idea and invested in several hand percussion instruments and a *cajón*, a box you sit on and slap or hit, like a drum. When he brought them home, the Tillers had their first musical jam. Out of the ensuing cacophony—experimenting with the sounds and possibilities of the instruments—their beats and rhythms began to synchronize. In total, they spent over an hour improvising and feeling connected by the music they were making together. Jace and Mariel both started talking about learning to play guitar, while Sara was secretly thinking of renewing her piano-playing skills. Parul went off to her room singing her favorite songs and preparing for their next family jam session.

Over the next couple of months, Sara gathered more of the family's songs into playlists that she would have ready to share when they all needed a boost of energy and connection. She also started thinking ahead to future transitions and ways to use their playlists to lighten the load of packing and moving.

Reflection

Most people think we must study music to be musical. Although lessons teach us about music and build specific skills, every person is innately wired for rhythm and song. Use these questions to invite more music into your family's life:

1. When could you use family playlists to enhance the connections between all of you?
2. Which favorite songs or musical pieces are popular with everyone in your family?
3. Which of your children is tech-savvy enough to create playlists to share with everyone?
4. What are your beliefs around being musical that might inhibit you and your children from using this Tool?
5. What Life Skills do you feel making music will nurture in your children?

TOOL #40
Online Career
Skill

"Going after what you want is a form of self-love. Teach your kids about loving themselves by loving yourself."

Catherine Reitman Actress and writer

Having an online career has never been easier

Purpose

To develop your skills and talents and to connect them with the world.

Life Skills

Self-efficacy, Self-esteem, Independence, Communication.

Online Mom

After Max and Sara's conversation about weekly allowances for the kids, Sara got to thinking of ways she could generate more income. She didn't have the right to get a paid job on their postings and so she donated her time to staying active in the local and expat communities. When the kids were younger, this was enough to satisfy Sara's need to keep growing. Later, she offered free yoga classes to other expats once she'd got her certification.

Now, she wanted to expand her reach to share her skills and experience. *The internet offers so many possibilities*, she thought. She turned on her laptop and started to explore.

In 2022, the number of Digital Nomads was 35 million, reported the WYSE Travel Confederation using statistics from New Horizons IV: A global study of youth and student travel. And that number is on the rise as more and more work-at-home options are available.

If you're an accompanying spouse, this opens opportunities anywhere there's internet. Whether working remotely for a company, creating marketing content, offering an online course, or setting up your own business, the internet and the modern mindset are primed for this new form of work and lifestyle.

What You Need

Materials: An idea to develop into a business, an internet connection

Time: Indefinite

Instructions

There are so many resources to choose from online. Here are some points to consider as you surf the internet for ideas:

- What's your goal? To build a business, connect with others, expand your reach, or to make money?
- What are your passions, skills, and talents?
- What kind of people would you want to connect with?
- What things *don't* you like to do? For example, sell products, write, or get in front of a camera.
- Which online forums are connected to your passions, skills, and talents?
- Who do you know that works online?
- How much time will you be able to commit to each week?

What Happened

Sara researched online work and discovered an overwhelming range of options, everything from coding to customer service, consultancy, content writing, marketing, betting, blogging, teaching, online therapy, and more.

As she explored, she also came across several expat writer blogs, which she subscribed to. Following a trail of interesting articles and links, Sara began turning her passion for "self-care in the whirl of expat living" into a blog. Writing about her experiences and the philosophical fruits that grew from them became both cathartic and reaffirming. She started including short videos about yoga, relaxation, and mindfulness. The more she wrote, the more she could feel a bigger project taking shape in her mind: a book.

Sara also learned about affiliate marketing, and a whole new mindset about making money unfolded in her thinking. Her vision to expand her influence was becoming a reality.

Reflection

Developing an Online Career takes time, but, more importantly, it requires a different way of seeing yourself and your contribution to the world of work. Consider these questions as you explore using this Tool:

1. How will having an Online Career affect your sense of identity and significance?
2. In what ways will having a larger community online help with your transitions to new locations?
3. What are you modeling for your children by developing your own Online Career?
4. How could an Online Career align with your *Personal Mission Statement Tool #37?*

TOOL #41
Organize Memories
Activity

"Memories are the key not to the past,
but to the future."

Corrie ten Boom   The Hiding Place

Photo albums are one way to organize memories

Purpose

To organize photos and other memorabilia for you and your children so you
have easier access to the memories from your journey.

Life Skills

Organization, Emotional Intelligence, Sense of Purpose, Reflection.

Overload!

The notification popped up on Sara's computer like an unwelcome guest pounding on her door and filling her with dread: "Disk almost full. No backup for 635 days."

"Just what I need!" she yelled. "Not!"

Jace popped his head in. "Are you OK, Mom?"

Sara explained to him that the computer disk was full, and he expertly started clicking around. "You've got too many photos and videos," he said. "There's no space for anything else. Do you need *all* of them?"

"Those are our memories from the past eight years. Of course I need them!" Even as she said it, Sara realized it was time to clean up and organize those memories. But the thought of going through all those files felt overwhelming. At the same time, she knew how important it was, not just for the computer, but for her family's journey.

Calvin Coolidge, the 30th president of the United States of America, once said, "The only difference between a mob and a trained army is organization." It's a perfect metaphor for the "mob" of digital photos stored on your various devices.

Consider a non-mobile child who has grown up in a monoculture, with family, friends, and neighbors serving as regular reminders of the child's experiences and memories. Their identity is continually affirmed by the links to family, community, and location that have been constant throughout their lives.

Compare this to a mobile child who is challenged to shape a myriad of multicultural influences and experiences into a Third Culture Kid identity. By creating, organizing, and accessing memories in the form of photos and other media, we structure and reinforce a child's internal store of experiences. Ultimately, this contributes to identity formation and becomes a valuable resource throughout their lives. Furthermore, as they continue along their own life journeys, this resource connects them with their past, their family and friends, and the places they've lived, like a welcome travel companion.

An example of the importance of memories is shown in the animated Pixar film *Inside Out*. It depicts what happens to a girl's brain when she loses connection to her memories and family during a major disruption—the family moves. She falls apart as her emotional and mental resilience are negatively affected. Her parents eventually help her restructure those memories and offer the support she needs to realign herself with the family.

What You Need

Materials: Photos, videos, printer, book binder

Time: Ongoing

Instructions

There are three parts to this Tool: Create, Organize, and Access. Use the ideas below to get you started.

Create memories

Whatever your family does, highlight the moment to make it memorable. For example:

1. Talk about what's interesting, different, cool, or unusual.
2. Express appreciation for the different aspects of an experience.
3. Take pictures and collect souvenirs and artifacts (or take pictures of them).

Organize memories

Going through old photos and videos can be tedious, but once it is done, you'll have a valuable resource for your family's journey. Set aside time to complete this task and then make a commitment to keep photo and video files organized from now on. For instance:

1. Put pictures into folders by date and location *soon after you take them.*
2. Create digital or physical albums and keep them accessible.
3. Older children may want to help choose and organize photos.
4. Start a family blog about your adventures abroad.

Access memories

This is a crucial piece for children who grow up in ever-changing locations. Read the suggestions below to think of ways to share memories once they are created and organized:

1. Leave the photo albums where your children can look at them.
2. Create and give away yearly calendars that record the highlights of your experiences.
3. Go through albums together and discuss the experiences with your kids and what they remember from them. Reminisce about feelings, tastes, smells, people, and so on.
4. Affirm the fact that your children are world travelers who have many different cultural influences that make up who they are.
5. Encourage your child to draw, write, dance to, or sing about their experiences to express what they mean to them.

What Happened

Sara set aside two hours a week to go through all the photos and videos of when the kids were very young. She created her own system, based on each child's developmental milestones, as well as pictures that showed the different cultures they lived in.

It was a monumental task that gave her strength as she persevered through the exciting memories as well as some of the more challenging ones. The real reward came when she saw her kids' reactions to the books she printed, each one devoted to a specific year or location.

Jace and Mariel got interested and started organizing the photos from the point Sara had stopped, getting rid of some and cataloging others. Soon, the old photos and videos were organized and stored on an external hard drive, and that pesky hard drive reminder disappeared. In total, Sara had ten books printed and they were shared on their living room table. For two months, the family went through them, reminiscing, laughing, and discussing some of the special moments they'd had on their mobile adventure. Sara put them back on the shelf eventually but would regularly find one of the books left open on the couch where one of the kids had been enjoying it.

She made a plan for her and the kids to organize their new photos into folders soon after they took them. She even put together a special book of "our life before kids" pictures as an anniversary present for Max. Not only was Max thrilled to take a trip down memory lane, but their children loved looking at Mom and Dad when they were young. In November, Mariel organized a family calendar with her favorite pictures and sent it to their grandparents and other relatives for Christmas.

Later, in high school, Mariel would use photos from her family's journey to inspire a dance project about life as a TCK. At university, Jace would use them to write essays about his experiences from different cultures and his search for self. In middle school, Parul would make up scenes and stories from different countries to act out with multicultural puppets.

Reflection

Creating and organizing memories can be done in a variety of ways and have a long-term effect on your family's sense of connection. Use these questions to consider how to get the most out of this Tool:

1. What other ways are there to organize your memories and experiences in each location for future reference?
2. How can you include organizing photos into your family rituals or regular planning sessions? Which of your children will be motivated to help?
3. Consider how your children will share their mobile life experiences with their children.
4. How can such photo albums support the activity *Life Journey Tool #32*?

TOOL #42
Packing
Activity

Packing can be overwhelming!

Purpose

To involve the whole family in the process of packing when preparing for your move.

Life Skills

Planning, Teamwork, Decision-making, Problem-solving.

Packing… Again 🙁

While preparing for the packers to come for their belongings, Sara was faced with convincing the kids to leave old toys, books, clothes, and knick-knacks behind. Parul fiercely protected her overpopulated "zoo" of stuffed animals. Jace and Mariel still had feelings of resentment about moving and were dragging their feet when it came to helping out with the packing. Max was out of town. Sara was so stressed with it all, she was ready to run off for a beach vacation with free cocktails and daily massages. After a break in her *Chill Out Space Tool #11* (aka "The Beach"), Sara recalled David Pollock's comment in *Third Culture Kids* about moving: "It takes six months to pack up one's heart, and six months to unpack it." She found an extra squeeze of energy, took a deep breath, and searched the Toolkit for inspiration. She also found some goodbye books to read to Parul.

Consider the first two levels of Maslow's Hierarchy of Needs discussed earlier: Physiological and Safety needs. Moving house puts our brains and bodies on alert to seek increased security and safety. It also signals disconnection from the third level, Love and Belonging. For children, this can translate into holding on to their belongings and other behaviors that help them feel a sense of control and security.

Children cannot choose to move. However, during the process of packing and unpacking, parents can give children choices that will help them feel a certain degree of control. When children have specific responsibilities during the packing process, they feel they're contributing to the family in positive ways.

To reinforce a sense of security, there are other Tools in this Toolkit that strengthen family cohesion and counterbalance some of the children's feelings of disruption during transition times:

Affirm the Positives Tool #6
Family Heirloom Tool #21
Family Meetings Tool #23
Family Night Tool #24
Music Tool #39
Rituals Tool #47
Routine Charts Tool #48

What You Need

Materials: Paper, pen, calendar

Time: 30–40 minutes

Instructions

Depending on the child's age and temperament, consider which of these options are the most appropriate:

- Use the *Limited Choices Tool #33* with younger children when going through toys, clothes, books, and so on. Here are some examples:
  - "Here are two boxes for your toys. Do you want to pack them, or do you want me to do it?"
  - "Do you want to give this to the orphanage or to a friend?"
  - "Do you want to get new toys when we move or keep the old toys?"
- Allow older children to choose what they will pack into a certain number of boxes.
- Ask them to pack two suitcases for items they will use now (the rest will be shipped).
- Younger children can choose books or activities to have on the plane or in the car.
- Designate which child or children will help with different areas of the house or with different chores that need to be completed.

- Older children can be asked to make a schedule and packing chart for everyone.
- Use the *Family Meetings Tool #23* or a ritual to pack the *Family Heirloom Tool #21* right before leaving (and after arriving).
- Turn on your family's playlist from the *Music Tool #39* during times you're all clearing out things to leave behind and when packing.

What Happened

Since Max was out of town, Sara sent him a list of agenda items to review before their *Family Meeting Tool #23*. Jace set up a Zoom session. Sara and Max started off with a review of their *Family Mission Statement Tool #2* before presenting the options on their list to their kids. They asked the kids to help out the family by organizing some of their belongings.

Jace and Mariel agreed they could give special objects to friends, donate clothes, books, and toys to the orphanage, and help their mom with the rest of the house. Jace got in touch with the contact person for the orphanage and planned for them to come for a pick-up. Mariel made a packing schedule for them all. One of the kids put on some music from their family playlist for leaving—*Music Tool #39*—and they all got in a positive mood. Parul brought out the instruments and got everyone jamming.

That night, Sara read Eric Carle's *A House for Hermit Crab* and some other books to Parul, while Jace and Mariel listened in. Parul agreed to let her old toys go to "Toy Heaven" but protected her menagerie like a mother lioness.

When they packed up the *Family Heirloom Tool #21*, Max was present on Zoom. They finished with their family motto, "Wherever we go, we learn and grow!"

Parul started chanting a catchy little song that everyone picked up and sang along to: "Stronger, Fun-ner, Happier Together." Everyone was smiling as they went off to bed that night. Sara gave herself a mental pat on the back and went into the living room to do some yoga.

Reflection

Use the questions below to reflect on how involving the children can help the transition process:

1. What are the different ways your children respond to leaving personal possessions behind when packing?
2. What ways are there to make packing enjoyable? For example, your family music playlist, a packing party, or ordering takeaway for dinner.
3. What books can you find in your school library about moving? (Also see the *Resources* section for a list of books.)
4. What skills do children learn through the packing process?

TOOL #43
Planning
Activity

"Once you've been supportive by engaging your children in planning and goal setting, have faith in them to carry out their plans and learn from their mistakes."

Jane Nelsen, Ed.D. Positive Discipline

The many-armed deity learns to delegate

Purpose

To build a sense of responsibility and teamwork through planning activities.

Life Skills

Organization, Responsibility, Thinking, Problem-solving, Self-efficacy.

Mutiny

Sara remembered back to when the Tillers first arrived in Belgium. School was starting in two days and Sara felt like the captain of a pirate ship in full mutiny, with undertones of "walk the plank" in the air.

"You can't make me go to the ballet class at school. It's for beginners!" declared eight-year-old Mariel.

"No way I'm going to the museums. You and Dad can take the girls," said pre-teen Jace.

Even Max was in a resistant mood. "Honey, how could you put my books in the living room? The kids will destroy them."

Only Parul seemed happy with what Sara had planned for her: a play-group with other mothers and young children. But back then, two-year-old Parul didn't really talk and was hardly in a position to give her opinion. It used to be so easy when Sara made the decisions and the kids went along with the plan. How could she get herself off the "plank" and back to keeping the family ship on course?

Jane Nelsen, author of *Positive Discipline*, recommends taking time to guide children through the process of planning and setting goals, then stepping back. "Be supportive without taking over, or some children will turn it into a power struggle."

It's common for parents to do most of the planning in a family. We might say or think things like: "We're in a hurry," "There's too much going on," or "Children have no experience of organizing things." However, when we take time for training, even young children can develop the skills to make a plan and put it into action. It's a meaningful activity that helps children contribute to the family—and an investment in their future.

What You Need

Materials: Pen, paper

Time: 20 minutes

Instructions

Once you and your partner have mentally prepared yourselves to allow your children to take some responsibility for Planning, consider these guidelines:

- Choose age-appropriate activities (see the lists below).
- Ask questions to guide their thinking.
- Support with advice only if you're asked.
- Agree to activities that don't have big consequences if they're not successful.
- If other people are involved, ask how your kids will contact them.
- Allow for mistakes and for time to talk about ways to improve.
- Use the Encouragement Tool #18:
  o "That was interesting. I learned something new."
  o "You put a lot of effort into the planning."
  o "It's hard to please everyone, but we had fun together."
  o "Thanks for taking the time to plan this."
- Stay calm and enjoy being together.

Age-appropriate ideas to start your thinking

Kids from two to six years old can help plan:

- Arrangement of toys
- Items in a school bag
- Inviting friends
- Daily menus
- Songs to sing together
- *Routine Charts Tool #48*

Kids from seven to ten years old can help plan:

- Restaurant outings
- *Family Night Tool #24*
- *Routine Charts Tool #48*
- Weekly menus
- Song playlists
- Playdates and activities with visitors
- Packing lists

Kids eleven years and older can help plan:

- School work
- Agendas for travel
- Travel destinations
- Parties
- Hotels
- New school connections
- Places to visit
- Family outings and activities
- Study plans

What Happened

Fast forward four years to their arrival in Turkey. Sara prepared herself to allow the kids to plan their activities and take responsibility for their choices, including mistakes. She talked with them separately.

First, she spoke with Mariel. "How are you going to keep up your ballet technique, Mariel?"

"I'll go to a real ballet studio, not the baby after-school activities," replied Mariel.

"Where is this real ballet studio?" asked Sara.

"I don't know, you can look it up and take me there," said Mariel.

"Where can you find this information? Shall we look together or can you do it, Mariel?" said Sara firmly.

Then she spoke to Jace. "Jace, I'm wondering what you would like us to do together as a family."

"I don't know. I'm new here, remember?" he snapped.

"We're all new here. How can you help us plan a family activity?" asked Sara gently.

Mariel and Jace weren't exactly thrilled with being given the responsibility of planning activities. However, they "took the helm" and started navigating different options. Sara unregistered Mariel from the ballet class at school. Unfortunately, by the time Mariel found a professional dance studio and realized it was too far for her mom to drive to, she couldn't re-register for the ballet class. It was full and the next group wouldn't begin for three months. Sara empathized with Mariel's frustration and let her deal with the disappointment—i.e., Sara didn't try to fix the problem. In the meantime, Mariel talked to the ballet teacher and found out she used more experienced dancers in the group to help choreograph. Mariel's three-month wait seemed long, but she was excited about the new possibilities. Sara commended Mariel on her patience and for reaching out to the teacher.

Jace came up with three outings he thought the family would enjoy: the trip to the zoo was a winner; a tour of the city was long and tiring, albeit interesting; the movie he chose was dubbed in Dutch, which, of course, they couldn't understand. He got angry when Mariel complained.

"Next time, *you* plan the activity, Mariel!" Jace shouted.

"What a great idea!" said Max.

"And maybe you can help your dad plan where to put his books, kids?" Sara added, smiling at her husband.

After this introduction to Planning, Sara and Max counted on their children to help plan more activities. To keep track of how much they liked the activities, the kids came up with their own "fun scale." The things they enjoyed most were marked "over the rainbow." Interesting activities were marked "one more time." Less interesting activities were voted "take it or leave it." And finally, things they didn't like got a "better luck next time" vote. Little Parul watched and absorbed everything, with inklings of how she would contribute to the crew already forming.

Reflection

1. Which age-appropriate activities are suitable for your children to plan?
2. Referring to Maslow's Hierarchy of Needs, in what ways does children participating in planning increase their sense of significance and belonging?
3. What kinds of questions and tones of voice can help children learn from their mistakes?
4. Which Life Skills are nurtured through participation in planning?
5. How can the *Encouragement Tool #18* be used with this Tool?

TOOL #44
Quest
Activity

"He who completes a quest does not merely find something. He becomes something."

Lev Grossman   The Magician King

What kind of quest will challenge you?

Purpose
To continue discovering and becoming more of yourself.

Life Skills
Risk-taking, Curiosity, Courage, Perseverance, Resilience.

Need to Stretch

Max had been keeping a regular exercise routine for more than a year and was feeling that he'd plateaued. He was ready to go to another level with his fitness, but not just by adding on more weights and repetitions.

He talked with Sara about this need to stretch himself in new ways. She understood this. She had just finished her yoga certification and was offering a class to expat parents. They discussed ways Max could start his own Quest. They looked in the Toolkit for some ideas and steps to use.

In *The Hero with a Thousand Faces*, Joseph Campbell describes the hero's journey as a quest that leads the hero through trials and tribulations to transformation. When a person hears the call of such a quest in their life, they may hesitate before accepting the challenge. However, an innate urge drives us past the borders of ourselves with purposeful intention, toward something larger than who we think we are.

Have you ever noticed the "quest" in *question*? A Quest leads us on an adventure that enriches, inspires, and uplifts us as we search for an answer to that inner query, *Do I have what it takes to do this?* With all the online options and resources at hand, it's easier than ever to embark on a Quest that will help you face new challenges with a fresh heart and mind.

What You Need

Materials: Ideas and resources for possible Quests

Time: Indefinite

Instructions

Use these ideas to clarify what kind of Quest you might take on and how to do it.

Types of Quests

Here are just a few examples of different types of Quests:

- Spiritual
- Professional skills in a new area
- Health and fitness
- Artistic
- Anthropological
- Geographical
- Political
- Social causes

Inspiration

How will Quests such as these impact your life? Why would you want to go on such a Quest?

- Take an area in your life to the next level.
- Create new connections with other skills and people in your life.
- Send yourself in a new direction.
- Contribute to a cause.
- Create more meaning in your life and clarify your purpose.
- Network with others who are doing Quests.
- Expand your influence to reach more people, new groups, or new markets.
- Develop your artistic skills.
- Expand your awareness.

Resources

Where can you find resources to help you on your Quest?

- Universities and colleges
- Online platforms, such as Coursera *www.coursera.com* and Mindvalley *www.mindvalley.com*
- Online communities and webinars
- Local libraries
- Local groups, such as yoga, martial arts, fitness, music, etc.
- Volunteer agencies
- Friends

Crafting your Quest

How to go about starting your Quest:

- Brainstorm ideas.
- Discuss with someone close to you.
- Explore resources.
- Choose a Quest.
- Choose ways to keep track of your journey.
- Celebrate your efforts and progress along the way.
- Mark the completion of your Quest with a ritual or celebration.

Some optional steps to take on your Quest:

- Share your journey with family and friends.
- Create a visual representation of the journey, i.e., a collage, a picture journal, a *Coat of Arms Tool #13*, a drawing, or a painting.
- Choose or create a theme song or motto for your journey.
- Re-enact your Quest in a one-man/one-woman show.

What Happened

Max and a university friend, Rollins, registered for a duathlon in Germany. They would be expected to run and bike for 42.1 km. It would be a real test of Max's strength and stamina. He was excited to take on the challenge but wondered if he had the willpower to stick to the demanding schedule Rollins had laid out for them.

Max kept data about his weight, muscle mass, strength, stamina, the distances he ran each day, his diet, and the supplements he used. He and Rollins kept a photo journal during the months that led up to the marathon. They created their own blog, *On the Run*, in which they shared their thoughts, their progress, and some advice. Every Friday, they celebrated by having a big dinner together and watching inspiring films about other famous sports people.

Rollins finished in the top 5% and Max in the top 20%. They put together a video that documented their preparation and the marathon itself. They each created their own photo collages and hung them in their offices. Their joint motto became a chant they would use for many challenges in the future: "Crawl, walk, run, fly; just keep moving forward."

Max celebrated his achievement with his family. Jace also got inspired to register for a marathon and asked his father for some tips. Mariel begged her parents to let her go on a two-week summer school for modern dance, something she was passionate about. Sara started thinking of new ways to expand her yoga skills to a bigger community. Perhaps she could use her blog...

Reflection

Whatever Quest you choose, consider these questions to expand your thinking about it:

1. How does pursuing Quests support your *Personal Mission Statement Tool #37*?
2. How can learning new skills help keep your marriage vibrant?
3. What can your children learn from seeing you pursue a Quest?
4. In what ways might your Quest connect with a community?

TOOL #45
Recognize Emotions
Skill

"The realization 'This is anger I'm feeling' offers a greater degree of freedom; not just the option not to act on it, but the added option to let go of it."

Daniel Goleman   Emotional Intelligence

We need to teach children the language of emotions

Purpose

To develop emotional language and emotional intelligence.

Life Skills

Communication, Emotional Intelligence, Self-awareness.

Out of Control

One evening, Parul was sobbing uncontrollably, unable to talk. Her family tried to figure out what the problem was but couldn't get much more than a combination of grunts, whines, and screams from her. Whatever they did to try and comfort her was met with greater and greater frustration from the unhappy six-year-old. One by one, they left her to cry it out. Sara offered her a hug, which Parul accepted, and gradually, over time, she calmed down. However, she was still unable to say what she was so upset about. Concerned, Sara took a look in the Toolkit to see if there was a way to address such strong, inarticulate emotions.

Emotional Intelligence is defined as understanding others' emotions and the ability to manage our own emotions; the first step toward this is self-awareness.

To highlight this in his book *Emotional Intelligence*, Daniel Goleman recounts the tale of a Zen master and a belligerent samurai. The warrior challenged the master to explain the concept of Heaven and Hell.

The monk insulted the samurai and said he refused to waste his time with the likes of him.

The warrior pulled out his sword and, in his rage, threatened to kill the monk.

"That is hell," replied the monk.

The realization of how his rage had overcome him moved the samurai to sheath his sword, bow to the master, and thank him.

"And that is heaven," said the monk.

Becoming aware of his strong emotion allowed the samurai to step out of its grip and into a new state of feeling and thinking. This is closely connected to the self-awareness needed for *The Amygdala: Fight, Flight, or Freeze Tool #7*. We can help our children develop this awareness in a similar way by recognizing emotions in *I-Statements Tool #28*.

As children develop this essential skill, they learn to harmonize head and heart for greater access to intellectual and social abilities. Interestingly, more and more companies are seeking employees with emotional intelligence and are investing in developing it in their teams. By nurturing "EI" in your children, you are arming them with soft skills for greater happiness and success in life.

What You Need

Materials: An emotions chart (online or homemade)

Time: 20 minutes

Instructions

Younger children will work best with a chart of six to nine emotions in picture form. Older children will relate to pictures of older kids or colored lists. Teens will appreciate this process by you just talking to them. Whether you print out a ready-made poster or have fun creating your own with your children, consider these ideas for using the emotions chart to develop self-awareness and the language to express emotions:

- Put the poster in a visible place.
- Chat about the different emotions, their names, and what to say when we feel that way:
  - "I feel sad when you're not around."
  - "I feel frustrated when I can't do something easily."
  - "I feel angry when you don't have time to play with me."

- Play matching games with extra copies of each emotion.
- Act out an emotion and get the other person to guess what it is.
- Express how you are feeling at different times:
  - "I feel happy about my new bag."
  - "I feel sad because I lost my keys."
  - "I feel angry because I broke the vase."
- Help your child articulate feelings:
  - "You feel disappointed because you want that new phone."
  - "You feel excited because we're going on vacation."
  - "You feel confused when your friend doesn't invite you out."
  - "You feel angry because you have to redo the project."

As your children grow older, you may want to change the poster to include more emotions.

What Happened

Sara printed out an emotions chart and asked Parul to help her put it on the magnetic board in the kitchen. Parul was curious to know what it was for. As her mom pointed to the different faces, she asked Parul what the person was feeling: "happy," "sad," "angry," and "surprised" were easy for her to recognize. However, she struggled when she had to name "afraid," "confused," "frustrated," "curious," and "disappointed." Sara gave examples of situations from her own life when she felt these emotions. Then she gave examples of situations where Parul might have experienced them herself. Sara reminded her that the *Chill Out Space Tool #11* they had created (Parul's Parlor) was a place where Parul could take time to calm down when she had strong emotions. Finally, they both put a magnet on the happy face that showed how they were feeling at that moment.

For the next week, mother and daughter had fun putting magnets on different faces and acting them out. After observing the fun they were having, Mariel and Jace started adding their magnets to the poster.

Finally, Max joined in with the game and everyone started talking more about their feelings. Sara planned to add an expanded version of the emotion chart for the older kids and made a mental note to refer to it before, during, and after their next move.

Reflection

Consider these questions to reflect on emotional language and expression:

1. How often do you recognize your emotions? How do you express them?
2. Which emotions can your children identify? Which emotions do they still need to learn to identify?
3. What are some of the reasons why children and adults don't express emotions?
4. In what ways can you nurture a richer emotional language and expression in your daily life?

TOOL #46
Reflective Listening
Skill

"To truly listen, you must listen not only with your ears but with your heart and soul."
Zen saying

Listen first

Purpose

To show support through listening, understanding,
and reflecting back to the speaker.

Life Skills

Communication, Empathy, Self-awareness.

Going Nowhere

Jace stomped into the house, threw down his bag, and holed up in his bedroom. Max went in to talk with him. The tenth graders had planned their end-of-year trip on the same dates as the Tillers' trip for a family wedding.

"I want to go to the wedding but I want to go out with my friends, too," said Jace.

"That can't be changed, Jace," Max replied. "This is family."

"I know that, Dad."

"It's just a class trip. Ask them to change the dates," Max suggested.

"Yeah, right. That's not going to happen."

Max tried to be positive. "There'll be more trips next year, right?"

"This is the end-of-the-year trip. It's a big deal." Jace was getting more and more frustrated with his dad's comments.

"I don't know what I can do to help, Jace," Max replied.

"Just forget it, Dad," said Jace, deflated.

Max wandered out feeling useless and confused. It was one of the few times he sought out the Toolkit to get more information and, hopefully, some guidance on how to deal with his teenager's emotions.

Reflective Listening is a combination of skills—essentially pausing your thoughts and comments to hear not only the words but also the emotions interlaced with the words. Why is this important? The authors of *The*

Parent's Handbook: Systematic Training for Effective Parenting summarize it this way: "It helps children know they are understood, to think about what they are feeling and why. It can help them think through a problem. It lets children know that talking about feelings is okay." It also helps the Amygdala to stay calm and let the cortex do its job: thinking.

Analyzing and talking about feelings is key to developing a sense of emotional intelligence that accompanies us throughout life.

What You Need

Materials: Two ears, one mouth

Time: 30–45 minutes

Instructions

Follow the steps below to start practicing and using Reflective Listening.

1. Focus your attention on the speaker with your body language, face, and mind.
2. **Encourage** as you listen:
   a. "Uh-huh," "mmm-hum," and "oh."
   b. "Right."
   c. "I see."
3. Name emotions:
   a. "How frustrating!"
   b. "You were worried!"
   c. "It sounds very overwhelming."
4. **Paraphrase** what you've heard, including emotions:
   a. "You were upset because they wouldn't help you."
   b. "You feel worried about the upcoming tests."
   c. "You felt confused when she said you're not the right person."

5. Open-ended questions:
    a. "Where were the organizers?"
    b. "Who could you ask?"
    c. "What are some options?"
6. **Summarize**:
    "You were upset when they wouldn't help you with the revision because you weren't on the list. Now you're confused about who to go to. I can see how that's frustrating."

What Happened

After reading through the Tool and practicing with Sara, Max invited Jace to talk.

Max apologized for not listening earlier. "Is now a good time to tell us more about it, or would later be better?"

Jace explained the situation again, albeit a bit more reasonably now that his emotions had calmed down.

"I want to go to Karl's wedding. But I also want to go on this trip with my friends."

"Mm-hmm," said Sara. (**Encourage**)

"I hear you," added Max. (**Encourage**)

"It's a final celebration before we start the IB program next year," explained Jace.

"How disappointing," said Max. (**Name emotion**)

"Yeah. But Karl's my closest cousin and I can't *not* go," said Jace.

"True," said Sara. (**Encourage**)

"But we have some cool stuff planned for the class trip and I don't want to be the one who didn't go," pleaded Jace.

"You feel conflicted because Karl's wedding and the school trip are both exciting events," said Max. (**Paraphrase**)

"Not conflicted. It just sucks," said Jace.

"Seems unfair, doesn't it?" his parents acknowledged. (**Name emotion**)

"Why did they both have to be on the same dates?" said Jace.

"That's hard when two things are happening at the same time," replied Sara. (**Paraphrase**)

"I wish I could be in two places at once," sobbed Jace.

"It's tough to deal with this kind of situation, Jace. Karl is important as he's family, and friends, well, are friends," said Sara. (**Summarize**)

"How can we help?" asked Max. (**Open-ended question**)

"You can't," said Jace.

"We know your friends will miss you *and* how much Karl will love having you there for his big day. Not to mention, for us, how nice it will be to be there together as a family," added Max. (**Summarize**)

"I guess so. Thanks for listening, Mom and Dad," said Jace in conclusion.

By listening to Jace's words and emotions, and reflecting them back to him, Sara and Max didn't fix his problem or try to cheer him up. They walked him through steps to analyze his thoughts and emotions separately from the "fight or flight response" that his brain was signaling with strong emotions.

Reflection

Our desire to help our children by discounting emotions or solving problems for them detours their learning processes. Consider the questions below to include a broader context in which they can develop their own skills:

1. When were there times in your childhood when you had to deal with strong emotions? What was helpful? What did you learn about yourself?
2. What is the hardest thing about listening to your child without offering solutions?
3. How can you tell if your child just needs to be heard? Or when they need help solving a problem?
4. What Life Skills is your child learning from *you* when you use Reflective Listening?

TOOL #47
Rituals
Activity

"Ritual and ceremony in their times kept the world under the sky and the stars in their courses. It was astonishing what ritual and ceremony could do."

Terry Pratchett   A Hat Full of Sky

Rituals can be traditional or personal

Purpose

To establish strong habits that give structure to your daily life, your family life, and your mobile lifestyle.

Life Skills

Organization, Perspective, Creativity.

A Surprise Welcome

When they had moved to India many years earlier, Max and Sara had been surprised to find the entrance to their new apartment in Delhi decorated with flowers, garlands, and small bells. Their two housekeepers and the Tillers' local contact through the embassy greeted them warmly and welcomed them into the new home. Max and Sara were slightly taken aback, but Fatima and Veda explained to the family that this was a typical Indian ritual.

They had also prepared some cakes and tea. The gesture was a lovely way to welcome them to India. However, when Veda was boiling milk for the tea, she intentionally let it overflow onto the counter and the floor. Incredulous, Sara quickly reacted and grabbed a towel to clean it up.

"Not to worry, missus," Fatima assured her. "Milk that has boiled over is good luck!"

"By defining beginnings and ends to developmental or social phases, rituals structure our social worlds and how we understand time, relationships, and change," writes Rebecca J. Lester in her *Psychology Today* article 'The Importance of Ritual: Marking life events in a socially distant world.' When describing "rites of passage"—from one social role to another—she highlights that the absence of rituals during such transitions can "produce a profound sense of dislocation and alienation that is existentially, psychologically, and even physically, painful and exhausting."

For Global Nomad Families, rituals also serve as scaffolding, upon which both children and adults can construct meaning from their experiences and the transitions they go through. By consciously marking important events, rituals create a connecting thread between the values, beliefs, and identities you carry with you against the background of change and growth.

There are various kinds of rituals. As a modern, mobile family, you can create your own rituals to underscore important moments in your life that affirm your family's values and identity.

What You Need

Materials: A list of known rituals, ideas for new rituals, and models for meaningful rituals

Time: One hour

Instructions

Use these steps when choosing rituals to include in your life:

1. Consider which rituals you already practice and in what areas of your life you can create rituals.
2. Choose rituals that have meaning for you and your family's lifestyle.
3. Learn about and adopt local rituals.
4. Practice your rituals for an extended period in order to incorporate them into your life.
5. Reflect on your rituals over time to decide if they're still meaningful.

Below are some ideas for rituals and how to use them.

General

- Religious and cultural practices, yearly celebrations
- Gratitude before meals or bedtime
- Weekly *Family Meetings Tool #23* to nurture communication, leadership, and teamwork
- *Family Night Tool #24* for connection, fun, and sharing
- Celebrating the successes of family members

Before Leaving

- Set up a Gratitude Jar (see the *Gratitude Tool #26*) the month before you leave, and then read the statements when you're all together.
- Have a final dinner at your family's favorite restaurant.
- Give gifts to neighbors and friends.
- Pack the *Family Heirloom* Tool #21.
- Play "leaving" songs from your family's *Music Tool #39* playlist.
- If you have hand percussion instruments, improvise a "goodbye" song.
- Walk through the house to say goodbye and take a final picture.

Arriving

- Walk through the house to say hello and take the first picture.
- Purify the house, using sage, incense, or another ritual.
- Play "arriving" songs from your music playlist as you unpack.
- Unpack the *Family Heirloom Tool #21* once you have completely moved in.
- Celebrate your first dinner in the house with candles, special food, and so on.
- If you have hand percussion instruments, improvise a "welcome" song.

Settling In

- Set up a Gratitude Jar the month you arrive. Read the statements once you're all together.
- Find a simple way to recognize your children making it through a week, a month, two months, and so on. (This is *not* related to school success and grades.)
- Celebrate settling in after six months and after a year.

What Happened

Over the next few years, Fatima and Veda enriched the Tiller family's life in India by introducing them to many of their traditions and rituals. Sara also shared some of the rituals she'd learned in Egypt with the two women. It was through this exchange that Sara and Max realized the importance of rituals for creating continuity in their mobile life.

When they went through the against-all-odds adoption of baby Parul, the rituals of welcoming a new being into their family and naming her gave deeper significance to their practice of rituals. However, Sara still had a hard time letting the milk boil over for good luck.

Reflection

Whether you already practice rituals or are interested in starting new ones, use these questions to reflect on the process:

1. Which rituals did you grow up with?
2. How did they influence your connection to family, religion, and culture?
3. What moments in your family's daily life would benefit from being highlighted by a ritual?
4. How can your children help create your family's own rituals related to a mobile lifestyle?
5. How does practicing rituals underscore your *Family Mission Statement Tool #2* and your *Personal Mission Statement Tool #37*?

TOOL #48
Routine Charts
Activity / Skill

"If you have good habits, time becomes your ally."
James Clear Atomic Habits

*Routine Charts can be in various forms, depending on
your child's age and input*

Purpose

To involve children more actively in their routines and make
mornings and bedtimes easier for parents.

Life Skills

Time Management, Independence, Responsibility, Self-esteem.

Hakuna Matata?

It was 7:45 am in the Tiller household. Jace was still on his computer and hadn't packed his things for school. Mariel was changing her clothes for the third time. Parul was playing with her cereal and singing one of her favorite Disney songs, "Hakuna Matata." By the time Max had to tell the kids to take their bags and get in the car to go to school for the tenth time, he lost his cool; not very "Hakuna Matata."

While waiting impatiently for the kids in the car, Max replayed the scene that happened almost every school night. Jace would start doing his homework around 8 pm and stay up too late. Mariel would be involved in some project, with stuff scattered around the living room. And Parul would keep popping out of bed to ask for something. By the time Max and Sara had nagged, coaxed, and finally ordered the kids to get to bed, they felt so exhausted they had little energy to enjoy some special time together. They wanted to change these scenarios to achieve a happy ending!

"Children feel more capable and confident when they learn to have faith in themselves instead of manipulating others," says Jane Nelsen about Routine Charts in her book *Positive Discipline*. Parents who stay "kind, firm, and consistent," as Jane Nelsen puts it, while using a Routine Chart, convey a sense of authority that stops kids from testing them and directs them to take more responsibility for themselves.

Parents will need to help younger kids prepare for and create their Routine Charts, but children should do as much as possible. Kids older than ten can make lists to remember what they need to do. The final product does not need to be a work of art, but rather a personal project that each child has created and "owns."

Morning and bedtime Routine Charts help everyone start the day off better and end it more calmly. This simple Tool has changed the mornings and evenings of many parents. Interestingly, children who have solid bedtime routines have fewer problems in school.

What You Need

Materials: Paper for preparation, poster paper, pens, pictures (computer-generated or photos)

Time: 20–30 minutes

Instructions

Follow these steps to create and use Routine Charts, appropriate for ages four to 14:

1. Discuss which activities need to be done in the morning or at bedtime.
   a. *Morning.* Younger and older kids use the toilet, get dressed, have breakfast, grab their lunch (if available), take their backpack, and go to the car/bus.
   b. *Bedtime.* Young kids: brush teeth, wash up, pajamas, toilet, water, read a story, turn out the light. Older kids: disconnect from devices, tidy up common areas, wash up, go to their room, lights out (time to be discussed).
2. Give choices. Do they want to draw pictures or take photos of themselves doing these activities? Do older kids want to make a list or a chart?
3. Your child chooses the order of the tasks (there might be some humorous discussion if they want to brush their teeth after getting into bed).
4. Younger children put the pictures and simple words on a big piece of paper. Ask your child where they will see it easily. Older kids can choose the format for their list.

5. Once it's time for a particular routine to start, ask them:
   a. "What do you need to do now? What's first?"
   b. "Do you want to do it by yourself, or do you need my help?" They might need extra support at the beginning, but should quickly become independent without reminders.
6. Follow up with Encouragement:
   a. "You're getting more independent." Younger kids: "How does that feel?" Older kids: "It's nice to have you on board."
   b. "It looks like you know what to do." Younger kids: "Come for a hug when you're ready." Older kids: "Glad we can count on you."
   c. "You got ready on your own." Younger kids: "You should feel proud of yourself." Older kids: "You're really responsible."
   d. "Thanks for helping the family."
7. Avoid:
   a. Reminding, directing, coaxing
   b. Rewards and punishments
   c. Getting angry

What Happened

Sara and Max read about Routine Charts in the Toolkit and got their kids together. They told them they needed their help in the mornings and evenings.

"More chores?" the kids asked in unison.

"More responsibility," Sara said.

"And independence," added Max.

They went through the steps and were surprised at how eager the kids were to create their personalized versions.

Jace made his lists for the evening and morning and put them on his door. Mariel created colorful charts that she put on her mirror. Parul asked Mariel to take pictures of her doing all the tasks for the evening and morning and then pasted them on poster boards, which she put on the wall outside her room. She added her own sticker system to put on the charts once she had completed a task.

It took a few days of "kindly, firmly, and consistently" redirecting the kids to their charts and holding them accountable for their actions. Max and Sara refused to respond emotionally; they let the chart "be the boss." Instead, they became like broken records, saying the following over and over:

"What did you say you were going to do?"

"How is what you're doing helping you follow your plan?"

"We know you're responsible enough to take care of yourself."

"This is Mom and Dad time, thanks for respecting that."

Soon they were playing different records:

"You're getting so independent. How does that feel?"

"Look at how responsible you are!"

"Thanks for helping the family."

If one of the kids "forgot" to follow the routine, Max or Sara would put an arm around them, gently guide them to the Routine Chart, and quietly point to the tasks before walking away. Mornings and evenings were calmer and more enjoyable. Despite himself, and to Parul's great delight, Max started singing "Hakuna Matata" as he got ready for work.

Reflection

Making the chart is an activity, and using it is a skill. Use these questions to reflect on the process:

1. What's the difference between your child making the chart and you creating it?
2. Once a Routine is in place, what will be *your* challenges when it comes to leaving your child to do it alone?
3. How does a young child respond to parental lectures in the mornings and at bedtimes?
4. Why do rewards and punishments only work short term when a child is learning to be independent?

TOOL #49
Self-Talk
Skill

"Of course I talk to myself. Sometimes I need expert advice."

Edward Henheffer   Computers R4U2

Which internal scripts are directing your brain and body?

Purpose

To use your inner voice for encouragement and a positive attitude.

Life Skills

Self-esteem, Self-efficacy, Positive Attitude.

Negative Self-Talk

"I suck. I'm never going to get this," Jace yelled from the other room.

"Jace, watch your language!" Sara called back. But she heard her son continue to mutter to himself. None of it sounded encouraging or helpful.

Mariel came home later and threw down her dance bag. "I'm going to quit the dance group. I'm so stupid, I couldn't even learn the new steps."

Sara was suddenly aware of a bad feeling in her gut as she listened to her children bad-mouth themselves. Henry Ford's quote popped into her head: *Whether you think you can, or you think you can't, you're right.* What could she do to get her kids on the I-can-do-it track?

We laugh about talking to ourselves, but self-talk is a normal part of developing language and cognitive skills. Self-regulation, self-criticism, self-encouragement, problem-solving, and other forms of dialogue are expressed through self-talk. This process usually becomes internalized around the age of six or seven, but it's still normal for us to talk to ourselves well into adulthood!

There are three types of self-talk: negative, positive (motivational), and instructional. Negative self-talk focuses on mistakes, insufficiencies, what's going wrong, things you don't like, and the impossibility of a task. This can lead to a negative self-concept, lack of motivation, and lower achievement. Unfortunately, several studies have shown that most of our self-talk is negative.

Positive self-talk is very much like the *Encouragement Tool #18*, which focuses on effort, progress, strength, and appreciation. It's a healthy way to keep your mind and mood positive, nurturing self-esteem, confidence, resilience, and willingness to take risks. In professional sports, the use of instructional self-talk has become a significant psychological tool to enhance performance. It can also be useful in other areas that require steps, such as learning a skill or when coaching oneself.

As we become more conscious of our thoughts, the challenge is to choose what kind of self-talk we want in our daily lives. If you choose to practice more positive self-talk, be prepared to face negative self-talk patterns that will insist on crashing your "positive" party. It takes patience and perseverance to change long-time habits.

What You Need

Materials: A notebook, pen, Post-its

Time: 30–60 minutes/ongoing

Instructions

Changing your self-talk is a serious undertaking. Use the steps below to start the process.

Step 1

Take note of your negative self-talk and record it in the notebook.

Step 2

Use the examples on the next page to help you change your negative statements to positive ones.

Negative	Positive and Instructional
"I'm horrible at this."	"This is going to take more time and effort. How important is it to me?"
"I'll never get it."	"I'll take a break and try again later."
I always mess up."	"I'm doing something wrong. What do I need to change?"
"This is too hard."	"I've never done this before. I love a challenge!"
"I'm such an idiot."	"Wow, this is hard. Step by step, I know I'll make it."
"I'm ridiculous."	"I'm a risk-taker and ready to make mistakes to learn something new."
"That's not how you do it, idiot!"	"This is hard. I know I can figure it out."
"Another fail. I'm worthless."	"I learned so much already in the past weeks. How did I do it?"

Step 3

Start verbalizing your positive statements so that your children hear *your* self-talk.

Step 4

When you hear your children's negative self-talk, adapt the positive and instructional statements in the table above to guide your children's talk toward positive.

What Happened

Once Sara became aware of how much negative self-talk was going on in her daily life, she started changing it. Max quickly caught on and began using more positive self-talk. They both modeled positive self-talk for their kids to overhear:

- "I don't understand why it's taking so long. I guess that's part of learning about the culture."

- "I'm struggling with Turkish. I've learned so many languages already; I'm sure I'll get it over the next year."

- "I keep making the same mistake on this document. I wonder what I need to do differently."

- "This is hard to understand. Let's look at the instructional video. I'm sure we'll figure it out."

When Sara and Max heard their kids using negative self-talk, they transformed their kids' statements into more motivational ones, like the ones in the examples above. Over the next couple of months, there was a lull in the self-talk the kids used. Gradually, it was replaced by new types of statements. For example:

- "This is hard. I think I need extra help."

- "Getting into this show isn't a priority. I'd rather just go to my dance lessons for now."

- "What do you think I need to do to make this work?"

- "I need a break before I try again."

- "I can't believe I did it! I rock!"

The next phase of this great transformation was filled with lots of Encouragement from Sara and Max:

- "That was hard and you persevered. Way to go!"

- "You took a big risk and learned a lot from it. How does that feel?"

- "I admire your ability to make decisions about your dancing. That's a real strength."

- "How did you do it? You should feel proud of yourself!"

Reflection

Changing Self-Talk from negative to positive is not always easy, but it has the power to change so many things in your life. Use the questions below to reflect on the process.

1. Can you trace negative Self-Talk statements to certain events in your life?
2. What difference do you feel in your body when using negative and positive Self-Talk?
3. How do people in your life respond differently when you use more positive Self-Talk?
4. Who can you get support from if working on this skill opens up too many powerful memories?

TOOL #50
Spa Day
Activity

"Take rest; a field that has rested gives a bountiful crop."
Ovid Roman poet

Breathe in. Breathe out. Say "Ahhhh."

Purpose

To incorporate pampering into your life!

Life Skills

Self-care, Self-regulation, Appreciation.

Something Different

Two of Sara's friends from university planned to visit her in Istanbul for a week in March. They were also Global Nomads, but she wanted to show them something different than the historical sites and the Grand Bazaar. Sara's new acquaintance, Ebru, suggested she book an afternoon at a traditional Turkish hammam. Intrigued by the idea, Sara arranged massages for her visitors and herself at the well-known and luxurious Cağaloğlu Hammam.

Moms are usually the hub of the family. When your family moves, moms are often the ones who are expected to take care of everyone's transition, while putting their own needs on hold. It's easy to get overwhelmed without realizing it. A day at the local spa, a weekly massage, regular pedicures, and other pampering sessions are essential to keep that hub strong and resilient.

Spa treatments can have many medical benefits. Apart from relaxing the body and mind, the heat, humidity, scrubs, and massages improve circulation as well as the skin's elasticity and health. Take your partner— or the whole family— for a weekend visit to a spa hotel, and enjoy some relaxing moments together.

What You Need

Materials: A list of spas

Time: 30–60 minutes (research), two to three hours (at the spa)

Instructions

Here are some ideas for organizing a regular Spa Day in your life:

- Create a list of spas you can get to regularly and a wish list of spas you'd like to try.
- Choose a block of time—either weekly, bimonthly, or monthly—and put it in your calendar.
- Prepay sessions to confirm your commitment to this use of time for yourself.
- Try other spas on your list.
- Create a spa group with friends.
- Schedule spa dates with your partner.
- Notice how you feel once this is a regular part of your life.

What Happened

Eliza, Marta, and Sara walked around Istanbul for three days visiting all the "must-see" places. When Sara surprised them with the spa invitation, they were delighted to give their feet and their minds a break. They were each handed a large cloth (*peştemal*) to wrap themselves in as they started with the hot steam room. Afterward, they had a foam and scrub treatment on a hot marble slab (*göbek taşı*) in a central space that was tiled with beautiful colors and patterns. They relaxed in a pool of hot water before more pampering. The scented oils and expert massages sent each of them into a deep state of relaxation.

By the time they left the hammam, their bodies and spirits were refreshed and rejuvenated! Afterward, the friends went to a juice bar and reviewed all the fun they had had that day.

Sara was already thinking about how to make hammams a regular part of her life while living in Turkey. She invited some friends to explore various hammams and included reviews in her growing blog. For their next *Date Night Tool #17*, Sara found a hotel where she and Max could enjoy a spa evening and a late dinner together.

Reflection

Sometimes, the most difficult challenge in taking time for pampering is convincing ourselves we deserve it. Use these questions to reflect on including a regular Spa Day in your life:

1. What kinds of pampering do you enjoy?
2. How can you schedule it into your life?
3. What are the changes in your mood and outlook when you go to the spa?
4. How can going to a spa with your partner strengthen your bond?
5. What are you modeling for your children when you take the time to rejuvenate and reset yourself?

TOOL #51
Stay in Touch
Activity / Skill

"The best mirror is an old friend."
George Herbert
The Temple: Sacred Poems and Private Ejaculations

*Technology makes it easy to stay in touch with
friends around the world*

Purpose

To build a long-term network of friends and acquaintances.

Life Skills

Communication, Appreciation.

Address Book

One day, Jace asked his mom about Koaru, a Japanese boy with whom he had been friends for four years in India. He reminisced about how they had shared a love of the computer game Minecraft, Cocoa Puffs breakfast cereal, and outer space. Koaru had taught Jace several words in Japanese and how to draw in a "manga" style. Jace had taught Koaru card tricks and his favorite jokes. They looked so different but they'd had so much in common. The two eight-year-olds had cried when it was time to move, and they'd promised to stay in touch. Unfortunately, after changing phones over the years, many such contacts had slipped through the cracks of their record-keeping.

Sara remembered the address book in which her parents used to keep the contacts of all the people they had met on their travels; the well-worn cover and overfilled pages testified to the thousands of kilometers they had journeyed, and the countless friendships they had forged. Compared with the ease of modern technology, Sara wondered how they had managed to stay in touch through snail mail and telephones.

Sara and Max's smartphones could spit out a telephone number on command, but it didn't help them stay in touch any more than the archaic address book system. In fact, given the vast amount of data that phones could collect, if anything, it felt more overwhelming. The question now was how to keep track of the data and organize it in a way that facilitated staying in touch.

Third Culture Families can easily relate to each other's shared experience of mobility and the strategies they deploy to connect and disconnect regularly. Staying in touch with fellow travelers, and other friends, remains one of their biggest challenges. Yet, it is a crucial piece that keeps the "moving puzzle" coherent over time and distance.

Not every person you meet will end up on your contact list, but the ones you share interests and similar values with are important "mirrors" that reflect who you are. As we discovered from Barbara Knuckles' model of "anchors and mirrors" in the earlier *Identity Formation* section, such mirrors affirm the image of ourselves that we use, in part, to construct our sense of identity. Against the background of mobility, staying in touch builds a network that contributes to an underlying structure amid the changing landscape of faces and places.

What You Need

Materials: Email account, address books, online calendar, phone reminders

Time: The span of many years!

Instructions

Everyone has their preferred way of organizing contacts and staying in touch. Here are a few ideas you might like to use:

- Create your own social media group.
- Blog about your life or create a family blog.
- Schedule calls into your monthly plans for yourself —and for younger children to contact their friends.
- Use your calendar to plan visits to international friends.
- Invite family and friends to meet at a vacation spot.

What Happened

Max and Sara stayed in touch with many of their friends over the years, but they needed to help their kids start building their own networks of long-term connections. Jace had an email account and phone to start organizing his contacts. Mariel could use Sara's accounts, but also had a small address book where she dutifully wrote down the contact information for all her friends.

As a family, they discussed upcoming vacations and how to plan with specific people and places in mind. Looking ahead in this way ensured they would stay in touch with friends who were important to them. It also gave the children a feeling of stability that would carry into future moves.

Sara had been working on her writing for several months, and her blog about living around the world was gaining momentum. As she made new friends in Turkey, she invited them to sign up for her blog. She would also share it with family members and other friends from her past locations.

Reflection

Whatever your preferred mode of staying in touch is, consider these questions to connect this Tool with other Tools in this Toolkit:

1. What are the differences between you making new connections as an adult and those your children are making during their developmental years?
2. What ways are there to guide your children to take more responsibility for staying in touch with friends as they grow older?
3. What can children learn about making and keeping friends as they move around?

TOOL #52

Take Time

Activity

"A connected relationship requires an investment that few folks make anymore – T-I-M-E."

David Ramsey More Than Enough

Shared moments create memories that children carry with them

Purpose

To build a stronger connection with your children.

Life Skills

Communication, Emotional Intelligence, Perspective, Patience.

No Time to Play

It was one of those extra-stressful days for Max. He was looking forward to relaxing at home and going to bed early. When he walked in the door, however, three needy children vied for his attention. Max told the kids he would change his clothes, and then they could do something together. However, when they tried to decide what to do, mayhem ensued. Jace wanted to shoot some baskets in the courtyard. Mariel wanted to show him the video from her dance composition. Parul wanted help building a house for her dolls.

"Let's look at Mariel's video and then shoot some baskets together. After dinner, we can all help Parul with her dollhouse," Max said, thinking it was a perfect plan.

Angrily, Jace bounced the basketball against the wall. "I'm going out after dinner."

"I hate basketball," said Mariel, as she walked away and pushed Jace's books off the table.

"You never want to play with me, Daddy," Parul sobbed, as she kicked over the Lego castle she had built.

Sara looked at Max from the kitchen, where she was unloading groceries and starting dinner, sending him a look of *I'm too busy right now!*

In her book *Positive Discipline*, Jane Nelsen links taking time with your children to a decrease in misbehavior. She writes, "Children feel a sense of connection when they can count on special time with you. This decreases their need to misbehave as a mistaken way to find belonging and significance."

This Take Time Tool is about more than just spending time together. It's an intrinsic aspect of the "Love and Belonging" piece in Maslow's Hierarchy of Needs covered earlier in the *Social Belonging* section. Giving your children special time creates strong "anchors" by affirming their importance and creates "mirrors" that serve as building blocks for their future identity. In addition, during these moments of uninterrupted time together, we offer models for their behavior through our actions, words, emotions, and reactions.

What You Need

Materials: A list of possible activities that you and your child have created together

Time: 15–20 minutes a day

Instructions

Using this Take Time Tool is different than being together out of obligation, or simply being at home together, or driving somewhere. Consider these ideas to underscore this special time with your children:

- Discuss several activities that both you and your child would enjoy doing. If you have more than one child, there will be individual lists for each of them.
- Make a schedule that is visible for your child (or children) to see; you and your partner can take turns in doing this.
- When you meet, take turns choosing one of the activities you have put on your list.
- In addition, you may plan regular dates with individual children to go to lunch, the hairdresser, sports games, or other activities that you can enjoy together.
- Bedtime and a nightly bedtime story are bonus times.

What Happened

After reading about the Take Time Tool, Sara and Max met with each child and made lists of the activities they could do together in 15–20 minutes. Once this was done, they decided on a set time that one of them would meet with each child, daily. They posted this schedule on the refrigerator and sealed the deal with a family banana split party after dinner.

Over the next few weeks, keeping this commitment became easier and easier, until they didn't need the actual schedule anymore. Somehow, Max and Sara's other tasks fell into place alongside this special time with the kids. And when the family was together, there was more sharing and more listening to each other. Even bedtimes and morning times went more smoothly. *Could it really be that simple?* wondered Max and Sara.

Reflection

1. What is the message you are sending to your child when you take special time with just them?
2. What is the message that is being sent to your child when you purposely turn off your phone during this special one-on-one time?
3. What Life Skills can a child gain from this regular special time with a parent?

TOOL #53
Therapy
Activity

"I couldn't afford therapy, so I just watched Frasier. Season Four was a breakthrough."
Cristela Alonzo   Cristela, ABC Sitcom

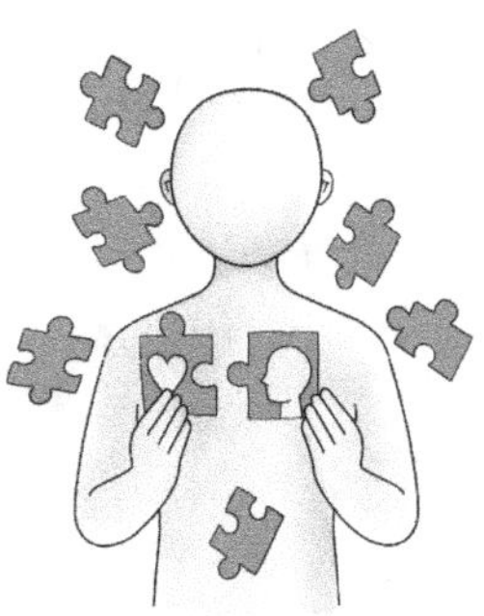

Sometimes, we benefit from professional support to put all the pieces together

Purpose

To find professionals who can support your mental health and fitness.

Life Skills

Self-awareness, Self-esteem, Problem-solving, Emotional Intelligence.

Max's Implosion

When they received the news that Max's father had passed away un-expectedly, Max seemed to recover from the shock unusually quickly. His grieving process was short, and he dove back into work with his usual enthusiasm. But when his boss announced their new posting, Sara noticed her husband closing himself off to the world around him. He separated himself from his family in the evenings and generally reacted with an emotional flatness that Sara recognized as one of the signs of depression.

It was hard for Max to verbalize what was wrong when Sara asked him. Her suggestion that they look for a therapist was met with objections and then dismissed. Nevertheless, Sara recognized the need for professional intervention. She started exploring options.

"The stigma associated with therapy has shifted. More people have come to understand that therapy is beneficial for a variety of situations and doesn't indicate sickness or weakness. In fact, seeking and utilizing therapy often takes a good deal of courage and strength," says BetterHelp, an online therapy platform. There are many different types of therapies and therapists to choose from, depending on what a client needs. Different approaches can address goals such as personal development, overcoming daily challenges, or making sense of your experiences for more meaningful living.

Global Nomads have to deal with an added layer of grief and loss that mobility creates, along with having to deal with the search for coherence in their multicultural life. An additional challenge you may face is establishing and affirming a sense of identity in the embrace of your family and workplace as you roam. Finding professionals in your home language can prove to be a tough task. But thanks to an increase in online possibilities, Global Nomads can connect with support around the world more easily.

Other professionals who provide such services are counselors and coaches. If we refer again to Maslow's Hierarchy of Needs, a counselor or therapist may help with issues in the middle sections, namely: Safety, Love and Belonging, and Esteem. A coach may help with the cap of the pyramid: Self-realization. If you're unsure which professional would be a good fit for you, consider the following:

Therapy is a longer-term process that addresses emotional and relational concerns—as well as trauma and mental illness—that may be present in the client's life or that affected them at various times in their past. Based on their training, a therapist chooses techniques to guide the client toward meaningful changes and solutions to live a more satisfying life. Global Nomads who have collected too many losses along the journey can address accumulated grief that may be affecting their lives in unexpected ways.

Counseling is usually a shorter-term process that focuses on a specific issue for which the client wants help. For example, emotion regulation, relationship and communication skills, stress management, or other challenges. The counselor and client work together to discover solutions and coping strategies that can help the client respond more adequately to situations and personal challenges. School counselors might also meet with children to build learning habits, organizational skills, and strategies for transitions, especially in the international scene.

Coaching is based on a client's goals to reach higher levels of achievement or performance. This could be in various areas of a person's life—career, sports, diet, the arts, and so on. In contrast to a therapist working with mental "illness," a coach trains mental "fitness."

What You Need

Materials: Paper, pen, a list of resources to investigate

Time: 30–60 minutes, ongoing

Instructions

Read through the lists below. You may find a phrase that applies to you, you might be inspired to write something that comes to mind as you read them, or you may decide to investigate working with a counselor or coach. For each question, write down your own answers to clarify your thoughts and beliefs about seeking out professional help.

What fears do you have around seeking help?

- "I don't want to tell my problems to anyone."
- "Others will find out I'm in therapy and judge me."
- "My problems aren't that serious."
- "Therapy is for crazy people."
- "I can get through my problems on my own."
- "It's a waste of time and money."
- "Deeper problems might surface."
- "I won't be able to return to my life afterward."
- "No one will understand my Global Nomad lifestyle."

What might the benefits be of seeking help?

- More awareness about your thoughts and feelings
- Better emotion regulation
- Clarity
- Increase in self-esteem
- More connection to self and others
- Clearer goals (and means to reach them)
- More positive mood
- A deeper sense of meaning
- Better functioning in daily life
- Improved coping mechanisms
- Healing past trauma
- Improved conflict-resolution skills
- More satisfying relationships
- Other

Other things to consider:

Finding the right fit

- Consult with your doctor for advice and referrals.
- Connect with others who have been or are in therapy to ask questions.
- Have at least one session to understand a therapist's approach and decide if you click with them.
- Check with your insurance provider about the kind of coverage they offer.

Online options

- American Psychological Association
- American Psychiatric Association
- American Association for Marriage and Family Therapy
- Better Help
- Families in Global Transition professional listings
- National Board for Certified Counselors
- *Psychology Today's* therapist search
- Truman Group

Check with your embassy and online forums for other suggestions.

What Happened

After a particularly tense situation in which Max blew up at the kids one evening, Sara found a calm moment to talk with him. "Honey, would you invest some time into our marriage by getting help for what you're going through?" This gentle nudge moved Max to agree. They tried one online agency, then another. Max seemed to prove his prediction that no one could understand what he was going through.

Sara asked around the expat community forums and they found an ATCK counselor with whom Max immediately clicked. He was also an ATCK and understood how the mobility in Max's life had set him up for an emotional implosion with the death of his father.

The original six sessions they had agreed on were extended to three months, then once a month for the rest of the year. Max was able to open up about many things Sara had never realized he was carrying around: guilt, resentment, feelings of uselessness, and more. Discovering this unknown—until now—part of her husband, Sara was grateful for the opportunities to work on herself through yoga, meditation, and several of the Tools she had tried.

She smiled to herself when she noticed Carl Jung's quote posted over Max's workspace:

"Who looks outside, dreams; who looks inside, awakes."

Reflection

Use the questions below to reflect on how working with a professional therapist, counselor, or coach could improve your well-being.

1. What areas in your life would you like to feel better about?
2. How can working on yourself affect your relationship with your partner and/or your children?
3. What might your children gain from knowing that you're working on yourself?
4. Which Life Skills are you nurturing in yourself through this Tool?

TOOL #54
Volunteer
Activity

---

*"If you think you are too small to make a difference,
try sleeping with a mosquito."*

The 14th Dalai Lama

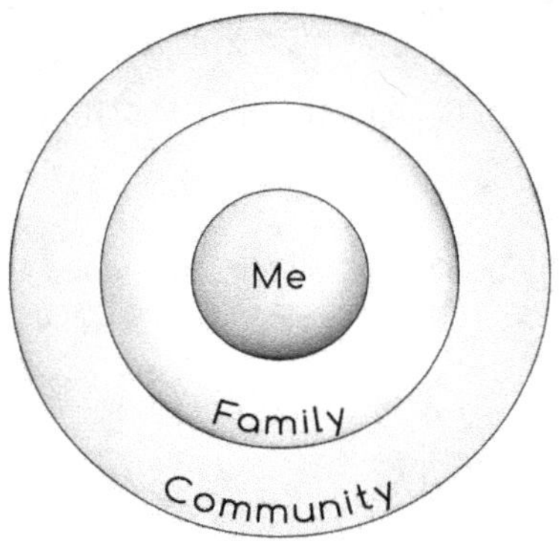

*Our positive actions ripple outward
in ways we may never know*

Purpose

To build connections and community.

Life Skills

Compassion, Being a Thinker, Leadership, Being Community-minded.

The Star Thrower

Sara attended the first Parent-Teacher Organization meeting of the school year. The father in charge of organizing volunteers for upcoming initiatives started his presentation with the story "The Star Thrower" by Loren Eiseley:

One morning, a woman was strolling along a beach where hundreds of starfish had washed up on the sand overnight. She began to pick them up one at a time and toss them back into the sea.

Another person came along and scoffed, "Why bother throwing some of them back when there are so many? What difference could it possibly make?"

The woman picked up another and cast it back into the water. "Well, it just made a difference to that one." She continued on her way.

Sara recognized the passerby's doubting comment in herself. She had volunteered for initiatives before because she knew it was a good thing to do, but often felt an overwhelming sense of helplessness. She took the organizer's contact to find out what volunteering opportunities were planned for the upcoming year.

Our need to feel a sense of significance and belonging lies at the heart of our well-being. Strong family bonds can fulfill some of this need, but as mobile families move and change communities every few years, greater fulfillment becomes a repeated challenge. International schools and their communities set up ways for Global Nomads to get involved with as little effort as possible. Volunteering is one way families can connect with locals. Offering our time and resources reaches beyond the borders of cultures and countries. Volunteering nurtures the hearts of both the giver and the receiver. When your children get involved, it creates strong memories of a place, not to mention new skills to include on their CVs later on.

What You Need

Materials: Connections with places to volunteer your time

Time: Indefinite

Instructions

Sometimes, opportunities come through everyday interactions with neighbors or residents. Once your family settles in, start investigating some of the places listed below.

- The Parent-Teacher Organization at your children's school
- School partners and projects
- Embassy partners
- Animal shelters
- Orphanages
- Women's centers
- Retirement homes
- Soup kitchens
- "Clean up" initiatives
- Church programs
- Neighborhood centers

What Happened

Once the kids had settled into a routine and Sara had set up the household, she investigated volunteering opportunities through the PTO. A newly established Single Mothers Association in Istanbul had a center that needed English teachers. Sara began giving lessons twice a week and later offered yoga for pregnant women.

In the past, Sara had helped sort clothes and deliver food, but having a regular group with the Single Mothers Association allowed her to get to know the mothers. She learned so much about the culture, the language, and the women.

When Sara shared stories about the English lessons she was teaching with her family, Mariel and Parul got inspired to volunteer somewhere. They built a relationship with the local vet clinic and pet shelter near their home. The girls spent one afternoon a week walking the dogs that were there for extended periods of time. This also satisfied the need to have animals in their life, without the logistics of moving a pet when the family left.

Reflection

Volunteering can happen through a variety of activities. It benefits us, as well as those we help, in unexpected ways. Use the questions below to reflect on the effects volunteering can have on our lives.

1. How does volunteering nurture the following:
   a. Self-esteem
   b. Independence from the family
   c. Creating one's identity
   d. Feeling grounded
2. What do your children learn when you volunteer your time in every location you move to?
3. What volunteering opportunities are in alignment with your *Personal Mission Statement Tool #37*?
4. How do you and your partner highlight the importance of volunteering to your children? For example, in light of your *Family Mission Statement Tool #2*, for religious reasons, as a community contribution, or something else?

TOOL #55

Write Your Own Story

Activity / Skill

"My story is, like yours, made up of many chapters. I have discovered the joy of bringing those seemingly fragmented and disjointed chapters together so that they tell one story; whole and complete and with the delicious anticipation of future chapters waiting to be written!"

Rachel Cason Life Story Therapies

Your story is waiting to be shared

Purpose

To reflect on your experiences and create your story to tell others.

Life Skills

Communication, Reflection, Sense of Purpose.

Sara's Story

As a child, Sara loved hearing her father's stories about "roughing it" in African countries, before he met her mom and after they married. She realized that she and Max also had tales to tell their children—about growing up as TCKs, a lifestyle that determined the choices they made to raise their own family as Global Nomads. They hadn't had that many opportunities to share their experiences, but the thought of Jace, Mariel, and Parul knowing and telling their children stories about Grandma Sara and Grandpa Max stirred a sense of creative adventure within her.

In his masterpiece, *Safe Passage*, Doug Ota gives three reasons why stories are essential in human lives:

1. We are wired to tell them.
2. Mental health requires a coherent life story.
3. Stories make Attachment Theory more tangible.

One of the traumatic things about moving is that your "storyline gets cut off," and with it, the attachment to those who know your story.

Bruce Feiler's article 'The Stories that Bind Us' cites research that confirms the importance of children hearing the stories of their parents and ancestors. Stories transmit values and morals through the generations, which reinforces a sense of belonging and significance. Not surprisingly, children who have knowledge of their family history have higher self-esteem and are more resilient when faced with adversity.

As a Global Nomad, recounting your story—the myriad of anecdotes that make up the fabric of your journey—connects the severed segments of your life to create coherence. The resulting narrative is as unique as your journey, affirming you, the "hero," at the core of an expanding adventure.

As Bruce Feiler's article explains, your narrative influences your children's sense of self as they carry your story with them. It helps them scaffold their personal narratives to pass on to your grandchildren and great-grandchildren—your family heritage and identity. What better gift to offer to future generations?

What You Need

Materials: Notebook or computer, examples of life stories,
a writing coach or group

Time: Indefinite

Instructions

Writing is an individual process where each person must discover what works best for them. Use the ideas below to support your journey.

Collect material

- Journal about your experiences, impressions, and reflections.
- Keep a record of your moves and details about the locations you've spent time in, things like information about the culture, customs, food, geography, places of interest, and interactions you've had with other TCKs as well as the locals.
- Take pictures to record places, people, and special moments.
- Talk to other TCKs as well as the locals about their impressions and reflections.
- Keep a record of the various ideas that come to you (both for fiction and non-fiction writing).
- Draw sketches to depict what you experience.

Develop your ideas

- Write short practice pieces about your experiences, impressions, and reflections.
- Join a writers' group.
- Work with a writing coach.
- Start a blog.

Take it further

- Decide which of your ideas to develop into a book or other project.
- Work with a coach, editor, and/or publisher to complete your project.
- Publish, print, and distribute your book or project to close family and friends, or market it to the broader public.

What Happened

One of the mothers talked about the online platform Families in Global Transition at a PTO meeting. Sara discovered a treasure chest of resources for Third Culture Families: blogs, webinars, groups, events, professional resources, and a bookstore.

Why haven't I heard of this before? she thought as she explored the website, impressed by the amount of literature for Global Nomads. After ordering at least a year's worth of reading material, Sara recognized that she, too, had something to write about from her journey. With a bit of research, she found an online writing group, which led to her connecting with a life story coach for ATCKs. A sense of excitement built within her as she explored and recorded her past stories through the framework her coach offered. Things started falling into place and Sara began a new journey, that of being a writer.

When insecurity about being a writer started battering her with excuses to give up the challenge, Sara used the *Encouragement Tool #18* to coach herself. *Look at how many new skills you've learned—you can do this!* When an inner critic tried to dissuade her, Sara countered it with positive thoughts. *Who knows where this journey will lead?* She gently repeated in her mind, *I have so many Tools to help myself succeed with this new skill.* The thought of sharing her stories with her children and others helped her keep her eye on the prize. She smiled, thinking of all the new skills she and Max had learned from the Toolkit over the past few years.

Reflection

Your children will have their own experience of your journey together, but they may never know the part that made you, you. Reflect on these questions to guide the process to Write Your Own Story:

1. What ways have you already used to create connections between the different pieces of your mobile lifestyle story? Think of your inner process as well as the countries, cultures, and experiences.
2. In what ways could writing your story help organize your feelings, thoughts, and experiences during your mobile lifestyle?
3. What possible reasons are there for you to *not* Write Your own Story? What are the reasons for doing it anyway?
4. How would you like to transmit your stories to your children, grandchildren, and beyond?

The Journey Continues

Between 70,000 and 100,000 years ago, Homo sapiens began migrating from what is now known as the continent of Africa into Europe and Asia. When a land bridge formed, the wanderers crossed to the North and South American continents. Later, they made it all the way to Australia, effectively populating most of the Earth. What initiated this urge for mobility? Food, climate changes, resources? As the hunter-gatherers found ways to grow their own food, settlements based on agriculture began to shape a new kind of lifestyle.

Mobility has continued through human history for more "modern" reasons—political and war refugees, work opportunities, religious missions, for a better life, or just for adventure. Crossing borders of culture, language, and religion, and the morals and values that go with all that, requires nomads and locals to open their hearts and minds. Connecting with people different from ourselves drives us to become more tolerant. It also puts more focus on the family to be the stable unit amid mobility.

As more and more people mobilize nowadays, there are even more opportunities to expand our awareness of other people and cultures. Perhaps the role of Global Nomads can be viewed through this lens in the continuing evolution of humankind toward more tolerance and understanding.

Now that you have traveled with the Tillers through the Toolkit, may your own journey be lightened by what you have gathered along the way. May you experience more connection within yourself and your family, with those you meet along the way, and with the journey itself.

APPENDIX

TOOL #1

Pitfalls and Perks of a Mobile Lifestyle

PITFALLS	TOOLS to transform Pitfalls to PERKS	PERKS

TOOL #3

Challenges and Gifts for Children

CHALLENGES	PARENT TOOLS	GIFTS

TOOL #4

The Temperament Assessment Scale

	Temperament Marker from *The Connected Mobile Family*
	Mark an X on the continuum, according to where you feel your child's temperament is.
1	**Activity Level** High Activity ____ Low Activity *Movement during daily activities and sleep.*
2	**Rhythmicity** Predictable ____ Unpredictable *Regularity of bodily functions; predictability of his/her response to daily schedule; regularity of organization and effort in school.*
3	**Initial Response** Bold ____Withdraws *Response to new people, places, foods, experiences, things.*
4	**Adaptability** Flexible ____ Rigid *How easily a child adapts after his/her first reaction to new people, places, foods, experiences, things.*
5	**Sensory Threshold** Very sensitive ____Non reactive *Level of sensory stimulation needed to elicit a response – (sight, hearing, taste, touch, and olfactory).*
6	**Quality of Mood** Optimistic ____Pessimistic *Overall positive or negative mood of a child.* **Intensity of Reactions** Intense reactions ____ Mild reactions *The strength of a child 's reaction to sensory stimulation and emotional response to situations and events (frustration, fear, anger, disappointment, surprise, etc.).*
7	**Distractibility** Highly focused ____ Easily distracted *The ability to tune out surrounding stimuli and stay focused without interruption.*
8	**Persistence and Attention Span** Persistent ____ Gives up *The ability to follow through on an activity despite feelings of frustration or external distractions; how long a child will stay focused with no interruptions.*
9	NOTE: Temperament is one factor in behavior. The younger the child, behavior is more closely linked to developmental level and needs. As children mature, their behavior also comes from their perceptions of worth and belonging. Permission: Adapted from *"Temperament and Development: Why Do They DO That?"* Jane Nelsen, *Positive Discipline: The First Three Years*

TOOL #4

Draw Your Child

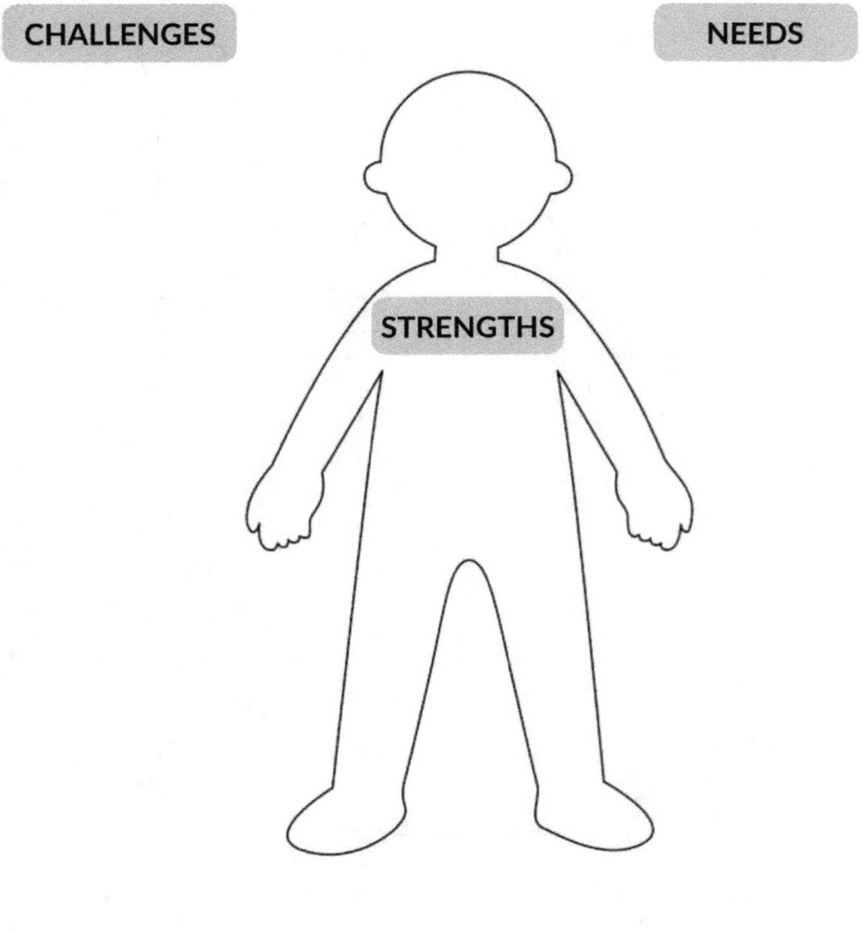

TOOL #13

Coat of Arms Template

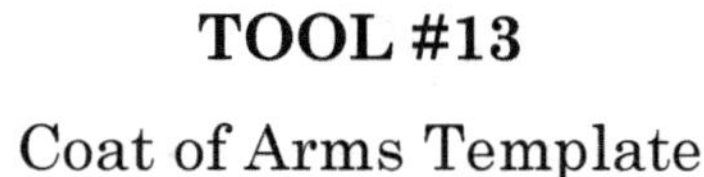

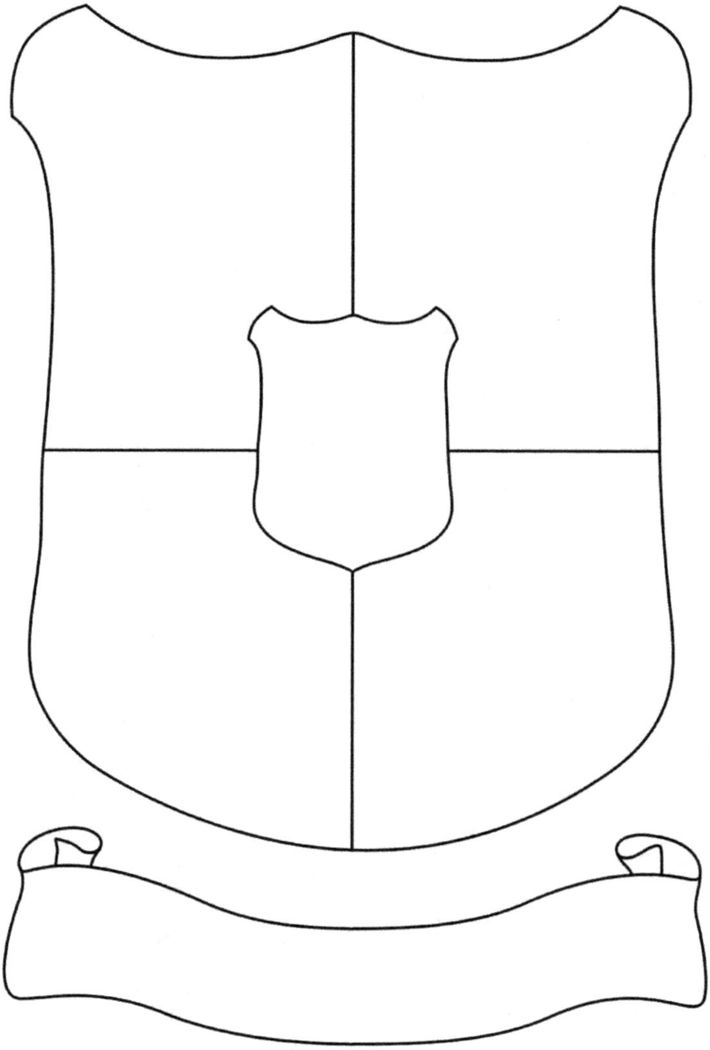

TOOL #23

Family Meetings Agenda

FAMILY MEETINGS	
Leader: Family Greeting:	
Kudos, Appreciation, Successes, Celebrations	
Tasks from previous meeting:	
New Agenda items: We will focus on:	
Action plan:	
Planning for upcoming events:	
Appreciation for the Leader:	
Family Greeting:	
Notes:	

TOOL #27

Feelings Chart

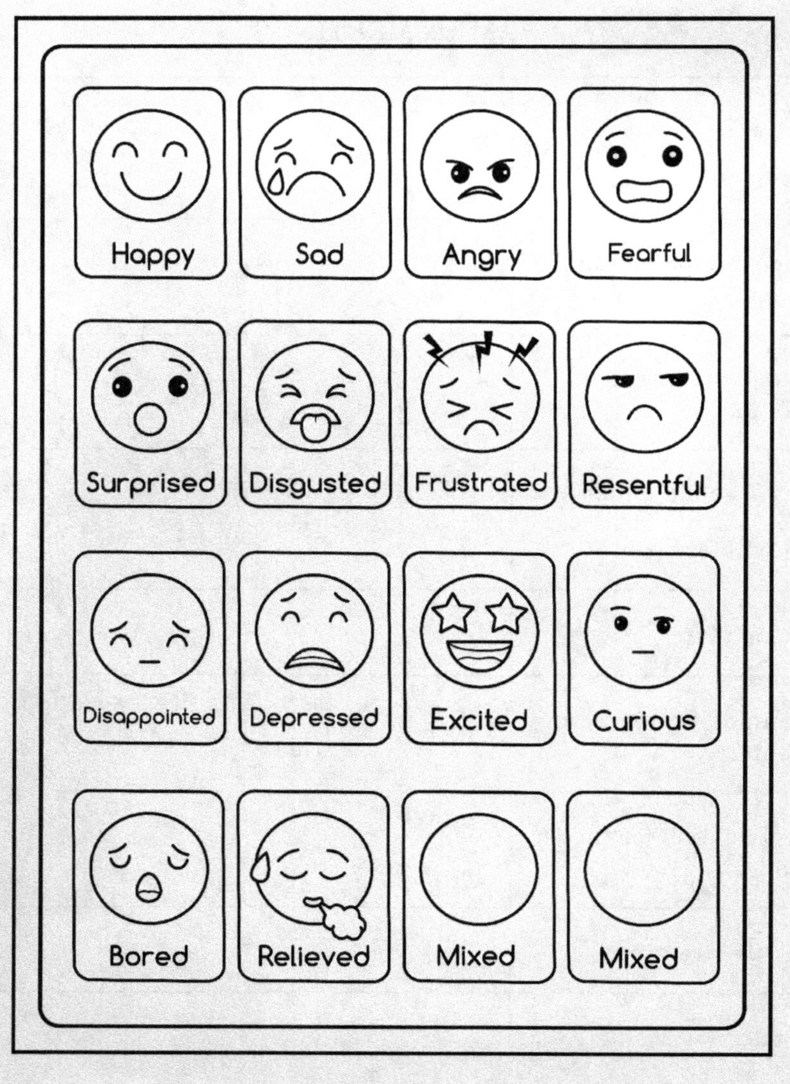

RESOURCES

Further Reading

Accumulated Lessons in Displacement: Poems, Rachel E. Hicks, Resource Publications, 2025

Arriving Well: Stories about identity, belonging, and rediscovering home after living abroad, Cate Brubaker, Doreen Cumberford, and Helen Watts, 2018

Awakening the Heroes Within, Twelve Archetypes to Help Us Find Ourselves and Transform Our World, Carol S. Pearson, Ph.D., Harper One, 1991

Beijing Tai Tai: Life, laughter and motherhood in China's capital, Tania McCartney, 2nd Revised edition, Exisle Publishing, 2015

Being a Distance Grandparent—A Book for ALL Generations, Helen Ellis, Summertime Publishing, 2021

Belonging Beyond Borders: How Adult Third Culture Kids Can Cultivate a Sense of Belonging, Megan C. Norton, Belonging Beyond Borders, LLC, 2022

Between Worlds: Essays on Culture and Belonging, Marilyn R. Gardner, Doorlight Publications, 2015

A Career in Your Suitcase, Jo Parfitt, Galen Tinder, et al., Summertime Publishing, 2008

China Blonde: How a newsreader's search for adventure led to friendship, acceptance ... and peroxide pandemonium!, Nicole Webb, Broadcast Books, 2022

Cultural Chemistry: Simple Strategies for Bridging Cultural Gaps, Patti McCarthy, Cultural Chemistry, 2016

Cultural Intelligence: Living and Working Globally, David C Thomas and Kerr Inkson, Berrett-Koehler Publishers, 2009

A Cup of Culture and a Pinch of Crisis: Tales from a Small Planet: The Food Edition, Leah Evans, Katie Jagelski, Patricia Linderman, and Nicole Schaefer-McDaniel, CreateSpace Independent Publishing Platform, 2016

Definite Articles: How to Write and Sell Winning Articles Based on Your Overseas Experience, Jo Parfitt, Summertime Publishing, 2010

Diplomatic Baggage: The Adventures of a Trailing Spouse, Brigid Keenan and John Murray, 2005

Dubai Dreams: Inside the Kingdom of Bling, Raymond Barrett, Nicholas Brealey, 2010

Dutched Up!: Rocking the Clogs Expat Style, Olga Mecking, 2014

Expat Life Slice by Slice, Apple Gidley, 2012

Expat Alien: My Global Adventures, Kathleen Gamble, CreateSpace Independent Publishing Platform, 2012

Find Your Passion, Jo Parfitt and Debbie Jenkins, Summertime Publishing, 2012

Global Coaching: An Integrated Approach for Long-Lasting Results, Philippe Rosinski, Nicholas Brealey, 2010

Global Grandmas, Kathleen McAnear Smith, Evangelista Media, 2004

The Globally Mobile Family's Guide to Educating Children Overseas, Karen A. Wrobbel, Wipf & Stock, 2022

Growing Up in Transit: The Politics of Belonging at an International School, Danau Tanu, Berghahn Books, 2017

The Guilty Can't Say Goodbye: Three Women. Three Secrets. Three Broken Lives., Mariam Navaid Ottimofiore, Springtime Books, 2004

Here Today There Tomorrow, Elisabeth Parker and Katharine Rumrill-Teece, Wesleyan Publishing House, 2010

Here We Are & There We Go: Teaching and Traveling with Kids in Tow (English Edition), Jill Dobbe, Ten16 Press, 2012

The Hero Within: Six Archetypes We Live By, Carol S. Pearson, Ph.D., Harper One, 1986

Home Keeps Moving, Heidi Sand-Art, McDougal Publishing, 2010

Homeward Bound: A Spouse's Guide to Repatriation, Robin Pascoe

Kids Like Me: Voices of the Immigrant Experience, Judith M. Blohm and Terri Lapinsky, Nicholas Brealey, 2006

Kids on the Move: 25 Activities to help kids connect, reflect and thrive around the world, Leah Moorefield Evans and Jodi Harris, MSW, CreateSpace Independent Publishing Platform, 2018

Letters Never Sent: A Global Nomad's Journey from Hurt to Healing, Ruth Van Reken, Summertime Publishing, 2012

Letters Now Sent: A Collection of Letters from the Globally Mobile, Megan Norton-Newbanks, Belonging Beyond Borders, LLC, 2025

Life in the Camel Lane: Embrace the Adventure, Doreen Cumberford, White Heather Press, 2020

A Map Is Only One Story: Twenty Writers on Immigration, Family, and the Meaning of Home, Nicole Chung and Mensah Demary, Catapult, 2020

The Means That Make Us Strangers, Christine Kindberg, 2019 (Young Adult)

Monday Morning Emails: Six months, twelve countries, a thousand thoughts: two mothers share the journey of living a global life, Terry Anne Wilson, Jo Parfitt, Summertime Publishing, 2018

The Newcomer's Dictionary, Joyce Agee, Springtime Books, 2022

Notes from a Traveling Childhood: Readings for Internationally Mobile Parents & Children, Karen C. McCluskey, Foreign Service Youth Foundation, 1994

Nothing Like a Dane: A real-life search for hygge in Denmark, Keri Bloomfield, Pembar Press, 2022

Once Upon An Expat, Lisa Webb, Canadian Expat Mom, 2016

Parents on the Move!, Kathleen McAnear Smith, Destiny Image, 2010

The Practice of Processing: Exploring our emotions to chart an intentional course, Elizabeth Vahey Smith, 2022

Raising Children At Promise: How the Surprising Gifts of Adversity and Relationship Build Character in Kids, Dr. Tim Stuart, Jossey-Bass, 2005

Raising Up a Generation of Healthy Third Culture Kids: A Practical Guide to Preventive Care, Lauren Wells, 2020

Relocation Workbook: Kids on the Move, Leah Moorefield Evans, CreateSpace Independent Publishing Platform, 2014

Sunshine Soup: Nourishing the Global Soul, Jo Parfitt, Summertime Publishing, 2011

The Toolbox for Multilingual Families, Ute Limacher-Riebold and Ana Elisa Miranda, 2020

Warrior Spirit Rising: A Native American Spiritual Journey, Dianna Good Sky, Good Sky Stories, 2020

The Worlds Within: An anthology of TCK art and writing: young, global and between cultures, Jo Parfitt, Summertime Publishing, 2014

Kids' Books

B at Home: Emma Moves Again, Valérie Besanceney, Summertime Publishing, 2014

Ben's Magical Journey to the Seven Wonders of the Modern World, Joni Kerr, 2024

Friends and Farewells: Kiya's Story, Joni Kerr, 2025

Home, James, Emily Steele Jackson, CreateSpace Independent Publishing Platform, 2018 (Young Adult)

Means that Make Us Strangers, Christine Kindberg, 2019 (Young Adult)

My Moving Booklet, Valérie Besanceney, Summertime Publishing, 2015

I'm New Here, Anne Sibley O'Brien, Charlesbridge Publishing, 2015

Little Bunny Dandelion discovers his favourite flower: or how to manage life in global transition, Angela Schreiner, 2018

25 Activities to Help Kids Connect, Reflect & Thrive Around the World: Kids on the Move, Leah Moorefield Evans and Jodi Harris, MSW, CreateSpace Independent Publishing Platform, 2018

Why Do We Have to Move?, Joy O´Neill, 2013

Goodbye Books for Children

Amber Brown is Not a Crayon, Paula Danziger, Puffin Books, 2006 (6–8 yrs.)

Alexander, Who's Not (Do You Hear Me? I Mean It!) Going to Move, Judith Viorst, Atheneum Books for Young Readers, 2012 (4–7 yrs.)

Bad Bye, Good Bye, Deborah Underwood, Clarion Books, 2014 (4–7 yrs.)

B at Home, Valérie Besanceney, Summertime Publishing, 2016 (6–8 yrs.) (Chapter book)

Gilbert the Great, Jane Clarke, Sterling, 2005 (4–7 yrs.)

A House for Hermit Crab, Eric Carle, Simon & Schuster, 1991, (4–18 yrs.)

I'm Moving, Sara Wallén, Summertime Publishing, 1991 (4–7 yrs.)

I'm Not Moving, Mama!, Nancy White Carlstrom, Simon & Schuster, 1990 (4–7 yrs.)

Ira Says Goodbye, Bernard Waber, Clarion Books, 1991 (4–7 yrs.)

Mitchell Is Moving, Marjorie Weinman Sharmat, Simon Spotlight, 1996 (5–8 yrs.)

My Best Friend Moved Away, Nancy Carlson, Viking Juvenile, 2001 (2– 6 yrs.)

My Moving Booklet, Valérie Besanceney, Summertime Publishing, 2015 (companion workbook to *B at Home*)

On the Move: Home Is Where You Find It, Michael Rosen, Candlewick, 2022 (10+ yrs.)

Pinky and Rex and the New Neighbors, James Howe, Simon Spotlight, 2016 (6–8 yrs.)

Sammy's Next Move, Helen Maffini, CreateSpace Independent Publishing Platform, 2011 (8–10 yrs.)

Saying Goodbye, Lisa Cooper, Xlibris AU, 2019 (5–6 yrs.)

We Are Best Friends, Aliki, Greenwillow Books, 1987 (4–8 yrs.)

Wilfrid Gordon McDonald Partridge, Mem Fox, Kane Miller, 1985 (2–8 yrs.)

The Year My Parents Ruined My Life, Martha Freeman, Holiday House, 1997, (4–8 yrs.)

Podcasts for Global Nomads

Holding the Fort Abroad, Rhoda Bangerter
Discover how families find creative ways to maintain relationships when one partner/parent works away more frequently, whilst the non-traveling parent juggles responsibilities at home amid their own pursuits.
https://podbay.fm/p/holding-the-fort-abroad-740457

Global Nomad Hacks Podcast, Dr. Heidi Forbes Ouste
Sharing stories and tips on life as a Global Nomad, Digital Nomad, expat, road warrior, and supporting third culture families and global migration.
https://www.globalnomadhacks.com

A Life Overseas is composed of a writing team.
Provides a place of online connection for Christ-following missionaries and humanitarian aid workers living in foreign countries.
https://www.alifeoverseas.com/about

The Mindful Muslim Podcast, Dina Aziz
The Mindful Muslim is an Inspirited Minds podcast that hosts raw, open, and honest conversations on various topics within the sphere of mental health, psychology, Islam, and spirituality.
https://open.spotify.com/episode/382dEHgVjcpN2BEseRcS2U

The Real Expat Wives of Arabia, Kim Haughton
https://podcasts.apple.com/au/podcast/the-real-expat-wives-of-arabia/id1611615644

The TCK Research Podcast, Mathieu Gagnon, Ph.D. and Andrea Schmitt, B.Sc.
https://www.youtube.com/watch?v=egARJqd2TBI

For more podcasts and blogs, visit the Expat Bookshop:
https://www.expatbookshop.com/extra-resources/directory-of-tck-cck-blogs-websites-a-to-m

Organizations

Looking for more support? Here's a list of places to look:

The embassy in your location.

The Expat Bookshop Resources for Expats, TCKs, and authors.

Families in Global Transition, a community of globally mobile individuals, families, and those who support them.

Global Nomads Group, connecting youth across difference and distance, Global Youth for Global Youth.

Positive Discipline Association, parent resources and training based on the work of Alfred Adler and Rudolf Dreikurs.

Safe Passage Across Networks (SPAN), a home to anyone committed to healthy transitions and attachment security.

Sea Change Mentoring, strengthening relationships in schools around the world Third Culture Kids International, providing Christian-based resources for expat families around the world.

Online Therapy

Better Help online therapists

Global Nomad's World

The Truman Group

Websites and Blogs

https://theblackexpat.com/the-important-questions-to-ask-before-you-move-overseas/

https://communicatingacrossboundariesblog.com/tck-resources/blogs/

http:/crossculturalkid.org

http://denizenmag.com

http://thedisplacednation.com

https://www.expatbookshop.com/extra-resources/directory-of-tck-cck-blogs-websites-a-to-m/

https://www.explorelifestory.com/

www.GlobalGrandmas.net

https://www.joparfitt.com

https://www.kldscp.org. TCK club providing consistent debriefing and ongoing friendships for kids on the move

http://www.tckworld.com

http://thirdcultureliterature.blogspot.ca/2014/07/an-ever-growing-list-of-third-culture.html

https://www.facebook.com/TCKWorldwide/

https://velvetashes.com/navigating-awkward-transitions-with-our-children/

https://purplecrayonyourworld.com/

https://rachelpiehjones.com/third-culture-kids/

https://www.seebeyond.cc. Support for individuals, couples, and organizations throughout North Africa, the Sahel, and the Middle East

BIBLIOGRAPHY

Books

The Alchemist, Paola Coelho, Harper Collins, 1993

Animal Spirit Guides: An Easy-to-Use Handbook for Identifying and Understanding Your Power Animals and Animal Spirit Helpers, Steven D. Farmer, Hay House, 2006

Arrivals, Departures, and the Adventures In-Between, Christopher O'Shaughnessy, Summertime Publishing, 2014

The Arts and Human Development, Howard Gardner, Basic Books, 1994

Attachment Theory Workbook, Annie Chen, LMFT, Althea Press, 2019

B at Home: Emma Moves Again, Valérie Besanceney, Summertime Publishing, 2014

Belonging Everywhere & Nowhere: Insights into Counseling the Globally Mobile, Lois J. Bushong, M.S., Mango Tree Intercultural Services, 2013

Burn-Up or Splash Down, Marion Knell, InterVarsity Press, 2006

The Celestine Prophecy, James Redfield, Warner Books, 1993

Children, the Challenge: The Classic Work on Improving Parent-Child Relationships, Rudolf Dreikurs, Plume, 1991

Definite Articles: How to Write and Sell Winning Articles Based on Your Overseas Experience, Jo Parfitt, *2010*

Discipline Without Tears, Rudolf Dreikurs, M.D., Pearl Cassel, M.Ed., Eva Dreikurs Ferguson, Ph.D., John Wiley and Sons Canada Ltd., 2004

Draw on Your Emotions, Second Edition, Dr. Margot Sunderland, Routledge, 2018

Emotional Intelligence, Daniel Goleman, Tenth Anniversary Edition, Bantam Books, 2006

Emotional Resilience and the Expat Child: Practical Storytelling Techniques That Will Strengthen the Global Family, Julia Simens, Summertime Publishing, 2011

The 5 Love Languages of Children, Gary Chapman, Moody Publishers, 2012

Guide to Raising Exceptional Expat Kids: A proven way to help kids assimilate to their new surroundings along with reducing the emotional stress due to moving abroad, Joni Kerr, 2022

The Guilty Can't Say Goodbye, Miriam N. Ottimofiore, Springtime Books, 2024

The Hero with a Thousand Faces, Joseph Campbell, New World Library; Third Edition, 2008

The Hidden Messages in Water, Dr. Masaru Emoto, Atria Books, 2005

The Hiding Place, Corrie ten Boom, Barbour, 1971

How Children Succeed: Grit, Curiosity, and the Hidden Power of Character, Paul Tough, Mariner Books, 2012

The How of Happiness, Sonja Lyubomirsky, Penguin Books, 2008

How to Talk so Kids Will Listen, and Listen so Kids Will Talk, Adele Faber, Elaine Mazlish, et al., Scribner, 2012

Kids on the Move: 25 Activities to Help Kids Connect, Reflect & Thrive Around the World, Leah Evans and Jodi Harris, MSW

Know Your Child: An Authoritative Guide for Today's Parents, Stella Chess, Jason Aronson Inc., 1996

The Last Lecture, Randy Pausch, Hyperion, 2008

Life is in the Transitions, Bruce Feiler, Penguin Books, 2020

The Light in the Heart: Inspirational Thoughts for Leading Your Best Life, Roy T. Bennett, Roy Bennett, 2016

The Magicians Trilogy, Lev Grossman, Viking Press, 2009

Mindset: The New Psychology of Success, Carol S. Dweck, Ph.D., Bernadette Dunne, et al., Random House, 2006

Misunderstood, Tanya Crossman, Summertime Publishing, 2016

More Than Enough, David Ramsey, Penguin Group, 1999

Nonviolent Communication, 3rd Edition, Marshall B. Rosenberg, Ph.D., PuddleDancer Press, 2015

Nurturing Spirituality in Children, Peggy J. Jenkins, Ph.D. Beyond Words Publishing, Inc., 1995

Parenting as a Spiritual Journey: Deepening Ordinary and Extraordinary Events into Sacred Occasions, Rabbi Nancy Fuchs-Kreimer, Jewish Lights Publishing, 1998

Parenting from the Inside Out: How a Deeper Self-Understanding Can Help You Raise Children Who Thrive, Daniel J. Siegel, MD, TarcherPerigee, 2004

A Parent's Guide to Raising Kids Overseas, Dr. Jeffery A. Devens, CreateSpace, 2017

The Parent's Handbook: Systematic Training for Effective Parenting, Don Dinkmeyer, Sr., Don Dinkmeyer, Jr., Gary D. McKay, Step Publishers, 1997

Parenting Toolbox, 125 Activities Therapists Use to Manage Emotions, Increase Positive Behaviors and Reduce Meltdowns, Lisa Phifer, Ded., NCSP, Laura K. Sibbald, M.A., CCC-SLP, Jennifer Roden, M.Ed., CAGS, PESI Publishing & Media, 2018

Parenting with Love and Logic: Teaching Children Responsibility, Foster Cline, Jim Fay, NavPress Publishing, 2006

The Pilgrimage, Paolo Coelho, Harper One; 32102nd edition, 2021

Playful Parenting: An Exciting New Approach to Raising Children That Will Help You Nurture Close Connections, Solve Behavior Problems, and Encourage Confidence, Lawrence J. Cohen, Ballantine Books, 2002

Pointing the Way, Martin Buber, Humanities Press, 1990

Positive Discipline, Jane Nelsen, Ed.D., Ballantine Books, 2006

Positive Parenting in the Muslim Home, Noha Alshugair, Munira Lekovic Ezzeldine, Izza Publishing, 2017

Positive Parenting: An Essential Guide (The Positive Parent Series), Rebecca Eanes, TarcherPerigee, 2016

Pride and Joy: A Guide to Understanding Your Child's Emotions and Solving Family Problems, 1st Edition, Kenneth Barish, Ph.D., Oxford University Press; 1st edition, 2012

Raising an Emotionally Intelligent Child: The Heart of Parenting, John Gottman, Ph.D., Simon & Schuster, 1997

Raising Global Nomads: Parenting Abroad in an On-Demand World, Robin Pascoe, RRLJ Investments LTD, 2006

Raising Global Teens: A Practical Handbook for Parenting in the 21st Century, Dr. Anisha Abraham, Summertime Publishing, 2020

Raising Resilient Children: Fostering Strength, Hope, and Optimism in Your Child, Robert Brooks, McGraw Hill, 2002

Release the Book Within, Joanna Parfitt, Summertime Publishing, 2007

Resilience and the Internationally Mobile Family, William Nicoll, Ph.D., Peggy Pelonis, Ed.D., Archway Publishing, 2019

A Rubric for Transition Among Cultures: To Assist and Inform Cross-culture Transition Progress, Rachel E Timmons, Summertime Publishing, 2022

Safe Passage: How Mobility Affects People and What International Schools Should Do About It, Douglas W. Ota, Summertime Publishing, 2014

The Secrets of Happy Families: Improve Your Mornings, Rethink Family Dinner, Fight Smarter, Go Out and Play, and Much More, Bruce Feiler, William Morrow, 2013

A Secure Base: Parent-Child Attachment and Healthy Human Development, John Bowlby, Basic Books, 1988

The Self-Talk Workout: Six Science-Backed Strategies to Dissolve Self-Criticism and Transform the Voice in Your Head, Rachel Goldsmith Turow, Shambhala, 2022

7 Habits of Highly Effective Families, Stephen R. Covey, Golden Books, 1997

7 Habits of Highly Effective People, Stephen R. Covey, Simon & Schuster, 1989

7 Habits of Highly Effective Teens, Sean Covey, Simon & Schuster, 2014

Short Thoughts for the Long Haul, Robert Brault, CreateSpace, 2017

The Star Thrower, Loren Eiseley, Harper Perennial, 1979

Start with Why, Simon Sinek, Portfolio Penguin, 2009

Secure Relating: Holding Your Own in an Insecure World, Sue Marriott, Harper, 2024

The Single Woman: Life, Love and a Dash of Sass: Embracing Singleness with Confidence, Mandy Hale, Thomas Nelson, 2013

The Six Pillars of Self-Esteem: The Definitive Work on Self-Esteem, Nathaniel Branden, Bantam, 1995

Third Culture Kids, Third Edition: David C. Pollack, Ruth E. Van Reken, and Michael V. Pollock, Nicholas Brealey Publishing, 2017

This Messy Mobile Life: How a Mola Can Help Globally Mobile Families Create a Life by Design, Miriam N. Ottimofiore, Springtime Books, 2019

The Total Money Makeover: A Proven Plan for Financial Fitness, Dave Ramsey, Thomas Nelson, 2013

25 Activities to Help Kids Connect, Reflect & Thrive Around the World: Kids on the Move, Leah Moorefield Evans, Jodi Harris, CreateSpace, 2018

24 Keys That Bring Complete Success, Paul J. Meyer, Bridge Logos Fndtn, 2006

When Abroad, Do as the Local Children Do, Hilly van Swol-Ulbrich, Bettina Kaltenhauser, X-Pat Media, 2002

Articles

'Adult Third Culture Kids,' Ruth Hill Useem and Ann Baker Cottrell, *Strangers at Home: Essays on the Effects of Living Overseas and Coming "Home" to a Strange Land*, Aletheia Publications, 1996, pp. 22–25
https://www.researchgate.net/publication/319289838_Adult_Third_Culture_Kids

'Allowance, Age by Age,' Scholastic.com
https://www.scholastic.com/parents/family-life/financial-literacy/allowance-age-age.html

'Can music improve our health and quality of life?', Lorrie Kubicek, MT-BC, *Harvard Health Publishing*, July 2022
https://www.health.harvard.edu/blog/can-music-improve-our-health-and-quality-of-life-202207252786

'Coaching vs. therapy: Do you need a coach, a therapist, or both?,' Madeleine Miles, *Betterup Blog*, July 21, 2022
https://www.betterup.com/blog/coaching-versus-therapy

'Connection Before Connection,' Lee Ann Jung, ASCD website article, November 2023
https://ascd.org/el/articles/connection-before-correction

'Digital nomads: rising number of people choose to work remotely,' Suzanne Bearne, *The Guardian*, November 2023
https://www.theguardian.com/money/2023/nov/04/digital-nomads-work-remotely-tech-visas

'Energy Levels, Electrons, and Covalent Bonding,' ACS Chemistry for Life, *Lesson 4.4 The Periodic Table and Bonding*, July 2024
https://www.acs.org/middleschoolchemistry/lessonplans/chapter4/lesson4.html

'The Essential Nature of Date Night for Parents,' Helene A. Miller, Family Psychiatry and Therapy, 2021
https://familypsychnj.com/2021/04/the-essential-nature-of-date-nights-for-parents

'Exercise: 7 benefits of regular physical activity,' Mayo Clinic Staff, *Healthy Lifestyle Fitness*, August 2023
https://www.mayoclinic.org/healthy-lifestyle/fitness/in-depth/exercise/art-20048389

'Factors Affecting Third Culture Kids' (TCKs) Transition,' Antonio Morales, QSI International School, China, *Journal of International Education Research*, First Quarter 2015, V. 11, N.1
https://files.eric.ed.gov/fulltext/EJ1051127.pdf

'Global Nomad, Third Culture Kid, Adult Third Culture Kid, Third Culture Adult: What Do They All Mean?', Barbara Schaetti, Ph.D., Families in Global Transition
https://www.figt.org/global_nomads

'Growing Up with a World View,' Norma McCaig, Keri Douglas, 9 Muses News, July 25, 2013
https://9musesnews.com/2013/07/25/growing-up-with-a-world-view-norma-mccaig/

'Growth and developments in the digital nomad market since COVID-19,' WYSE Travel Confederation, January 2023
https://www.wysetc.org/2023/01/growth-and-developments-in-the-digital-nomad-market-since-covid-19/

'Identifying child temperament types using cluster analysis in three samples,' Amanda Prokasky, *Journal of Research in Personality*, Volume 67, April 2017, Pages 190–201
https://www.sciencedirect.com/science/article/abs/pii/S0092656616301805

'Identity and Belonging Between Worlds,' Elena Moroni, *Global History Dialogues*, 2022
https://globalhistorydialogues.org/stories/identity-and-belonging-between-worlds

'The Importance of Ritual: Marking life events in a socially distant world,' Rebecca J. Lester, Psychology Today, May 2020
https://www.psychologytoday.com/us/blog/anthropology-in-mind/202005/the-importance-ritual

'Music Can be a Great Mood Booster,' Sara Elizabeth Adler, *AARP Magazine*, June 2020
https://www.aarp.org/health/brain-health/info-2020/music-mental-health.html

'Pets and Children,' Facts for Families, American Academy of Child and Adolescent Psychiatry, May 2008
https://www.aacap.org/AACAP/Families_and_Youth/Facts_for_Families/FFF-Guide/Pets-And-Children-075.aspx

'Positive thinking: Stop negative self-talk to reduce stress,' Mayo Clinic Staff, Healthy Lifestyle – Stress Management
https://www.mayoclinic.org/healthy-lifestyle/stress-management/in-depth/positive-thinking/art-20043950

'Prayer and healing: A medical and scientific perspective on randomized controlled trials,' Chittaranjan Andrade and Rajiv Radhakrishnan, *Indian Journal of Psychiatry*, October-December 2009
https://www.ncbi.nlm.nih.gov/pmc/articles/PMC2802370/

'The Psychology of Compliments: A Nice Word Goes a Long Way,' Abigail Fagan, Psychology Today, September 14, 2021
https://www.psychologytoday.com/intl/blog/evidence-based-living/202109/the-psychology-compliments-nice-word-goes-long-way

'Reflections on Identity and Belonging in Times of Coronavirus,' Global Nomad's World website, 29 May
https://www.globalnomadsworld.com/psychology-and-coaching/reflections-on-identity-and-belonging-in-times-of-coronavirus

'Science of Family Activities, United Nations Office on Drugs and Crime,'
https://www.unodc.org/unodc/en/listen-first/science-of-care/video/the-science-of-family-activities.html

'The Science and Research on Gratitude and Happiness,' Erika Stoerkel, *Positive Psychology Journal*, 2019
https://positivepsychology.com/gratitude-happiness-research/

'A Simple Compliment Can Make a Big Difference,' Erica Boothby, Xuan Zhao, and Vanessa Bohns, Harvard Business Review, February 24, 2021
https://hbr.org/2021/02/a-simple-compliment-can-make-a-big-difference

'The Stories That Bind Us,' Bruce Feiler, New York Times, This Life, March 2013
https://www.nytimes.com/2013/03/17/fashion/the-family-stories-that-bind-us-this-life.html

'10 Good Reasons to Keep a Journal: From stress reduction to creativity, here's why you should start writing today,' Kevin Bennett, Psychology Today, January 2023
https://www.psychologytoday.com/intl/blog/modern-minds/202301/10-good-reasons-to-keep-a-journal

'10 Tips for Successful Family Meetings', R.J. Fetsch and B. Jacobson, Colorado State University Extension
https://archives.mountainscholar.org/digital/collection/p17393coll94/id/4705

'Therapy vs. counseling: Is there a difference? Which is right for you?,' Jessica Lammers, M.D., *Ohio State Health & Discovery*, March 14, 2022
https://health.osu.edu/health/mental-health/therapy-vs-counseling-is-there-a-difference

'This is your brain on prayer and meditation,' Nicole Spector, *NBC News*, October 2017
https://www.nbcnews.com/better/health/your-brain-prayer-meditation-ncna812376

'Three Reasons Why the Best Leaders Ask Rather Than Tell,' Sinive Seely, Forbes Magazine, October 2019
https://www.forbes.com/councils/forbescoachescouncil/2019/10/01/three-reasons-why-the-best-leaders-ask-rather-than-tell

'Totem Pole,' Editors of Encyclopedia Britannica, Britannica website
https://www.britannica.com/art/totem-pole

'Utilizing Animal Metaphors in Child Psychotherapy: An Integrative Approach for Therapists,' Tricia J. Gordon, Bridgewater State University, *The Graduate Review*, 2018, Volume 3, Article 21
https://vc.bridgew.edu/cgi/viewcontent.cgi?article=1072&context=grad_rev

In this article, the following reference was used: 'Metaphor with an attitude: The use of the mighty morphin' Power Rangers television series as a therapeutic metaphor,' Dr. Avi Rose, *International Journal of Play Therapy*, 4(2), 59–72, 1995.

'Why and How Music Moves Us,' Jennifer L.W. Fink, Pfizer Journal, (no date)
https://www.pfizer.com/news/articles/why_and_how_music_moves_us

Quotes

"Friendship is the only cement that will ever hold the world together." Woodrow Wilson:, speech at Metropolitan Opera House, New York, 17 May 1918

"The family that prays together, stays together." Address of John Paul II to the Plenary Assembly of the Pontifical Council for the Family, October 2002: https://www.vatican.va/content/john-paul-ii/en/speeches/2002/october/documents/hf_jp-ii_spe_20021018_pc-family.html

Websites

The Black Expat
https://theblackexpat.com/the-important-questions-to-ask-before-you-move-overseas

Life Story Therapy, Rachel Cason
https://www.explorelifestory.com

Insigniam – Transformational Leadership Company, Gregory Trueblood
https://insigniam.com/our-people/gregory-trueblood

www.terraamericanart.org
The Terra Foundation fosters intercultural dialogues and encourages transformative practices to expand narratives of American art.

Podcasts

'No.1 Neuroscientist: Stress Leaks Through Skin, Is Contagious & Gives You Belly Fat!' *The Diary of a CEO podcast*, Steven Bartlett, September 2023

Interviews

Orie Medicinebull, Northern Cherokee tribe: animal spirits and totems in Native American tribes

Parul Diwan: adoption of Indian children

Wafaa' Mosa: Muslim traditions

Acknowledgments

To all the parents and students who entrusted themselves to my care. Getting to know you and working together is the reason for this book.

I thank the colleagues who first read through the basic manuscript—Wafaa' Mosa, whose enthusiasm drove me forward in those first doubtful moments, as well as Carrie Turissini, Joni Kerr, Christine Milner, and Teodora Zlatareva for your support as readers.

Wafaa' Mosa generously shared information about Muslim culture to give me details to use for Sara's life. Parul Diwan sent me information about adopting children in India. Fatma Ustun shared Turkish customs, and Orie Medicinebull helped clarify the terminology and usage of animal spirits and totems in Native American culture.

The support of my worldwide Positive Discipline colleagues has been invaluable both directly and indirectly. Our online meetings and trainings have kept me connected to like-minded souls on a similar path of self-improvement and contribution to something greater than ourselves. Jane Nelsen's work has been a guiding force in my personal and professional development with children, parents, and colleagues. The clarity and guidance gained from her books and videos have given me the certainty that I can offer something of practical value in the world.

The upbeat expats and Global Nomads at Families in Global Transition have reminded me that my identity is more complex than I realized (and suffered from!). I have taken great inspiration from our discussions that there is no "normal" lifestyle once you leave your birthplace. Our conversations across multiple time zones have been a lifeline that nurtures that multicultural part of my identity.

In the sphere of Global Nomads, David Pollock and Ruth Van Reken's *Third Culture Kids* is a source of continual support and revelation. Ruth Van Reken's continuing work with CCKs has added an important piece to my work and my reflection on my own identity. Doug Ota's *Safe Passage* was motivational for my work as a counselor in the international school scene. So many other authors in the world of TCKs, ATCKs, and CCKs have enriched my understanding of the phenomenon of global mobility and its effect on individuals and families. Thank you all.

My Daughter, My Teacher

Our daughter, Nicole, grew up with almost no extended family in Bulgaria and far from my small family in the US. In first grade, she started at the international school where I taught. By sixth grade, it was evident that such a school was not the right environment for her. She felt neither Bulgarian nor American, and clearly had her own learning style that would not be well-accommodated by the high school IB Diploma Program.

When she was in eighth grade, our family discussed other possibilities for her schooling. Nicole chose to do online homeschooling through an American program. We embarked on a very stressful path that was full of teachable moments and opportunities to learn from mistakes. Although we sometimes wondered if her choice to do homeschooling was the right one, those life lessons formed the most valuable part of her high school education, and the "cementing" of my parenting tools. She became more organized, independent, and resourceful. She had to accept help, learn how to communicate her needs, and be responsible for her own learning—skills she hadn't previously demonstrated. She received positive feedback for her creativity and humor from her online teachers (something that had not been formerly recognized in school). She came to enjoy learning and passed with good grades—something she took great pride in, having done it by herself.

She was a talented athlete and competed in track and field in a club at the Bulgarian National Sports Academy. This covered fitness training and making social connections, and also affirmed her identity as Bulgarian, a crucial piece at that moment in her life. She walked and talked differently than just a few months before—more confident, cheerful, and integrated as a person.

It was through this difficult passage that I realized the importance of keeping our nuclear family "tight." We found ways to affirm Nicole's identity, particularly in that pivotal moment from middle school onward. Our approach to parenting also went through a transformation that required examining our values, taking time to listen and guide, working as a team, while staying kind and firm.

Perhaps the most valuable realization from my parenting journey is that our task is to find ways to nurture each child's individuality, instead of trying to mold it to our visions and expectations. Ultimately, school success should not be the measure of a child's success or value as a person; the love and sense of belonging they receive at home is the foundation for success and happiness as they journey into life.

About the Author

Laura Giosh-Markov, B.A. Music, M.Ed. School Counselor

Laura lived with her family in Chicago until the age of 17, then moved 25 times in the following 10 years, exploring the US. Her sojourn continued to England, Spain, Germany, and France, where she discovered very different lifestyles from her homeland. She met her husband-to-be, a Bulgarian rockstar, and moved to Bulgaria, during a time of transition from communism to democracy.

She has been in international education for more than 30 years, first as a teacher of French, music, and theater, and later as a school counselor. Social and emotional themes became an integral part of her teaching. As a transition counselor, she helped parents and students with transition strategies to support their arrivals and departures. She initiated a program for host country students and families to support their transition when joining an international school community—so different from their local culture.

Laura leads Positive Discipline parent and teacher workshops and offers consulting services. She is also a certified music therapist in Bulgaria, using the expressive arts to help clients discover their inner resources for personal growth and healing. She has composed several school songs which inspire and affirm the school identity and students' experiences while attending those institutions.

It was through her own challenges—coping and thriving without family and a long-term support system—that she initiated transition meetings for parents. She acknowledges that these meetings and, later, parent workshops, were a form of self-help with witnesses. Learning while teaching was her way of contributing to the community while expanding her skills and friendships.

Bulgaria, where she lives with her daughter, is still her home. Recently widowed, her work with children, teachers, and parents, along with new projects in writing, music, and learning foreign languages, keeps Laura busy. Currently, she is co-director of a private kindergarten in Sofia, where she uses the principles from Positive Discipline to build a strong school environment and community. As an active member of Families in Global Transition, she stays connected with friends and colleagues around the world.

With these Tools, it is her hope that Global Nomad parents will be able to "connect more dots" in their journey and help their children build life-long skills to navigate their own journeys better.

About the Illustrator

Achini Madhushika Jayarathna

Achini is a young Sri Lankan illustrator whose talent and illustrations bring life to books, children's stories, and personal projects.

Contact: psdachinimadhushika@gmail.com

Get in Touch

It would be a great pleasure to hear more about your journey,
the challenges you encounter, and the strategies you use to
keep your family connected and growing.

Websites

www.lauramarkov.com

https://lauragmarkovauthor.pubsitepro.com

Email

gioshmarkov@gmail.com

For workshops and supplementary materials,
contact Laura at this email.